Guide to Analysis of Language Transcripts

Guide to Analysis of Language Transcripts

FOURTH EDITION

Kristine S. Retherford
Linda R. Schreiber
Rebecca L. Jarzynski

800-897-3202
Fax 800-397-7633
www.proedinc.com

© 2019, 2007, 2000, 1993, 1987 by PRO-ED, Inc.
1301 W. 25th St., Suite 300
Austin, TX 78705-4248
800-897-3202   Fax 800-397-7633
www.proedinc.com

All rights reserved. **Except as indicated below**, no part of the material protected by this copyright notice may be reproduced or used in any form or by any means, electronic or mechanical, including photocopying, recording, or by any information storage and retrieval system, without prior written permission of the copyright owner.

This product includes reproducible pages. PRO-ED, Inc. grants to individual purchasers of this material nonassignable permission to print the reproducible pages in the Appendixes, Form 1.1, and Table 3.3. This license is limited to you, the individual purchaser. This license does not grant the right to reproduce these materials for resale, redistribution, or any other purposes. Permission to reproduce these materials for any other purposes must be obtained in writing from the Permissions Department of PRO-ED, Inc.

Library of Congress Cataloging-in-Publication Data

Names: Retherford, Kristine S., 1950- author. | Schreiber, Linda
    R. (Linda Rose), 1952- author. | Jarzynski, Rebecca L.,
    author.
Title: Guide to analysis of language transcripts / Kristine S.
    Retherford, Linda R. Schreiber, Rebecca L. Jarzynski.
Description: Fourth edition. | Austin, Texas : Pro-Ed, [2019] |
    Includes bibliographical references.
Identifiers: LCCN 2018045678 (print) | LCCN 2018046617
    (e-book) | ISBN 9781416410942 (e-book) | ISBN
    9781416410935 (print)
Subjects: LCSH: Children—Language—Evaluation.
Classification: LCC RJ496.L35 (e-book) | LCC RJ496.L35 R475
    2019 (print) | DDC 618.92/855—dc23
LC record available at https://lccn.loc.gov/2018045678

Art Director: Jason Crosier
Designer: Tina Brackins
This book is designed in Proxima Nova and Sina Nova.

Printed in the United States of America

4 5 6 7 8 9 10 11 12   29 28 27 26 25 24 23 22 21

To Em and David, my ever and always inspirations

Contents

Preface ix

CHAPTER 1 GETTING STARTED WITH *GUIDE* 1

Overview 1
Target Population 2
Target Users 2
The Rationale for Learning Language Sample Analysis 2
Computer-Based Analysis Procedures 4
Using *Guide* to Learn Language Transcript Analysis 6
Obtaining Language Samples 6
    Factors Affecting Sample Representativeness 7
    Guidelines for Interaction 10
Transcribing Language Samples 11
Numbering Language Transcripts 15

CHAPTER 2 SEMANTIC ANALYSIS 23

Introduction 23
Analyzing the Semantic Content of One-Word Utterances .. 23
    Bloom's One-Word Utterance Types 24
    Nelson's One-Word Utterance Types 29
    Comparison of Bloom's and Nelson's One-Word Utterance Types ... 33
Analyzing the Semantic Content of One-Word and Multiword Utterances ... 34
    Semantic Roles 34
    Brown's Prevalent Semantic Relations 55
Analyzing Vocabulary Diversity 60
    Calculating the Results 61
    Interpreting the Results 62
Implications for Intervention 66

CHAPTER 3 SYNTACTIC ANALYSIS 69

Introduction 69
Analyzing Mean Length of Utterance in Morphemes 69
Analyzing Variations in Utterance Length 76
Analyzing Use of Grammatical Morphemes 78
Analyzing the Complexity of Negation 83
Analyzing the Complexity of Yes/No Questions 85

Analyzing the Complexity of *Wh-* Questions 90
Analyzing the Complexity of Noun Phrases 93
Analyzing the Complexity of Verb Phrases 95
Analyzing the Complexity of Complex Sentences 98
Summary and Interpretation 106
    Comparison of Most Typical Stage to MLU Stage 111
    Comparison of Most Typical Stage to Most Advanced Stage 112
    Comparison of MLU Stage to Child's Chronological Age 113
Implications for Intervention 113

CHAPTER 4   PRAGMATIC ANALYSIS 115

Introduction 115
    Language as Communication 115
    Pragmatic Language Disorders 116
    Narrative Analysis Procedures 117
    Pragmatic Analysis Procedures 118
Dore's Primitive Speech Acts 119
Dore's Conversational Acts 127
Martlew's Conversational Moves 135
Retherford's Appropriateness Judgments 141
    Referent Specificity 141
    Contributional Conciseness 145
    Communication Style 149
Implications for Intervention 153

APPENDIX A: Transcription Form (available at www.guidepractice.com)
APPENDIX B: Semantic Analysis Forms (available at www.guidepractice.com)
APPENDIX C: Syntactic Analysis Forms (available at www.guidepractice.com)
APPENDIX D: Pragmatic Analysis Forms (available at www.guidepractice.com)
APPENDIX E: Sara's Transcript and Analyses 157
APPENDIX F: Unanalyzed Transcripts Analyses, Paul and Luis 193
Glossary 215
References 219
About the Authors 227

Preface

Guide to Analysis of Language Transcripts evolved from the frustration experienced when attempting to teach undergraduate- and graduate-student clinicians to analyze language production in children. While many procedures are available, most failed to meet my needs as an instructor; they lacked explicit directions and offered limited interpretation of results. The procedures included in *Guide* attempt to improve existing procedures by providing explicit directions, guided practice, and principles for interpretation of results.

Guide takes readers from the data collection stage through the organization and analysis of data to the early stages of treatment planning. The selection of procedures to include for semantic analysis was influenced by my familiarity with an elaborate set of semantic categories for describing children's productions varying from approximately two to five morphemes in length. Procedures for analyzing productions of children in the one-word stage are included, as is a procedure for analyzing vocabulary diversity. Of the many syntactic analysis procedures available, Jon Miller's procedures for assigning structural stage were selected for inclusion in *Guide*, with modifications as deemed appropriate. The selection of procedures for analyzing pragmatic aspects of language production was difficult. Sets of procedures for describing the functions of utterances are included, as are procedures for analyzing turn taking and appropriateness judgments. We make no attempt to describe procedures for analyzing narrative abilities or phonological aspects of language. Overall, the semantic, syntactic, and pragmatic procedures described in *Guide* provide an organized, systematic approach to the analysis of language production.

The procedures consolidated in *Guide* have been applied to transcripts of the language of preschool and early school-age children. An understanding of the variability in the productions of children developing typically is essential before accurate diagnosis of children with language delays and/or disorders can occur. The relevance of the procedures must be learned by first applying them to transcripts such as those included in *Guide*. We have developed a companion online program—*Guide Practice*—to give clinicians and students some additional practice making the judgments demonstrated in *Guide*. Students are encouraged to use the web-based program, along with the practice items included in each chapter of *Guide*, before attempting the full transcripts included in the book.

I am grateful to many individuals for their assistance in the preparation of *Guide to Analysis of Language Transcripts*. My students provided inspiration; for their criticism of and confusion over existing procedures, I extend my sincere thanks. Nancy McKinley provided the original encouragement and contributed many hours of careful editing in earlier editions; I still miss you, Nancy. My reviewers of the first edition—Marc Fey, Vicki Lord Larson, Linda Maro, and Susan Schultz—offered insightful suggestions; I am grateful for their input. I could not have completed this fourth edition of *Guide* without the dedication of my co-authors of this edition, Linda Schreiber and Rebecca Jarzynski. Linda had served as editor of the three previous editions and Becca was a student of mine and now teaches many of the courses I used to teach! I am so very grateful for their willingness to take on this project! For this edition, I enlisted assistance from a graduate student in Communication Disorders here at Mankato State University in Minnesota, my new home. Thank you, Mariah! My children have now grown into beautiful, talented, successful adults since the first edition was published. In fact, I made final edits to the first edition just 3 weeks after Emily was born! She is now 30 years old and my baby boy turns 28 this year. I thank Emily and David for their patience, understanding, and encouragement. You are the best!

The revisions to *Guide* have been in the works almost from the time the first edition was in print. Some revisions have evolved from class discussions and serve to clarify ambiguity. Other revisions have grown out of suggestions offered by instructors who use *Guide* and add information or additional interpretation. To both these groups, I extend my gratitude. Ken Ray made the web-based program fully functional; his vision is much appreciated.

And Jessica and Krista, as 4-year-olds, provided priceless examples of rich sentence elaboration. These utterances were central to my in-class discussions long before the first edition of *Guide*. These examples have found their way into the Glossary. I am grateful for their willingness to talk about anything and everything. Although these two are adults now, when I use one of their utterances as an example, I will always remember their fourth summer. One of my all-time favorite utterances described the search for "Jellies what have holes for your toes." Thanks, Jess and Krista

CHAPTER 1
Getting Started With Guide

Overview

Guide to Analysis of Language Transcripts provides guidelines for (a) identifying three aspects of language production: semantics, syntax, and pragmatics; (b) analyzing the identified structures' developmental levels; and (c) interpreting these analyses' results. Blank analysis sheets and summary forms are available online (at www.guidepractice.com), and practice in making crucial judgments is incorporated into each procedure's discussion. *Guide* differs from other sources in that it includes an integration of procedures for analyzing three of the multiple components of language production (semantics, syntax, and pragmatics) and includes a framework for gaining experience in making judgments before applying the procedures to sample transcripts.

Although phonology is considered to be a primary component of language, no procedures for describing or analyzing spontaneous sound systems of children are included in *Guide*. An experienced speech–language pathologist (SLP) may be able to complete some type of phonologic analysis of transcripts obtained and transcribed using conventions described in *Guide*, such as an inventory of sounds used by a child while engaged in conversation or a summary of phonological patterns using procedures described by Hodson (2010); Watson, Murthy, and Wadhwa (2003); Shriberg and Kwiatkowski (1980); and Ingram (1981). However, *Guide* will not demonstrate any type of phonologic analysis. Nor has any attempt been made to describe procedures for analyzing narrative abilities. The analysis procedures described in *Guide* are based on spontaneous conversational interaction. To analyze narration, sampling procedures would differ greatly from those described here.

Guide is intended for use with undergraduate and graduate students in communication sciences and disorders clinical education programs. It is a tool for teaching students how to obtain quality language production transcripts and how to analyze the semantic, syntactic, and pragmatic aspects of those transcripts. *Guide* may also be helpful to the practicing SLP who is looking for a comprehensive set of procedures for analyzing all three conversational components of the language production system. In addition, *Guide* can be used as a tool to enhance appropriate development of intervention goals and objectives based on results of the analysis procedures described in this resource. *Guide* is helpful in developing goals and objectives for intervention even when the analysis procedures described are not used, as would be the case if computer analysis procedures were used.

As a companion web-based program, *Guide Practice* has been developed and access is included to give additional opportunities to make the judgments demonstrated in *Guide*. We encourage readers to use the exercises provided online (using the code provided), along with the practice examples included in each chapter of this book, before attempting to use analysis procedures on the full transcripts included in *Guide*.

The glossary in *Guide* serves as a useful tool for students to quickly look up puzzling or unfamiliar terms. Appendixes containing all the forms used throughout the book are available online. Appendix E includes an analyzed transcript (Sara); and Appendix F contains two unanalyzed transcripts for further practice (Paul and Luis; Answer keys are available to professors only).

Target Population

Guide to Analysis of Language Transcripts is designed to provide analysis procedures for use with language transcripts obtained from children at the one-word level through Stage V++ of linguistic production (Miller & Chapman's [1981] extension of Brown's [1973] original five stages), or ages 12 months through 6 years for children who are developing typically. Some procedures are appropriate for use with children older than age 6; however, the focus is on analysis of semantic, syntactic, and pragmatic aspects of language production during Brown's stages of linguistic development, and minimally beyond. Within each chapter are procedures appropriate for use within a more limited age range than 1 to 6 years, and guidelines are provided for determining which procedures to use with a particular child.

A word needs to be said about the use of language production measures to identify children with language delays and/or disorders. The procedures described in *Guide*, when combined with other information about a child (e.g., chronological age, developmental level, comprehension level), can identify a child whose productive-language level differs from that expected on the basis of chronological age and/or developmental level and comprehension level. Whether such children are language delayed or language disordered may not be clinically relevant. Various criteria have been used to determine language delays and language disorders, including performance at least 1 standard deviation below the mean, performance 1.5 standard deviations below the mean (Spaulding, Plante, & Farinella, 2006), 2 standard deviations below the mean (Bloom & Lahey, 1978), performance below the 10th percentile (Lee, 1974; Rizzo & Stephens, 1981), and delays greater than 6 months (Crystal, Fletcher, & Garman, 1976). For the purposes of *Guide*, the child whose productive language is at least one production stage below expectations or 1 standard deviation below the mean (whenever available) based on either chronological age or developmental level (whichever is lower) or whose language behaviors are penalizing to him as a conversational participant is considered a candidate for language intervention. Language production measures alone cannot be used to determine the existence of a language disorder. It is not these authors' intent to resolve the debate regarding the definition of *language delay* and/or *language disorder*, but rather to make it clear that *Guide* adheres to a developmental perspective in that once a level of language performance has been determined, and the decision has been made that a child is a candidate for intervention, the accomplishments of the next developmental level (whether that be semantic, syntactic, or pragmatic) may be targeted during intervention.

Target Users

Guide to Analysis of Language Transcripts is intended for use in teaching undergraduate and graduate students in communication sciences and disorders clinical education programs to obtain quality language production transcripts and to analyze the semantic, syntactic, and pragmatic aspects of those transcripts. The terminology used assumes minimal clinical background, and the extensiveness of the practice sections, both in the book and in the online web-based practice, are designed to provide the speech–language pathologist-in-training with introductory exposure to the types of judgments necessary for successful analysis of language transcripts.

Guide may also be helpful to the practicing SLP who is looking for a comprehensive set of procedures for analyzing these three components of the language production system. While the use of practice examples in the book and the web-based exercises may not be necessary for those familiar with similar analysis procedures, an examination of all the practice sections is encouraged since many of the judgments may not be clear in the discussions of the procedures alone.

The Rationale for Learning Language Sample Analysis

One goal of an SLP is to identify children with language delays and/or disorders. To identify such children, an evaluation battery must include the two major processes of language performance—language comprehension and language production—plus the interaction of these two processes in ongoing conversation. Numerous formal assessment procedures that have statistically documented validity and reliability measures with diverse sample populations are available for the evaluation of comprehension abilities. Among these are the *Peabody*

Picture Vocabulary Test–Fourth Edition (PPVT-IV; Dunn & Dunn, 2007), the *Boehm Test of Basic Concepts–Third Edition* (Boehm-3; Boehm, 2001), the *Montgomery Assessment of Vocabulary Acquisition* (MAVA; Montgomery, 2008), the *Bracken Basic Concept Scale–Third Edition: Receptive* (BBCS-3: R; Bracken, 2006), the *Comprehensive Receptive and Expressive Vocabulary Test–Third Edition* (CREVT-3; Wallace & Hammill, 2013), the *Test of Auditory Comprehension of Language–Fourth Edition* (TACL-4; Carrow-Woolfolk, 2014), the *Preschool Language Scale–Fifth Edition* (PLS-5; Zimmerman, Steiner, & Pond, 2011), the Test of *Early Language Development–Fourth Edition* (TELD-4; Hresko, Reid, & Hammill, 2018), the *Clinical Evaluation of Language Fundamentals–Preschool: Second Edition* (CELF: P-2; Semel, Wiig, & Secord, 2004), and the *Test of Language Development–Primary: Fifth Edition* (TOLD-P: 5; Hammill & Newcomer, 2019).

While many of these formal procedures also include cursory measures of language production, few result in a thorough description of production abilities. A few standardized tests of spoken language are available, including the *Comprehensive Assessment of Spoken Language–Second Edition* (CASL-2; Carrow-Woolfolk, 2017), the *Expressive One-Word Picture Vocabulary Test* (EOWPVT; Brownell, 2000), the *Test of Expressive Language* (TEXL; Carrow-Woolfolk & Allen, 2014), and the *Oral and Written Language Scales–Second Edition* (OWLS-2; Carrow-Woolfolk, 2011).

Inventories of language are also available, including the *Sequenced Inventory of Communication Development–Revised* (SICD-R; Hendrick, Prather, & Tobin, 1975), *LanguageLinks to Literacy: Expressive Syntax Assessment* (Wilson & Fox, 2015), and the *Test of Children's Language* (TOCL; Barenbaum & Newcomer, 1996). The language production information obtained from these measures, however, is contrived and not necessarily a reflection of conversational abilities. In addition, formal measures for the analysis of communicative interaction are relatively few in number. There are the *Test of Pragmatic Skills–Second Edition* (TOPL-2; Phelps-Terasaki & Phelps-Gunn, 2007) and the *Let's Talk Inventory for Children* (Bray & Wiig, 1985).

To analyze language production, one must compare various aspects of production with data obtained from the language of children who have typical development. Determining the appropriate linguistic behaviors to compare to normative data may be difficult, and comparison under conditions identical to those under which the data were collected may be impossible. In addition, it may be difficult to efficiently manage data leading to synthesis for the development of intervention goals and objectives.

Historically, language sampling has been considered the cornerstone of assessment in communicative competence. "One of the greatest strengths in language sampling is seen to be its direct representation of a person's language production system as opposed to the secondary representation afforded by elicitation procedures such as standardized procedures" (Klee, 1985, p. 183). Language sample analysis (LSA) has greater ecological validity than formal testing because it evaluates a child's actual use of language, making the assessment more authentic; it has been considered a crucial component of a comprehensive language assessment (Evans, 1996).

The benefits of using language sample analysis (LSA) have been explored over time by numerous researchers (Bloom & Lahey, 1978; Brown, 1973; Heilmann, Nockerts, & Miller, 2010; Miller, Andriacchi, & Nockerts, 2015; Nelson, 1973; Owens & Pavelko, 2017; Pavelko & Owens, 2017; Price, Hendricks, & Cook, 2010; Ratner & Brundage, 2016; Ratner, Fromm, MacWhinney, 2017; Templin, 1957) who have found it to be a powerful tool for documenting and describing communication in naturalistic speaking situations. Unlike standardized testing, LSA allows for flexibility in obtaining a representative language sample and advocates observation of communication in naturalistic settings, thereby being a more effective measure for distinguishing between children who are typically developing and those who have a language disorder. Dunn, Flax, Silwinski, and Aram (1996) also found evidence that mean length of utterance (MLU) and error analysis of a spontaneous language sample may be more sensitive than a standardized test to the language deficits that are common in children with language impairment. Other researchers have shown that standardized tests and language sample analyses of MLU and number of different words (NDW) are highly correlated (Berstein & Haynes, 1998; Ukrainetz & Blomquist, 2002). Owens and Pavelko (2017), who examined the correlation of standardized test measures to several measures of communication (e.g., mean length of utterance, total number of new words, clauses per sentence, words per sentence) using language sample analysis, concluded that conversational language samples complement norm-referenced tests.

Condouris, Meyer, and Tager-Flusberg (2003) and Koegel, Koegel, and Smith (1997) provided evidence for use of language sample analysis rather than standardized testing for students with autism spectrum disorder (ASD) for whom compliance to standardized testing can be an issue and because of the demands of standardized testing. Additionally, children with high-functioning autism can do well on standardized tests but may struggle with language use in context. A group of experts on ASD assembled by the National Institute on Deafness and Other Communication Disorders (NIDCD, 2010) strongly encouraged language sampling to be part of the comprehensive assessment of children suspected of being on the autism spectrum.

In addition, standardized procedures do not always address the sensitivity and specificity required to eliminate cultural and linguistic bias (Betz, Eickhoff, & Sullivan, 2013; Craig & Washington, 2000), which can result in overidentification of students who are nonstandard-English speakers or English-language learners. Chase and Johnston (2013) suggested that LSA provides for occurrences when a speech–language pathologist may not have available a standardized instrument that is sensitive to the needs of the child (especially his or her linguistic and cultural needs).

In addition, federal laws require the use of multiple data (formal and informal) to determine a student's eligibility for exceptional educational services. LSA can serve as one source of data and is considered a valid source by the American Speech-Language-Hearing Association (ASHA), as well as one that ASHA feels student clinicians should show competence in administering.

Guide to Analysis of Language Transcripts provides LSA guidelines for (a) the identification of three aspects of language production (semantics, syntax, and pragmatics), (b) the analysis of the identified structures' developmental levels, and (c) the interpretation of these analyses' results. Summaries of the data relevant to each analysis procedure are provided, and methods for comparing analysis data to normative data are described. Once each component of language production is analyzed, strategies for synthesis of data as the foundation for intervention are discussed. In addition, practice in making the necessary judgments is provided for each of the analysis procedures described. With practice, the task of analyzing language transcripts becomes easier and more efficient.

Many sets of procedures are available for the analysis of specific aspects of language production. Commercially available procedures are typically designed to analyze one aspect of language production. For example, the *Developmental Sentence Analysis*, described by Lee (1974), provides a procedure for analyzing subject + verb complete utterances on the basis of the developmental level of eight grammatical categories: indefinite and personal pronouns, primary and secondary verbs, negation, conjunctions, interrogative reversals, and *wh-* questions. Although some of the categories analyzed would be considered semantic, the major intent is to provide a syntactic analysis of language production. The *Language Assessment, Remediation, and Screening Procedure* (LARSP), developed and described by Crystal, Fletcher, and Garman (1976, 1991), provides for analysis of sentences, clauses, phrases, and word types. Again, some semantic information can be gleaned from this analysis procedure, but the primary result is analysis of syntax production.

In addition to commercially available procedures, procedures described in the literature may make reference to syntactic and semantic aspects of language production, but no guidelines for the integration of these two components are described. For example, the Assigning Structural Stage procedure described within Miller's (1981) *Assessing Language Production in Children* includes identification of the developmental level of a variety of grammatical forms for syntactic analysis. Miller also identified a variety of semantic analysis procedures and Chapman (1981) summarized a variety of pragmatic taxonomies. Application of semantic, syntactic, and pragmatic analyses to the same language transcript is not provided. The procedures described in *Guide*, however, have been developed to be used together to analyze semantic, syntactic, and pragmatic aspects of the same language transcript.

Computer-Based Analysis Procedures

One might ask, "Why should I learn to analyze language transcripts when computers can do the work?" It is true that a variety of software programs have been developed for analyzing of language transcripts. However, available programs differ in the types of analyses performed and the ease with which the coding procedures are learned and the analyses accomplished. For example, SALT: Systematic Analysis of Language Transcripts (SALT 16) has evolved since the early 1980s to become one of the most flexible yet complicated software programs available (Miller & Chapman, 2000; Miller, Andriacchi, & Nockerts, 2015). Three types of analyses can be performed. First, morphologic analysis can be accomplished, resulting in MLU in morpheme and word measures. Second, semantic analysis is accomplished, by measuring NDW. Third, structural analysis is possible with several grammatical categories. Fourth, utterance analysis can be performed, resulting in, among other things, preceding and following utterance–match summaries. In addition, many other options can be selected and/or created by the user. Because of its sophistication, the SALT program takes considerable practice to master. However, a tutorial program is included to facilitate coding. Again, interpretation of results is dependent on a comparison of the results to developmental norms and/or the user's knowledge and experience.

Another example of a software program used for language transcript analysis is Computerized Profiling (CP), developed by Long, Fey, and Channell (2003). It contains several analysis systems, including many traditional manual analysis procedures. Among these are LARSP, found within The Grammatical Analysis of Language Disability (Crystal, Fletcher, & Garman, 1976, 1991); PRISM, found within Profiling Linguistic Disability (Crystal, 1992); and Developmental Sentence Scoring (DSS), found within Developmental Sentence Analysis (Lee, 1974). Pragmatic and phonological analyses are possible as well. Depending on the type of analysis performed, complex manual coding is necessary and time-consuming. Only the DSS and Conversational Acts Profile found within CP contain normative data for interpretation.

A third example of a computerized language sample analysis program is CLAN/KidEval (Ratner & Brundage, 2016; Ratner, Fromm, & MacWhinney, 2017). Among the more than 20 measures that can be obtained using this free software are: MLU, morpheme count, lexical diversity (e.g., type-token ratio [TTR]), DSS, grammatical classes, and Brown's morphemes. The CLAN procedure loads the measures into an Excel file; however, as with SALT, knowledge of specific coding procedures is required.

The Parrot Easy Language Sample Analysis (Weiner, 2000) is another software program that provides analysis of numerous grammatical forms. However, it is useful only on Windows-based platforms.

Although the development of software programs represents a major advance in resources available to the speech–language pathologist, without a thorough understanding of what each program does or does not accomplish, a knowledgeable development of intervention programming is impossible. Software programs used for the analysis of language production are only as accurate as the coded transcriptions on which they are based. In other words, accurate analysis can be obtained only if the language sample is representative of the child's production abilities, has been transcribed correctly, and has been coded appropriately. Obviously, these same criteria apply to manual procedures as well. The time-saving advantage of computer software comes with the frequency-of-use summaries. Responsibility for interpretation of the results obtained from either software programs or manual procedures continues to be dependent on the knowledge and skill of the speech–language pathologist. The procedures described in *Guide* can aid in understanding what computer analyses accomplish and can assist in the interpretation of computer analyses' results.

In addition to being dependent on user skill for coding and interpretation, software programs have a number of analysis limitations. Software programs are not capable of accomplishing semantic roles analyses that rely on nonlinguistic context for making these judgments. Second, with the exception of the conversational context search provided by SALT (Miller & Chapman, 2000; Miller, Andriacchi, & Nockerts, 2015), no existing program can perform analyses of pragmatic aspects of language production, including speech act analysis, topic maintenance analysis, and appropriateness judgments. Third, existing programs are incapable of analyzing nonverbal variables that may influence interpretation of an utterance, such as eye gaze, gestures, and intonation. Finally, software programs available at this time do not provide analysis of stylistic variations in speakers that may influence a listener's judgments of the speaker.

Thus, judicious use of software programs for the analysis of language production can save time in tallying the frequency of occurrence of specific structures. In addition, software programs can permit the speech–language pathologist to accumulate sufficient data so that, over time, local norms for specific behaviors can be developed. *Guide to Analysis of Language Transcripts* can facilitate use of software programs by familiarizing the beginning speech–language pathologist with a set of structures to be identified and coded for computer analysis and summary. The practice provided in *Guide* facilitates more accurate coding of target structures and assists in the interpretation of results of computer analysis. In addition, the procedures delineated in *Guide* can provide analysis of structures and/or aspects of language production currently not available through computer analysis. Finally, the development of intervention goals and objectives from computer analysis may be enhanced with *Guide*.

Using *Guide* to Learn Language Transcript Analysis

Guide to Analysis of Language Transcripts provides a comprehensive set of analysis procedures encompassing semantic, syntactic, and pragmatic components of language production. Examples and a sample transcript (Bridget) accompany each analysis procedure. Blank analysis forms and summary forms are provided (online at the *Guide Practice* website) and practice in making crucial judgments is incorporated into the discussion of each procedure. Working through the practice examples for each procedure should increase accuracy in identifying and coding targeted structures and should increase the reliability of the resulting analyses. The accompanying *Guide Practice* online exercises include in-depth practice for many of the procedures. No other source currently available includes a framework for gaining experience making judgments before applying the analysis procedures to sample transcripts. Three additional transcripts also are provided in appendixes (one analyzed—Sara, and two not analyzed— Paul and Luis) for continued practice.

In the analysis of a single child's language production, the developmentally appropriate procedures from each chapter should be applied to thoroughly describe the child's production abilities. In some cases, the developmental level of the child precludes the use of syntactic analysis procedures; typically, however, examination should proceed from semantic to syntactic to pragmatic analysis. For example, some form of semantic analysis will be performed for all language transcripts. Depending on the child's age and/or developmental level, that semantic analysis may be an analysis of the meanings expressed in one-word utterances, analysis of semantic roles and relations expressed in multiword utterances up to approximately four words in length, and/or analysis of vocabulary diversity using Templin's (1957) Type-Token Ratio. If a child's MLU is over 1.0 morphemes, analysis of syntactic aspects of the transcript must be performed. Such analysis may be cursory in that very few target structures are present; however, analysis is necessary to document emergence of early structures. The child whose MLU exceeds 6.0 morphemes may be at a level beyond which the structures analyzed with procedures in *Guide* can be documented. However, unless the structures described here are present in the child's production, and the highest level for each is observed, that conclusion cannot be drawn. In all cases, some form of pragmatic analysis must be performed. Again, depending on the child's age and/or developmental level, such analysis may be limited to the function of one-word utterances or may be as extensive as a conversational acts analysis with measures of appropriateness. In nearly every case, thorough analysis of language transcripts involves semantic, syntactic, and pragmatic analyses.

Clinical experience has demonstrated the effectiveness of proceeding with analysis in the order mentioned above. This order is consistent with the ordering of chapters in *Guide*. Rules for deciding which of the three sets of procedures (i.e., semantic, syntactic, or pragmatic) to use with any particular child are discussed in each chapter. An interpretation of each analysis procedure's results is incorporated into the discussion of that procedure and can be used as the foundation for intervention.

These procedures have proved to be helpful in identifying children with language production delays and/or disorders evaluated in university and school settings, and intervention programs have been based on the results of the described procedures. *Guide* should be used as a manual to learn each of the analysis procedures presented. Clinical use of the procedures should be supplemented with the practice exercises online in *Guide Practice* and with readings on the theoretical foundation of each procedure, for which sources are provided in Chapters 2, 3, and 4.

Obtaining Language Samples

The first step in analyzing language production transcripts is to obtain samples of the child's productive language. When collected appropriately, this language sample may be the best picture of the child's production abilities. In fact, Gallagher (1983) contended that "spontaneous language sampling is the centerpiece of child language assessment" (p. 2). However, the communicative interaction often is contrived to such an extent that the resulting sample is anything but representative of the child's usual productive language.

The term *representative* has been used in various ways in the literature. Miller (1981) supported the notion that a representative sample is one that is reliable and valid. McLean and Snyder-McLean (1978) suggested that a representative sample reflects the child's optimal performance. Gallagher (1983) reported that throughout the years, a sample is considered to be representative if it portrays the child's usual performance. In *Guide*, the term *representative* is used to describe a child's usual productive language, including language that may be somewhat below or somewhat above his usual language performance.

Factors Affecting Sample Representativeness

Miller (1981) contends that a number of aspects of the communication interaction affect sample representativeness and that each aspect can be controlled to ensure representativeness. Examining each factor and then taking steps to optimize conditions in each will improve the quality of the sample. High-quality representative samples are the foundation for accurate production analysis.

NATURE OF THE INTERACTION

The first variable, the *nature of the interaction*, refers to the person with whom the child is interacting and to whether that participant asks questions or engages in conversation during interactive play. Miller (1981) supported obtaining a number of language samples of the child's interactions with a variety of people, including the speech–language pathologist, a parent, and a sibling or peer. While the general assumption has been that a child will produce language that is most representative when interacting with his mother, studies comparing mother–child and SLP–child interactions have been inconclusive. Olswang and Carpenter (1978) found that the only variable of 21 lexical, grammatical, and semantic measures that was significantly different in the two interactions was the total number of utterances. Children produced significantly more utterances when interacting with their mothers than they did with familiar SLPs, but other length and complexity measures were not significantly different. Other studies comparing mother–child interactions obtained at home and SLP–child interactions obtained in the clinic have found that some children produce longer utterances with the SLP, other children produce longer utterances with their mother, and still other children produce utterances of equal length with both conversational co-participants (Kramer, James, & Saxman, 1979; Scott & Taylor, 1978). Gallagher (1983) suggested that the numerous research design differences between these studies may have contributed to the differences in results.

Studies comparing fathers to mothers as interactive partners also are fraught with inconsistencies in their conclusions. Gallagher's (1983) sampling of relevant studies found some research that indicated that no significant differences existed between the interactive style of mothers and fathers (Golinkoff & Ames, 1979; Smith & Daglish, 1977; Wilkinson, Hiebert, & Rembold, 1981). Gallagher also found studies supporting the contention that the language fathers use with children is different from the language mothers use with children. Gallagher supported the contention that the "most facilitating communication partner" may be one or the other of the parents, or neither. None of the studies cited by Gallagher compared fathers interacting with children to speech–language pathologists interacting with the same children.

Peer and/or sibling interaction may result in some language differences; however, the exact differences are not easy to predict. For example, some studies document length and complexity adjustments when children are interacting with a younger child (Sachs & Devin, 1976; Shatz & Gelman, 1973). Other studies emphasize differences in conversational acts, including more responses to adults' questions (Martlew, Connolly, & McCleod, 1978) and more repetitions, attention holders, and directives with peers than with adults (Wilkinson, Hiebert, & Rembold, 1981). Gallagher (1983) concluded that child–child communicative behavior has not been described sufficiently with regard to a single variable to predict the effects on communicative interaction.

Results of studies comparing children interacting with various conversational partners are mixed. Although it is possible to predict that a range of differences will occur, it is not possible to predict which differences will occur with a particular child and a particular conversational co-participant. Therefore, instead of pairing the child with only one conversational co-participant to obtain a language sample, it is prudent to obtain samples with the child interacting with various partners. Differences in samples add to the picture of the child's overall communicative abilities.

Miller (1981) included conversational act variables, such as questioning and responding, as aspects of the nature of the interaction. He suggested that in attempting to obtain a representative sample, SLPs should keep question asking to a minimum. The assumption is that children will produce longer and more complex utterances when spontaneously conversing than when responding to questions. However, in a study in which children were asked to retell a story as they acted it out with toys, to tell what they were doing while playing with toys, and to respond to questions about toys as they played with them, Stalnaker and Craighead (1982) found inconclusive results. General group trends followed the order mentioned previously for language complexity, but these authors concluded that none of the methods of language sampling was superior to the others.

Overall, it is apparent that a conversation in which one partner asks questions and the other responds is not a natural interaction. As conversational partners, speech–language pathologists should try to reduce the number of questions asked, especially yes/no and one-word-response questions, and to permit the child to take the lead in the interaction. However, a complete absence of questions on the part of the SLP would be impossible to attain and may not result in a representative sampling of the child's production abilities. To reduce one-word or minimal responses, Pavelko and Owens (2017) suggested avoiding questions that answer themselves and questions that test the child's knowledge. Refer to the earlier discussion for more detailed information on gathering a language sample that represents a child's communication abilities.

SETTING

The second variable that Miller (1981) indicated may affect sample representativeness is setting. Miller specified a number of alternative settings to an intervention or therapy room and asserted that using more than one setting is optimal. He suggested that samples be obtained in a variety of locations, such as at home, at school, in a residential facility, or at a clinic. Although Miller contended that "representative samples can be collected almost anywhere" (p. 11), differences may arise in the language of the child because of the setting. For example, the differences found in the mother–child versus SLP–child studies previously mentioned (Kramer, James, & Saxman, 1979; Scott & Taylor, 1978) may have been due primarily to the differences in setting. The mother–child samples were obtained in the home, and the SLP–child samples were obtained in the clinic. In two other studies, the effects of two settings on the language use of 3- to 4-year-old children were compared (Dore, 1978; Hall & Cole, 1978). Results indicated that a supermarket setting did not elicit more complex language than the classroom, and that the differences, again, were related more to the interactive style of participants than to the setting (Dore, 1978).

While it may not be possible to predict which setting will result in representative language for a particular child, obtaining samples in more than one setting is optimal. The resulting differences, if any, add to the description of the child's communicative abilities.

MATERIALS

The third variable that Miller (1981) believed may affect sample representativeness is the materials that are present. Numerous authors have found that different types of materials result in different language behaviors. Miller, Andriacchi, and Nockerts (2015) reported that children with language disorders talk more about new and unique toys than they talk about familiar toys and suggested that older children may converse without an object present. Nisswandt (1983) reported the opposite for children with typical language. Longhurst and File (1977) examined the effect of single-object pictures, multi-object pictures, toys, and no materials present on the language complexity of 4- to 5-year-old children. While group data supported increases in complexity in the order above, individual data indicated that increases in complexity could occur in any ordering of the stimulus conditions. Cook-Gumperz and Corsaro (1977) reported differences in the communicative demands placed on 3- and 4-year-old children with three different sets of materials: those for a playhouse, a sandbox, and an adult-directed arts-and-crafts activity. Results indicated that there were language differences across conditions, with very few initiative turns in the arts-and-crafts activity, adherence to role-play conventions in the playhouse, and unpredictable fantasy interactions in the sandbox. Cook-Gumperz and Corsaro (1977) concluded that the sandbox was the most difficult of the three settings in terms of interactive demands and resulted in an increased use of repetition and expansion, semantic typing, and verbal descriptions of behaviors.

Again, different materials may result in differences in language frequency and complexity. The differences, however, do not appear to be predictable for children. Therefore, it is wise to provide a variety of developmentally appropriate materials and to encourage the child to interact with as many materials as possible. Differences, again, will contribute to the overall picture of the child's communicative abilities.

SAMPLE SIZE

The fourth variable that Miller (1981) indicated may affect sample representativeness is sample size. Various authors have suggested numbers of utterances ranging from 50 to 200 for the sample to be representative (Casby, 2011; Crystal, Fletcher, & Garman, 1991; Eisenberg, Fersko, & Lundgren, 2001; Lee, 1974; Miller, 1981; Owens & Pavelko, 2017; Pavelko, Owens, & Johnson, 2016; Pavelko & Owens, 2017; Rice et al., 2010). Guo and Eisenberg (2014) found diagnostic accuracy values for longer (100-utterance) samples for typically developing children and a high correlation for 10-minute samples for children with a range of language abilities (Guo & Eisenberg, 2015). Heilmann, Nockerts, and Miller (2010), who studied the effects of transcript length on different measures of language, suggested that a blanket statement regarding sample length would be inappropriate; longer samples are usually more reliable than shorter samples, but some measures (e.g., MLU, NDW) can be determined using shorter samples. They further suggested that longer samples may be more appropriate when the purpose of the analyses is to determine a language disorder versus to monitor progress. Miller, Andriacchi, and Nockerts (2015) suggested that children who are younger or who have language difficulties will require more time to elicit a representative sample of language, and Rice et al. (2010) found it challenging to gather samples of more than 150 utterances for children below 4 years of age.

Owens and Pavelko (2015) suggested that if a language sample is robust, a shorter sample of 50 utterances may be sufficient; however, their research examined only four measures of language: mean length of utterance, total number of new words, clauses per sentence, and words per sentence. However, the authors maintain that a 100-word utterance sample is critical to capture the nuances in conversation for pragmatic analyses as well as to capture numerous grammatical and semantic features to determine the presence of a language disorder.

One option for gathering the sample size required is to obtain a specific number of utterances from the child (or transcribe that number from a sample containing a larger number). An alternative is to obtain utterances during a particular duration of time—for example, 30 minutes—regardless of how many utterances occur during that period. This 30-minute period is likely to result in 100 to 200 utterances for children functioning at a 2-year level or older (Miller, 1981). Longer periods of time will be necessary to obtain 100 utterances from children younger than 2 years of age, and it may be prudent to supplement a sample with diary accounts from parents.

The obvious conclusion is the more utterances, the better. However, in an effort to be realistic, practical, and efficient, 100 utterances gathered under various conditions typically result in a respectably diverse sample.

METHOD OF RECORDING

A fifth variable that Miller (1981) contended could affect sample representativeness—the method of recording—is really a variable affecting the overall quality of the resulting transcription. The optimum method is videotaping, because it permits the SLP either to interact freely with the child or to watch undistracted as others interact with the child. Mobile phones, tablets, and computers have video- and sound-recording features and can be taken anywhere. Transcription from videotape recordings is considered to be the most reliable method and permits detailed delineation of changes in nonverbal contexts (Heilmann, 2010; Price, Hendricks, & Cook, 2010).

Another method of recording is strictly audio recording and is likely the most common (Pavelko, Owens, Ireland, & Hahs-Vaughn, 2016). When audio recording, the SLP is free to interact with the child, but must make notes about the child's activities during the taping to provide the nonverbal context for transcription. The quality of recordings can be improved by using an external microphone.

An additional method of recording suggested by Miller (1981) is online transcription (i.e., transcribing what the child says, as the child says it)—also referred to as real-time transcription. This method is useful in settings where videotaping and/or audiotaping is not practical for younger children who are producing one- or two-word utterances. Real-time transcription is not recommended if the conversational partner is also the transcriber, as attention to and active involvement with the child may be affected and consequently the sample may not be representative of the child's language (Owens, 2014).

Real-time transcription may be useful to record a child's productions on field trips or other outings away from the clinical setting. The major criticism of real-time transcription is that it results in transcriptions that underrepresent or overrepresent the child's actual productions. The key to obtaining reliable online transcriptions may be to use one of the procedures suggested by Miller: time sampling. Using this procedure, the SLP transcribes for a few minutes, then rests for a few minutes before continuing. This method maximizes attention during transcription. The alternative—writing down every single thing the child says—can be cumbersome and exhausting. As in audiotaping, nonverbal context notes should be made during online transcription.

Regardless of the method of recording the interaction, quality transcripts can be obtained. Miller (1981) reported a high reliability for MLU computations based on real-time transcriptions and transcriptions from both video and audio recordings. Phones, tablets, and computers have speech-to-text (dictation) features that in some cases can be helpful later when transcribing the sample. Each method has its own problems and advantages, and each relies on accurate representation of the child's productions for valid and reliable transcripts.

SPECIFICATION OF CONTEXT

The final variable, which also affects the quality of the obtained language transcript, is the specification of context. This includes the conversational co-participant's utterances as well as the nonverbal or situational context. The utterances preceding and following a child's utterances may dramatically affect the interpretation of the child's utterance. In addition, the objects that are present and the events that are taking place as the child produces an utterance greatly influence interpretation of the child's utterance. Research has shown that different contexts place differing demands on the speaker and may give different results (Miller, Andriacchi, & Nockerts, 2015). Miller, Andriacchi, and Nockerts suggested that up through age 5 or for students with developmental disabilities, conversation during play is the best platform for collecting a sample of an individual's language use, and as children enter the elementary school years, personal narratives, story retells, and exposition may give a better representation of a child's language use. It becomes obvious in the following chapters that semantic and pragmatic analyses require the specification of nonverbal context; such specification is also helpful with syntactic analysis. Overall, a quality transcription must include a detailed account of both the linguistic and nonlinguistic context.

Guidelines for Interaction

The preceding discussion highlighted numerous variables that are important to consider when obtaining representative language samples and producing quality transcripts. The following guidelines for interacting with a child are offered as a synthesis of the preceding discussion. The first four guidelines should be adhered to in sequence to establish the conversational interaction. The remaining guidelines are general and are to be followed throughout the interaction.

1. Begin with parallel play and parallel talk. With a very young child at the one-word stage, imitate his or her verbalizations and use many animal sounds and vehicle noises. With a child older than 2 years, talk about what you are doing as you play using role-playing dialogue (e.g., "I'm gonna make my guy drive. Here's the tractor for him. Wow, what a big tractor. I'm gonna go fast!").

2. Pay attention to the child's interests to discover a topic he or she might want to talk about (Pavelko & Owens, 2017).

3. Move into interactive conversation. With the young child, use some routine questions (e.g., "What's a doggie say?") and elicit fingerplays (e.g., "Let's play pat-a-cake"). With the older child, invite him or her to participate in play (e.g., "You be the service station guy. I'll bring my car in. It needs fixing"). Continue in role-playing dialogue unless establishing rules for play. Encourage the child to participate in plans for play, including what toy people/animals will be doing (e.g., "Hey, how about having a picnic?").

4. Continue the child's topic. If he or she is role-playing, stay in the role. If the child shifts out of this role, follow the lead. Respond to questions, acknowledge comments, and solicit more information about a topic.

5. Restrict your use of questions to approximately one question for every four speaking turns. Eliminating the use of questions is unnatural, but too many questions may reduce the length of the child's utterances. The often-suggested prompt "Tell me about this" can also break down the conversation and result in descriptive strings from the child. Instead, carry on a conversation with the child at the child's level.

6. Avoid questions that answer themselves and questions that test the child's knowledge (Pavelko & Owens, 2017).

7. Use process-type questions or comments, such as "What happened?" "How did . . . ?" "Why did . . . ?" "Tell me more," and "I wonder . . ." (Pavelko & Owens).

8. Give the child options that are presented as alternative questions (e.g., "Should we play gas station or have a picnic?"). While children under 3 years of age may not comprehend the alternative-question form (Beilin, 1975), pointing to each option provides contextual support for the choice prior to full comprehension of the question form. By using alternate question forms, the shy or uncooperative child does not have the option of saying no, but can feel in control by choosing one of your options.

9. Match the child's pace; give the child time to think about his or her response (Pavelko & Owens, 2017).

10. Cue the child when it is his or her turn by using body language or via comments (Pavelko & Owens, 2017).

11. Use utterances that are, on average, slightly longer than the child's utterances. Keep the number of utterances per speaking turn to approximately the same number as the child's.

12. Match the length of the child's turn (Pavelko & Owens, 2017).

13. Learn to be comfortable with pauses in the conversation. If you are too quick to take a speaking turn in order to fill a pause, you deny the child the opportunity to take a turn. In addition, the child may come to expect you to fill pauses and thus feel no obligation toward continuing the conversation. If a pause becomes too long (longer than eight seconds), continue with parallel play and parallel talk until the child moves back into interactive conversation.

14. Do not be afraid to be silly and have fun. Many shy children have been brought into the interaction by asking silly, obvious questions (e.g., "Those are great shoes. Can I wear them?") or by making silly comments (e.g., "There's a mouse in your pocket!"). Enjoy the child and the child will enjoy the interaction.

Transcribing Language Samples

The next step in obtaining a language transcript for analysis is to transcribe the interaction recorded. Table 1.1 summarizes a number of conventions that are helpful in transcribing language samples obtained from videotape recordings, audiotape recordings, and real-time interactions. These conventions are adapted from Bloom and Lahey (1978).

Adult and child utterances can be transcribed in Standard English orthography except when utterances are unintelligible or when the child's approximation deviates substantially from expectations. Conventions for specifying the nonlinguistic or situational context are described, since this information is crucial for each analysis procedure delineated in *Guide*. When transcription from videotapes is not possible, audio recordings or real-time transcriptions may be used. However, it is important that you have made context notes during the interaction so that the situational context may be specified in the transcript.

For those who find transcription time-consuming, technology is available to shorten the time required to transcribe video- or audiotaped language samples. Remember that while your phone, tablet, or computer may have dictation capability, you will still need to enter some information (e.g., international phonetic alphabet [IPA] symbols, rising intonation symbols, etc.) by hand.

TABLE 1.1.

Transcription Conventions for Child Language Samples

Style Conventions

1. Fully transcribe all speech produced by the child and to the child (or within the child's auditory field) in Standard English orthography. Transcribe words that appear to function as one word for the child as one word (e.g., *lookit, alldone, goodnight*). (Note that in Bridget's transcript, *look it* is written as two words because there is evidence elsewhere in the transcript that she has productive control over *look* and *it*.)

   For adults, use Standard English segmentation. Whenever possible, transcribe unclear or mispronounced words using the International Phonetic Alphabet (IPA). Common familiar pronunciations, such as *ya* for *you*, *da* for *the*, and *'em* for *them*, need not be transcribed phonetically. Transcribe the child's utterances in the right-hand column and utterances produced by other speakers in the left-hand column. Place information about the situational context in the middle column and enclose it in parentheses. Identify individuals within the situational context by an initial (e.g., M for Mom, D for Dad, J for Jane).

	(M takes toy from boy and offers it to J)	
Look at this/		
	(J takes toy)	
		puppy/

2. Capitalize proper names within utterances. Do not capitalize the initial letter of a child utterance. The initial letter of an adult utterance typically is capitalized.
3. Place an action or event that occurs simultaneously with an adult or a child utterance on the same line as that utterance.

	(J banging cars together)	boom/
A new car/	(M handing car to J)	

4. When an utterance precedes or follows an action or event, transcribe the utterance on the preceding or succeeding line. When in doubt about the situational context, use separate lines for young children.

	(J eats cracker)	
		allgone/
		more cracker/
	(J reaches for bag)	

5. Different verb tenses should be used to describe situational context: Use the present progressive tense for simultaneous action; use the simple present tense for actions or events that precede or follow an utterance.

Punctuation Conventions

6. Use a slash (/) to punctuate an utterance boundary. The boundary is determined by length of pause before the next utterance and apparent terminal contour. Pauses greater than 2 seconds prior to the next utterance typically mark utterance boundaries, with or without rising or falling terminal contour. Specification of pauses of any length to mark utterance boundaries is viewed as secondary to other criteria.
7. When emphasis or exclamation is apparent, follow utterances by an adult with an exclamation mark and no slash. When a child utterance is exclamatory, it should be followed by both an exclamation mark and a slash.

Wow!	(J taking wheel off car)	
		there!/

TABLE 1.1. (*continued*)

8. Indicate adult questions with question marks. For child utterances, one of two procedures should be used:

    (1) For *wh-* questions, use a question mark and a slash.

	(J looking in bag)	where's da cracker?/

    (2) When a child utterance seems to be a question because of its rising intonation, use a rising arrow (↑) instead of a question mark and follow it with a slash.

	(J shaking empty bag)	no more in there↑/

    Even for a well-formed yes/no question (i.e., one with subject–verb inversion), use the arrow to indicate rising intonation, since it is more informative than a simple question mark.

	(J meeting K at door)	do you have cookies↑/

9. Use a dot (•) to indicate a pause of less than 2 seconds within an utterance.

	(J trying to fit wheel on car)	put • this one on/

10. Indicate a long pause either between speakers or between utterances of the same speaker by placing three horizontal dots in the context column. Only use this convention if the situational context remains the same.

	(J trying to get wheel on)	wheel go there/
	...	
	(J succeeds)	
		there!/

    If the situational context changes, indicate a long pause by placing three vertical dots in the context column.

	(J playing with blocks)	make a tower/
	•	
	•	
	•	
	(J running to bathroom)	potty/

11. Use a colon to indicate that an utterance or word is drawn out.

	(J trying to fit large peg into	no:/
	small hole)	

12. Use a curving arrow (↰) when there seems to be an utterance boundary but the utterance is drawn out, such as when the child is counting or listing.

	(J pointing to raisin)	one↰/
	(J touching next raisin)	two↰/
	(J touching next raisin)	three↰/

(*continues*)

TABLE 1.1. (continued)

13. Use stress marks to indicate strongly emphasized words.

Do you want this´ one?	(M giving J a blue crayon)	
		no!/
	(J reaching for red crayon)	that´ one/

14. An utterance should be followed by a falling arrow (↓) when it is important to emphasize the fact that the utterance has falling terminal contour.

	(J looking in box)	cow↓/
	(J pulls out cow)	
		cow↓/

15. Use a line (_____) to indicate an abrupt stop when the child interrupts him- or herself or when another speaker suddenly interrupts (either verbally or nonverbally) leaving the utterance unfinished.

Do you want some _____ /		
	(J picks up cup and spills milk)	

16. Use a self-correct symbol ($_{s/c}$) when the child interrupts himself or when another speaker interrupts to change or correct it.

Those are your $_{s/c}$ my cookies/		
		more cookie $_{s/c}$ cracker/

17. Use three Xs (XXX) to indicate an unintelligible utterance or a portion of an utterance. Whenever possible, use a phonetic transcription instead and, if possible, provide an interpretation in brackets.

	(J reaching for bag)	XXX/
	(J pointing to sky)	/ʌpə/ [airplane]

18. The following abbreviations may be used to indicate the manner in which an utterance was produced:

(lf) = laugh   (wh) = whisper
(cr) = cry   (wm) = whimper
(wn) = whine   (yl) = yell
(gr) = grunt   (sg) = sing

The abbreviation should follow the utterance in parentheses.

	(J holding finger to mouth)	she's sleeping/ (wh)

A sample transcript for a girl named Bridget has been provided (at the end of this chapter) to demonstrate the transcription conventions used in *Guide*. In addition, a blank transcription form is provided in Appendix A, found online at the *Guide Practice* website for convenient printing.

Numbering Language Transcripts

The final step in preparing language transcripts for analysis is to number the utterances. Each fully intelligible utterance to be analyzed should be assigned an utterance number. If an utterance is repeated with no intervening activity or utterance by the other speaker, the utterance is considered a repetition and does not receive an utterance number. In addition, totally or partially unintelligible utterances should not be assigned an utterance number. Finally, incomplete utterances resulting from self-interruptions or overlapping speakers are not assigned utterance numbers. The alternative would be to number all child utterances and exclude repetitions, unintelligible utterances, and incomplete utterances from analysis. The convention of not numbering these utterances has been selected to aid in managing the process of coding individual utterances and computing percentages.

Obviously, there may be times when a repetition or an incomplete utterance is erroneously assigned a number. If that happens, it should not be included in analysis. Utterances do not have to be renumbered; additional utterances should simply replace repetitions or incomplete utterances if additional sequential utterances are available following the original 100 utterances (i.e., add one or more lines to the transcript form and label the utterances as 101, 102, etc.). If replacement utterances are not available, percentage and mean computations must be adjusted to reflect the number eliminated from 100 utterances.

All analysis procedures described in *Guide to Analysis of Language Transcripts* are based on 100 child utterances. As previously discussed, there is considerable variability in the literature regarding the number of utterances recommended for analysis. While it may be difficult to obtain 100 utterances from children less than 2 years of age (Miller, 1981), for the purposes of the analysis procedures described in *Guide*, a minimum of 100 utterances collected under a variety of conditions has been judged necessary to capture the variability in performance present in spontaneous language. Utterance numbers appear handwritten on the sample transcripts to demonstrate the conventions for numbering described in *Guide*. The same conventions should be followed in numbering adult utterances for the pragmatic analyses described in Chapter 4. Although you may end up with more or less than 100 adult utterances, these surrounding adult utterances are important for interpreting the 100 child utterances.

One final word about transcribing of samples of children's productive language: Transcription is a time-consuming task that becomes easier and faster with practice. The validity of the analysis procedures that are applied to language transcripts is contingent upon the quality of the transcriptions. Therefore, an investment of time and energy in transcribing and numbering the utterances is necessary to ensure that quality transcripts are being used for analysis. The remaining three chapters present how to apply semantic, syntactic, and pragmatic analysis procedures following accurate transcription.

A sample transcript of a 28-month-old child (Bridget) follows as Form 1.1. Review the transcript to study the transcription conventions described in Table 1.1. Bridget's transcript will be analyzed throughout Chapters 2, 3, and 4, so it may be helpful to photocopy the transcript or print it from the *Guide Practice* website at this time.

Guide to Analysis of Language Transcripts

FORM 1.1

TRANSCRIPT (BRIDGET)

Name of Child	Bridget		Chronological Age	2-4
Type of Situation	free play in living room		Date	3-12
Length of Recording	1 hr 20 min	Length of Transcript	100 utterances	Time of Day 1:30 pm

Materials Present   circus set, dolls, doll buggy, tea set, kitchen set, toy telephone

People Present   M = Mom; B = Bridget (Bill, camera operator, & Kay, context transcriber)

	ADULT	CONTEXT	CHILD	
1	What happened to the lion?	(B trying to put lion on bar by tail)	/wƱp/ [whoops]	1
2	Did he get hurt?		fall down/	2
3	He did?	(B looks at M)	no/	3
4	What happened to him? What happened to him?		yes/	4
		(B reaches to lion)		
		(B pointing to tail of lion)	hurt his tail there/	5
			see*/	6
5	Uh-huh/	(B looking back)	XXX/ (If)	
			what else?/	7
6	What else? How about _____/			
7	Yes/	(B taking giraffe from box)	giraffe/	8
8	What is that?		giraffe/	9
9	That's right/	(B giving giraffe to M)		
10	What's that?		here/	10
11	Put him upside down too?		put upside down/	11
			yeah/	12

FORM 1.1

	ADULT	CONTEXT	CHILD	
12	Okay/	(B taking back giraffe and pointing to bar)	bar/	13
13	Up there/		here/	14
14	You do it/	(B tossing giraffe to M)		
15	Don't you want to do it honey?	(M holding out giraffe)	Mommy you do it/	15
16	You make him stand up here/	(B looks in box)		
17	You wanna see if he can go like this maybe/	(M placing giraffe; B watching M hold box)		
18	Oh/	(B looking in box)		
19	What else?		what else?/	16
20	Find something/	(B reaching in box)		
21	The monkey's right here/	(B pulls out two toys)	lookie in the box/	17
22	The monkey's right here/	(B looks where M points)	XXX/	
23	Find something/	(B looks back in box)	that's not enough/	18
			what else?/	19
24	Where did you put the elephant this morning? Where did you put the elephant this morning?	(B pulling toys out of the box and setting them on the floor)		
25	You were playing with him/			
26	Where is he?	(B scans the floor with her eyes)	he's not here/	20
27	Where did you put him?			
28	What?		I don't know/	21
29	Where did you put him?	(B pushes toys on the floor)		

FORM 1.1   TRANSCRIPT (BRIDGET)

ADULT	CONTEXT	CHILD	
30 Find him?		find him/	22
	(M pointing to picnic table)	where it is?/	23
		where that elephant go?/	24
31 I don't know/			
Did you put him in with —/			
32 Oh what's that?			
33 What's that over there?	(M points to a toy on other side of the room; B looks)		
34 Will you get it?		the elephant/	25
	(B stands up)		
	(B walks over and gets the elephant, brings it back to M)		
	(B holding legs of elephant)	stand up/	26
		legs/	27
		stand up/	28
35 Oh I think he might be too heavy/	(B stoops, stands up, stoops again to stand up elephant)		
36 Let's put another one of these up here/	(M pulling box around B and over to her)		
Let's put another one of these up here/	(B stands, pulls ladder from box)		
37 How does this work?		huh↑/	29
38 Do you know how this works?			
	(M attaches ladder)		
39 Like this?			
40 Oh okay/		yeah/	30
41 Put him up on top/	(B stooping)		
42 Is he too big?			
43 Up here/			
44 Put him up there/	(B sitting on floor holding toy)	you do it upside down/	31
45 Oh:/	(B putting elephant on ladder)		

FORM 1.1

ADULT	CONTEXT	CHILD	
46 There's another one/	(B pointing)	there's a elephant/ (lf)	32
47 Do you want to put him up there too?		no it's heavy/	33
48 Oh it's heavy/	(B wipes nose on shirt sleeve)		
49 Okay/			
50 Is he too heavy?	(M pointing to toys on floor)		
51 He's just a baby one/		yeah/	34
52 How about the circus man?	(B looking around floor)	where's another one?/	35
53 Woo: what happened here?	(B turns and kicks toy structure)		
54 What happened?	(M catching toy structure)		
55 You kicked him?		I kick 'im (lf)/	36
56 You know what you need?		yeah/	37
57 You need a Kleenex/	(M turns and brings back tissue)		
58 Can I help you?	(B reaching for tissue)	gimme/	38
	(B wipes nose and gives tissue to M)		
	(M wipes B's nose)		
59 Look/	(B turns head away)		
60 Let me see that/		ick/	39
61 Okay/	(B looking at hand)	owie/	40
62 What happened?			
63 Did you fall down?		owie/	41
	(B looks at M)		

(continues)

FORM 1.1   TRANSCRIPT (BRIDGET)

ADULT	CONTEXT	CHILD	
64 Oh:/	(B holding her own hand)	yeah/	42
65 How does it feel?			
66 It feels better/		pretty better/	43
67 Okay/	(B kisses finger)		
68 Can I kiss it too?			
	(B extends finger so M can kiss it)		
	(M kisses finger)		
69 Okay/			
	(B extends arms and pulls toy structure back into lap)		
	(M rebuilds structure)		
70 You wanna put 'em back up again?			
71 Let's put 'em back up again/			
72 You gonna make them fall down again?			
73 Why did you kick him?	(B watching M)	he fall/ (lf)	44
	(B elevates body and returns ot sit)		
74 Aw:/		I kick him/	45
	(B leans forward and with a wave of her hands, knocks the toy over)		
75 Is that funny?		fall down • boom/	46
76 You think so?		yeah/ (lf)	47
77 Are you done playing with this?		yeah/	48
78 Should we do something else?		yeah/	49
79 You want to take this man for a ride in the buggy?	(M pulls buggy over)		

FORM 1.1

ADULT	CONTEXT	CHILD	
80 You want to take him for a ride in the stroller?			
81 Hmm?	(B pulling buggy)	/sokə/ [stroller]	50
	(M stands bed up and moves toys away, then points to bed)		
82 Can you bring him over here and put him in bed?			
83 Okay/	(B places man in bed)	yeah/	51
		go to sleep/	52
		shh/	53
84 Shh/			
85 Did you give him a kiss and tell him good night?	(B bending over bed)	goodnight/	54
86 There he is/	(B points to bed and whispers to M)		
87 Is he tired? (wh)		yeah/ (wh)	55
	(B squeals as she turns man over)		
	(B lifts man out of bed)		
88 Oh you woke him up/	(B puts man in bed and touches nose with finger; M puts finger to her lips)		
89 Shh/			
90 What else should we do?	(B picks man up; M leans over her)	I wake him up/ (yl)	56
What else should we do?			
91 How about having some coffee?	(B puts man in bed)		
92 Should we go get some coffee?			
93 Will you go get me a cup of coffee please in your kitchen?	(M pushing aside toys)		
94 Can you go get me a cup of coffee in your kitchen?			

GETTING STARTED WITH *GUIDE*

FORM 1.1   TRANSCRIPT (BRIDGET)   FORM 1.1

ADULT	CONTEXT	CHILD		ADULT	CONTEXT	CHILD	
95 I want some coffee/				117 Can I have a plate please?		welcome/	63
96 Can I have some coffee?	(B stands up and walks to kitchen)			118 I want to eat something too/	(B reaching for a plate)	okay/	64
97 Oh I'll have some milk too/		all right/	57			here's yours/	65
98 What's that?				119 This is mine?			
99 Who makes the milk?		cow/	58	120 What about yours?			
100 Who makes the milk?		huh↑/	59	121 Do you want some too?			
101 Woo:/					(B puts pot down on cabinet and moves dishes around)	/wʌzət/ else?/ [what else?]	66
102 The dishes are dirty/						else/	67
103 Yeah but I want to have some coffee/	(B picking up a ball and turning toward camera)	there's a ball↑/	60			else/	
	(B walking with ball and milk carton in hand)	d•d•d•dere's a ball/	61	122 Bridget?			
		dere's a ball/		123 You mean those?			
104 Okay come on/				124 The other ones are over there/			
105 Let's have some coffee/				125 Huh•uh-oh•	(B walking, banging pot and cup together)	huh↑/	68
106 Come on/				126 You're going to give some coffee to Bill and Kay?			
107 Come on Bridget/				127 Is that what you're going to do?			
108 Can I have a cup of coffee please?				128 Let's sit down and have some first okay?	(B walking back to M)	yeah/	69
109 Here's the milk/				129 You sit down okay?			
110 Get me a cup of coffee/	(B moves hands in air and walks back to cabinet)			130 Sit down/	(B sits down)		
111 You have one too/				131 Tastes good			
112 Okay?	(B stooping at cabinet and pulling out a cup)	this yours/	62	132 How does yours taste?			
113 Okay here's mine/	(M extends arm)			133 How does yours s/c yes please/		more↑/	70
114 Thank you/				134 Thank you/	(B pours from pot into M's cup)		
115 Can I get a plate too?	(B holds teapot in position to pour into cup and hands cup to M)			135 You want some more?	(B standing up, extending arm toward camera, but Bill just winks and continues filming)	Bill/	71
116 Thank you very much/							

©2019 by PRO-ED, Inc.

(continues)

FORM 1.1

TRANSCRIPT (BRIDGET)

ADULT	CONTEXT	CHILD	
136 I think Bill's full/		take 'em Bill/	72
137 I don't think he's hungry/		take 'em Bill/	73
138 I don't think he's hungry/	(B sitting down)	huh↑/	74
139 But I'd like some more please/			
	(M places her cup on floor in front of B, then B pours from her cup to M's cup)		
140 How does yours taste?		taste good/	75
141 Does it taste good?	(B hitting her cup against her foot)	yeah/	76
142 What else?			
143 Does it taste delicious too?		yeah/	77
144 Could I have some cookies please?			
Could I have some cookies please?	(B shaking head back and forth)	no cookies/	78
145 Hmm?		allgone/	79
146 Are they?		yeah/	80
147 Who ate them?			
Who ate them?			
148 Who ate the cookies?		somebody ate the cookies/	81
	(B claps pot and cup together, then takes a drink from cup)		
150 Can I have a piece of toast please?	(B shakes head and drops pot and cup)		
151 There's some in there/	(M points to cabinet)		
152 See it?	(B looks toward cabinet)		

FORM 1.1

ADULT	CONTEXT	CHILD	
153 Get some toast please/	(B crawls to cabinet)		
	(B takes something from cabinet and looks toward M)		
154 Uh-huh/		XXX/	82
	(B stands and walks to M)	okay/	83
		way up here/	84
		plate/	
155 A plate/			
156 Oh/			
157 Oh you're going to give me toast on a plate/	(M extends plate)		
158 Can I have one piece please?			
159 Thank you/	(B turns her plate over M's plate)		
160 Tastes good/	(M tastes "toast")		
161 Could I have some peanut butter on it?		yeah/	85
162 Will you put some peanut butter on it?	(B waves her plate near M's "toast")		
163 Please?	(B drops plate)		
164 Here put some peanut butter on my toast/	(B takes "toast" from M, puts hand in mouth, then behind her back)		
165 Oh you ate mine/			
166 You ate mine/	(B giggles and then points to mouth)		
167 Oh give me that/	(B points to mouth again)	ate mine/	86

GETTING STARTED WITH *GUIDE*

FORM 1.1   TRANSCRIPT (BRIDGET)

ADULT	CONTEXT	CHILD		ADULT	CONTEXT	CHILD	
168 Oh/				186 Want to talk on the telephone?			
169 I'm going to eat up your tummy/				187 I think I'll play with the other telephone/		yeah/	95
170 A rum rum rum/	(B walks toward M, extends her tummy)			188 You want to talk on the phone/?			
171 A rum rum rum/	(B backs off and returns)			189 Here you sit down and I'll get it/			
172 I see it/	(B holding M's head to tummy, talking to camera)	look at it/	87	190 I'll get it/	(B turns around; M stands up)		
173 A rum rum rum/		look at it/	88	191 Uh-oh!	(B walks over to M)		
174 A rum rum rum/		look it Bill/	89	192 Where did it go?		what happened?/	96
175 A rum rum rum/		look it Bill/	90	193 Here it is/		in that box/	97
176 Want me to eat you all up?	(B releases M's head and puts hand on tummy)			194 I found it/	(M picks up phone)		
177 Would you like me to eat you all up?		huh↑/	91	195 There/			
178 Why?		yeah/	92	196 You want to talk?			
179 Why?	(B walks to M's face, tummy extended)			197 Why don't you call Grandma?	(M puts phone on floor)		
				198 Turn around/	(B sits on floor)		
180 Why would you like me to eat you up?				199 Call up Grandma?	(B picks up receiver)		
181 Hmm?				200 Dial first/	(B dials phone)	hello/	98
182 What are you doing now?	(B lies on floor and holds toy)					Grandma here/	99
183 Hmm?					(B holds out phone to M)	you talk/	100
184 What are you doing now?							
185 Let's see here/	(B getting up)	telephone/	93				
		telephone/	94				

©2019 by PRO-ED, Inc.

CHAPTER 2
Semantic ANALYSIS

Introduction

Semantic analysis of language transcripts provides valuable information for determining the developmental level of children with potential language delays. A variety of procedures are appropriate, including analysis of individual semantic roles (Bloom, 1973; Nelson, 1973; Retherford, Schwartz, & Chapman, 1981), analysis of prevalent semantic relations (Brown, 1973), and analysis of vocabulary diversity (Templin, 1957). Most of these analyses are based on data obtained from transcripts of children who are typically developing, interacting with their mothers. While these procedures have not been standardized, results of semantic analysis may support other judgments regarding the presence of language delays, including syntactic and pragmatic analysis results. In addition, semantic analysis procedures yield data that are crucial for developing intervention goals and objectives.

The following analysis procedures have been selected on the basis of clinical relevance. The majority of the procedures are appropriate for use with children who produce utterances primarily between one and three words in length. The type-token ratio (Templin, 1957), however, is applicable for children up to 8 years of age. The procedures delineated in this chapter have been selected to work in conjunction with each other, resulting in a complete analysis of the semantic content of a child's productions. Each procedure may also be used separately to provide an analysis of a single aspect of the semantic content. All procedures are described in detail with directions and examples, and all procedures are demonstrated using Bridget's transcript from Chapter 1.

When analyzing the semantic content of child language transcripts, an important distinction must be made between the referential and the relational aspects of the child's productions, since analysis of these two aspects yields different results. *Referential analysis* describes the child's use of individual words to refer to objects or classes of objects and events in the environment. *Relational analysis* describes the meaning relationships expressed by words in relation to aspects of objects or events in the environment, or by words in relation to other words. This distinction can be seen in the difference between the child's use of a word to label (or refer to) an object in the environment (e.g., "ball") versus the child's use of a word to describe the relationship between a previous situation and a current situation (e.g., "All gone" after eating a cookie) or two object labels in combination to describe the relationship between the two objects in the environment (e.g., "Daddy ball"). This chapter examines five types of analysis procedures: (1) Bloom's one-word utterance types, (2) Nelson's one-word utterance types, (3) Retherford et al.'s semantic roles, (4) Brown's prevalent semantic relations, and (5) Templin's type-token ratio. These analysis procedures are organized by the length of the utterances being analyzed.

Analyzing the Semantic Content of One-Word Utterances

When children are predominantly using one-word utterances (i.e., more than 50% of their utterances are one word in length), it is appropriate to analyze the semantic content of the utterances. The first step, then, is to identify the prevalence of one-word utterances in the transcript. To analyze the semantic content, two different procedures can be used: (1) a categorization of one-word utterance types described by Bloom in 1973, and (2) a classification scheme provided by Nelson, also in 1973. While both types of analyses are appropriate for use with productions one word in length, each provides slightly different information. Each will be considered in detail before examining the differences in results.

Bloom's One-Word Utterance Types

Bloom's (1973) categorization scheme describes the three types of words that children use in their one-word utterances. The first type is a **substantive word**. A **substantive word** refers to a generic object or event, like *ball* or *cookie* or *chair*. At times, children refer to particular objects or events, and these words are part of the second type: **naming words**. The child might use a **naming word** to refer to a family pet, parents, siblings, or other important people in the environment.

It is important to be familiar with the names of significant people and animals in the child's environment before attempting to categorize the child's utterances as either of these two types. The third type of word in Bloom's categorization scheme is a **function word**. **Function words** refer to conditions shared by many objects or events and make reference across classes of objects or events. A word like *up* is not just a direction; it may refer to the desired relationship between a child, and a parent or it may describe the location of an object in relation to another object. A word like *more* does not only refer to an object but also indicates the recurrence, or desired recurrence, of an object. By describing the child's use of these three types of one-word utterances, we can build a picture of how the child uses words to convey meanings.

A few typical one-word utterances are provided in Example 2.1 for practice in using Bloom's categorization scheme before attempting to categorize Bridget's utterances. Cover the right side of the page with a sheet of paper, categorize each example utterance, and then check your answers with those provided in the shaded section. An explanation for each utterance is included to help clear up any discrepancies.

EXAMPLE 2.1

BLOOM'S ANALYSIS

(C picks up toy horse) horsie/	**SUBSTANTIVE WORD** This utterance refers to a real or pretend object.
(C hears door opening) Dada/	**NAMING WORD** This utterance refers to a particular person, the child's father.
(C reaches for cup on table) cup/	**SUBSTANTIVE WORD** This utterance labels an object.
(C picks up car with no wheels) broke/	**FUNCTION WORD** This utterance does not label an object, but refers to its condition.
(dog barking in background) Dee Dee/	**NAMING WORD** This utterance refers to the family pet and names it. Remember, it is important to be familiar with the names of significant people and animals in the child's environment before attempting to categorize the child's utterances.
(C takes a drink from cup) juice/	**SUBSTANTIVE WORD** This utterance provides a label for the liquid refreshment.
(M says, "Where is that shoe?"; C points to chest of drawers and says) there/	**FUNCTION WORD** This utterance refers to the condition or location of an object.

EXAMPLE 2.1 (*continued*)

(C points to picture of a baby in picture book) baby/	**SUBSTANTIVE WORD** This utterance provides a generic label for a person.
(C points to self in mirror) Baby/	**NAMING WORD** Here, the child is referring to himself, not just labeling a baby. The nonlinguistic context is crucial for making judgments like this. If the child had been labeling the object, the utterance would have been categorized as a **substantive word**.
(C picks up music box an looks at M) no/	**FUNCTION WORD** While it is impossible to determine the type of negation being expressed without the additional nonlinguistic context, various types of negation are coded in this way to make reference across classes of objects or events.
(C carries cup to sink while holding it out for more juice) drink/	**SUBSTANTIVE WORD** Again, the nonlinguisitc context is crucial for differentiating the labeling of the liquid refreshment from the description of an activity. In the second case, the utterance would have been categorized as a **function** word.

At this point, the one-word utterances in the sample transcript need to be identified and categorized. Using Bridget's transcript from Chapter 1 and Bloom's One-Word Utterance Types Analysis form, put each one-word utterance into the appropriate column on the form. If a particular word occurs more than once, tally additional instances of that word next to the original recording (e.g., ball ℍ𝕀𝕀𝕀 means the word ball occurred nine times in the transcript). After you finish, check your analysis against Form 2.1.

CALCULATING THE RESULTS—BLOOM'S ONE-WORD UTTERANCE TYPES

Following the identification of each one-word utterance and the categorization of each one-word utterance into one of Bloom's (1973) three categories, you can calculate the frequency of occurrence of each type. Proceed as follows:

1. Count the number of words in each column, including additional instances of each word, and put the total for each type in the blank space provided. (Keep in mind that short phrases such as *goodnight*, *allright*, and *allgone* are listed as one word because they typically function as such for children this age.)
2. Add all instances to obtain the total number of one-word utterances and write that number in the blank provided. Double-check this number by returning to the transcript and counting the one-word utterances.
3. Return to each one-word utterance type and compute the percentage of total one-word utterances accounted for by each type. This is accomplished by dividing the number of instances of the type by the total number of one-word utterances, using the fourth decimal place to round up or down to the nearest thousandth, and multiplying that number by 100.
4. Determine the percentage of total utterances accounted for by one-word utterances. Do this by dividing the total number of one-word utterances by the total number of utterances.

In the sample transcript, there were 11 substantive words, which, when divided by 52 total one-word utterances, yields .2115. After rounding this off to .212 and multiplying by 100 to convert to a percentage, this means that 21.2% of the one-word utterances were categorized as **substantive words**. (See Form 2.1 and note

FORM 2.1　　　　　　　　Name of Child __Bridget__

BLOOM'S ONE-WORD UTTERANCE TYPES ANALYSIS

Substantive Words	Naming Words	Function Words
giraffe l	Bill	whoops
bar		no
legs		yes
owie l		see
stroller		here l
cow		yeah |||| |||| ||||	
plate		huh ||||
telephone l		gimme
		ick
		shh
		goodnight
		allright
		welcome
		okay l
		else
		more
		allgone
		hello

Although "shh" does not have syllable structure, it clearly carries semantic content. Bloom probably would not have included this as a word, but it now appears in dictionaries and so is counted here.

__11__　　Substantive Words = __21.2__ %　　of Total One-Word Utterances

__1__　　Naming Words = __1.9__ %　　of Total One-Word Utterances

__40__　　Function Words = __76.9__ %　　of Total One-Word Utterances

Total Number of One-Word Utterances __52__

Total Number of Utterances __100__

% of Total One-Word Utterances __52__

where this number is filled in on the analysis form.) One instance of a **naming word** divided by 52 yields 1.9%. There were 40 **function words**, which, when divided by 52 total one-word utterances, yields 76.9% of the one-word utterances. Finally, divide the total number of one-word utterances (52) by the total number of utterances (100), which yields 52%. This means that 52% of Bridget's total utterances were one word in length.

But look again at Bloom's function-word category on the completed analysis form (see Form 2.1). The most striking thing about the words listed is the preponderance of the word *yeah*. A look at each function word listed reveals that there are several variations of yes/no responses and many routine responses (e.g., *hello, goodnight, welcome*). These types of responses can be called *conversational devices* and *communication routines* respectively (and are presented in detail later in this chapter). If these responses are eliminated, six words are left, one of which occurs twice. (Those are checked ✔ on the adjusted analysis form [Form 2.2]). This changes the total number of one-word utterances to 19 and the individual computations to 57.9% substantive words (11 substantive words divided by 19 one-word utterances), 5.3% naming words (1 naming word divided by 19 one-word utterances), and 36.8% function words (7 function words divided by 19 one-word utterances). Exclusion of certain one-word utterances from the analysis may appear to be an arbitrary decision; however, an examination of Bloom's examples of function words will indicate that this is an appropriate decision. Finally, the percentage of total utterances accounted for by one-word utterance types must be calculated. In the sample transcript, there were 19 one-word utterances, which, when divided by 100 total utterances, reveals that 19% of the total utterances were one-word utterance types, allowing for the exclusion of conversational devices and communication routines.

INTERPRETATION OF RESULTS—BLOOM'S ONE-WORD UTTERANCE TYPES

Now the results of the semantic analysis can be interpreted. To begin, note that only 19% of Bridget's total utterances were one word in length. This indicates that more than half of the child's utterances with semantic content in this sample were longer than one word in length. At this cursory level, one might suspect that the child is beyond the one-word stage. Thus, it could be concluded that the child's lexicon exceeds 50 words (Bloom, 1973), because a child's lexicon containing less than 50 words would have a greater percentage of total utterances accounted for by one-word utterances, even after exclusions. Consequently, the analysis of one-word utterance types may not be the most important analysis regarding this particular child's semantic abilities.

However, we can draw some conclusions about the types of words used. Note that Bridget used more substantive words than either function or naming words. Various authors have described the proportion of one-word utterances accounted for by various types of one-word utterances. Some authors contend that the first 50-word lexicon is composed primarily of nouns, or in this categorization scheme, substantive or naming words (Benedict, 1979; Gleitman, Gleitman, & Shipley, 1972; Huttenlocher, 1974; McNeill, 1970). Only later in the one-word stage do children add function words. That Bridget uses more substantive words would suggest that she is in an early stage of language production.

On the other hand, Bloom, Lightbown, and Hood (1975) described a nominal–pronominal continuum in children at the one-word utterance stage. Children whose one-word utterances refer predominately to nouns are considered to be on the nominal end of the continuum. Children whose one-word utterances refer predominately to nouns but are in the pronominal form (e.g., *this, it, that*) and to relations between objects and events are considered to be on the pronominal end of the continuum. This apparent tendency is reported to persist into the preschool years (Horgan, 1979). From Bridget's transcript, one may conclude that, with regard to this particular sample, this child tends to be predominately nominal. In addition, considering that 19% of the total utterances were one-word in length, one may conclude that this child has progressed beyond a simple labeling stage and is cognizant of the functional relations that exist between objects and events.

More data are necessary to substantiate this hypothesis. For example, would this same distribution occur in another transcript from this child obtained under variations in the conditions described in Chapter 1? This example points out the need for multiple samples of the child's productions. Overall, the results of this analysis indicate that examination of more diverse aspects of the child's productions is necessary to accurately assess the child's semantic abilities.

FORM 2.2   Name of Child ___Bridget___

BLOOM'S ONE-WORD UTTERANCE TYPES ANALYSIS—ADJUSTED

Substantive Words	Naming Words	Function Words
giraffe l	Bill	~~whoops~~
bar		~~no~~
legs		~~yes~~
owie l		see ✓
stroller		here l ✓
cow		~~yeah llll llll llll l~~
plate		~~huh llll~~
telephone l		gimme ✓
		~~ick~~
		~~shh~~
		~~goodnight~~
		~~allright~~
		~~welcome~~
		~~okay l~~
		else ✓
		more ✓
		allgone ✓
		~~hello~~

Although "shh" does not have syllable structure, it clearly carries semantic content. Bloom probably would not have included this as a word, but it now appears in dictionaries and so is counted here.

___11___   Substantive Words = ___~~21.2~~ 57.9___ %   of Total One-Word Utterances

___1___   Naming Words = ___~~1.9~~ 5.3___ %   of Total One-Word Utterances

___~~40~~ 7___   Function Words = ___~~76.9~~ 36.8___ %   of Total One-Word Utterances

Total Number of One-Word Utterances   ___~~52~~ 19___

Total Number of Utterances   ___100___

% of Total One-Word Utterances   ___~~52~~ 19___

Nelson's One-Word Utterance Types

The second categorization of one-word utterances that we use was developed by Nelson (1973) to describe the first 50-word lexicons of children approximately 18 months of age. The five categories that Nelson used to analyze one-word utterances are listed and defined in Figure 2.1.

Nelson's (1973) data were obtained from diary accounts of children's productions that were analyzed to provide a frequency distribution of five categories. When using Nelson's One-Word Utterance Type analysis, one-word utterances produced in a 100-utterance language transcript are used. Such an analysis procedure may not be appropriate for language transcripts, but we completed it for Bridget's transcript for the purpose of demonstrating Nelson's analysis. Thus, data from the Bridget's transcript cannot be compared directly to Nelson's data; only diary accounts of the productions of a child being assessed can be compared directly to Nelson's normative data.

Miller (1981) described a format for obtaining diary accounts from parents. Miller's description includes directions to parents regarding the format for what to record, what contextual information to specify, and when to collect data. Concerns regarding accuracy of recording will always exist, but diary accounts can be very helpful in obtaining samples from children at the one-word stage.

One-word utterances are provided for practice (in Example 2.2) before attempting to categorize the utterances in the sample transcript. As before, cover the right side of the page, categorize each example utterance, and then check your categorizations with those provided in the shaded section. The explanations may help clear up discrepancies. As shown in Example 2.2, some of the same practice examples used for Bloom's categories are also used for Nelson's, along with a few new ones.

The translation of utterances previously coded using Bloom's one-word utterance types into Nelson's categorization scheme is fairly straightforward. The category posing the greatest difficulty is probably that of function words. In the practice examples, the types of words coded function words using Bloom's coding scheme were quite different from those coded as function words using Nelson's coding scheme. Bloom's function words were more closely aligned with Nelson's modifiers, although some of Bloom's **function words** overlap with Nelson's **personal-social words** category, and others overlap with Nelson's **action word**s category. Keeping that in mind, return to the one-word utterances identified and categorized for Bridget's transcript using Bloom's One-Word Utterance Types Analysis form. This time, code them on the Nelson's One-Word Utterance Types Analysis form. Put each one-word utterance in the appropriate column. Again, if a particular word occurs more than once in the transcript, tally additional instances next to the original recording of the word. After you finish, check your analysis against Form 2.3.

(Text continues on p. 32.)

---

1. **Nominal:**
   - **Specific nominal:** Word used to refer to a particular instance of a person, an animal, or an object (e.g., *Mama, Bill*).
   - **General nominal:** Word used to refer to a general instance of an object, a substance (e.g., *snow*), an animal, a person (including pronouns), an abstraction (e.g., *birthday*), a letter, or a number.
2. **Action words:** Words used to refer to an action through a description (e.g., *bye-bye, go*), an expression of attention (e.g., *look, see*), or a demand for attention (e.g., *up, out*).
3. **Modifiers:** Words used to refer to a property or quality of a thing or an event, including expressions of recurrence, disappearance, attribution, location, and possession (e.g., *there, little, pretty*).
4. **Personal-social words:** Words used to express an affective state (e.g., *want, feel*) or a social relationship (e.g., *please, thank you, yes, no*).
5. **Function words:** Words used to fulfill a grammatical function (e.g., *what, where, is, for*).

FIGURE 2.1. One-word utterance types.

EXAMPLE 2.2

NELSON'S ANALYSIS	
(C picks up toy horse) horsie/	**GENERAL NOMINAL** This utterance refers to a real or pretend animal.
(C hears door opening) Dada/	**SPECIFIC NOMINAL** This utterance refers to a particular person.
(C reaches for cup on table) cup/	**GENERAL NOMINAL** Again, this is an example of a general instance of an object.
(C picks up car with no wheels) broke/	**MODIFIER** This utterance describes the quality of the car.
(C reaches up to M, who has entered bedroom) up/	**ACTION WORD** This utterance provides a description of an action or a request for an action. In either event, it is coded **action** word.
(dog barking in background) Dee Dee/	**SPECIFIC NOMINAL** Since Dee Dee is the family pet, this is an example of a particular instance of an animal.
(C takes a drink from cup) juice/	**GENERAL NOMINAL** This utterance refers to a substance that is general in nature.
(M says, "Where is that shoe?"; C points to chest of drawers and says) there/	**MODIFIER** This utterance describes the location of something and therefore refers to a property of that object.
(C points to picture of a baby in picture book) baby/	**GENERAL NOMINAL** This child's utterance provides a general label for a person.
(C points to self in mirror) Baby/	**SPECIFIC NOMINAL** It is important to know that this child refers to himself, but no one else, as "baby" to determine that this is an example of a particular baby.
(C picks up music box and looks at M) no/	**MODIFIER** This particular utterance refers to the previous prohibition of an object; therefore, it is coded **modifier**. If the context had revealed that the child was responding to a question (e.g., "Do you want to go night-night?"), the utterance would have been coded personal-social word.
(C carries cup to sink while holding it out for more juice) drink/	**GENERAL NOMINAL OR ACTION WORD** Depending on the nonlinguistic context for the next utterance, this utterance could be referring to a general substance (**general nominal**) or to an activity (**action word**). The next utterance by the mom would determine how to code this utterance, presuming she accurately interprets the child's intent.
(C holds up larger half of cookie) big/	**MODIFIER** This utterance describes a property (attribute) of an object.
(M says, "What do you say?" as she holds out cookie; C says) please/	**PERSONAL-SOCIAL WORD** This utterance reflects a convention used in social relationships.
(clock on wall makes buzzing sound and C looks at M) what?/	**FUNCTION WORD** This utterance fulfills the grammatical function of requesting the label for something.

FORM 2.3   Name of Child __Bridget__

NELSON'S ONE-WORD UTTERANCE TYPES ANALYSIS

Specific Nominals	General Nominals	Action Words	Modifiers	Personal-Social Words	Function Words
Bill	giraffe I	whoops	here I	no	huh IIII
	bar	see	ick	yes	shh
	legs	gimme	more	yeah IIII	else
	owie I		allgone	IIII IIII I	
	stroller			goodnight	
	cow			allright	
	plate			welcome	
	telephone I			okay I	
				hello	

__1__	Specific Nominals = __1.9__	% of Total One-Word Utterances
__11__	General Nominals = __21.2__	% of Total One-Word Utterances
__3__	Action Words = __5.8__	% of Total One-Word Utterances
__5__	Modifiers = __9.6__	% of Total One-Word Utterances
__25__	Personal-Social Words = __48.1__	% of Total One-Word Utterances
__7__	Function Words = __13.5__	% of Total One-Word Utterances

Total Number of One-Word Utterances __52__

Total Number of Utterances __100__

% of Total One-Word Utterances __52__

CALCULATING THE RESULTS—NELSON'S ONE-WORD UTTERANCE TYPES

Once again, the frequency of occurrence of each one-word utterance type needs to be calculated. Proceed as follows:

1. Count the number of words in each column and write that number in the blank space provided.
2. Add all instances to obtain the total number of one-word utterances, and write that number in the blank provided. Double-check this number by returning to the transcript and counting the one-word utterances.
3. Return to each one-word utterance type and compute the percentage of total one-word utterances accounted for by each type. Do this by dividing the number of instances of the type by the total number of one-word utterances, using the fourth decimal place to round up or down to the nearest thousandth, and multiplying that number by 100.
4. Determine the percentage of total utterances accounted for by one-word utterances. Do this by dividing the total number of one-word utterances by the total number of utterances.

Nelson specified that yes/no responses (conversational devices) and routine responses (communication routines) should be included. Consequently, there is no need to adjust for such one-word utterances and to re-compute percentages as we did for Bloom's analysis of one-word utterance types.

In the sample transcript, there were 11 **general nominals**, which, when divided by 52 total one-word utterances, yields .2115. After rounding this off and multiplying by 100 to convert to a percentage, this means that 21.2% of the one-word utterances were categorized as **general nominals**. One instance of a **specific nominal** divided by 52 yields 1.9%. There were three **action words**, which, when divided by 52 total one-word utterances, yields 5.8% of the one-word utterances. Five **modifiers** divided by 52 yields 9.6%. Twenty-five **personal-social words** divided by 52 yields 48.1%. There were seven **function words**, which, when divided by 52, yields 13.5% of the one-word utterances. Again, the final step is to determine the percentage of total utterances accounted for by one-word utterances: Divide 52 by 100 total utterances, then multiply by 100 to obtain 52%.

Unlike Bloom's categorization scheme, normative data on the frequency of occurrence of Nelson's categories are available. Figure 2.2 indicates the percentage of the child's first 50 words accounted for by each of Nelson's categories.

Keep in mind that Nelson's data are based on the percentage of the child's first 50 words accounted for by type. In other words, one word might have been used in 50% of all word attempts, yet in Nelson's data, it would contribute only 2% to a type category (i.e., 1 divided by 50 equals 2%). Data from Bridget's language sample are based on percentages of how often a word type appeared in a sample of 100 utterances. Thus, it is not possible to compare these results directly to Nelson's data. To compare Nelson's normative data directly, a diary account of the first 50 words Bridget produced would be needed. As previously mentioned, it may be productive to obtain diary accounts using Miller's (1981) procedures.

INTERPRETATION OF RESULTS—NELSON'S ONE-WORD UTTERANCE TYPES

So how are our data to be interpreted? Cautiously. If one erroneously compared Bridget's frequency data directly to Nelson's data, the distribution would be quite different. One might conclude that the sample is too

---

Nominals
- **Specific** 14%
- **General** 51%

Action words 14%

Modifiers 9%

Personal-social words 9%

Function words 4%

FIGURE 2.2. Percentage of first 50 words accounted for by Nelson's (1973) one-word utterance types.

limited and that diary analysis is needed. However, what the analysis does reveal is that approximately half the utterances were longer than one word in length, warranting not a diary analysis but an analysis of the semantic content of the longer utterances.

In addition, the sample data can be considered in relation to a continuum similar to the nominal–pronominal continuum described by Bloom et al. (1975). Nelson referred to this continuum as a *referential–expressive continuum*. Children whose first 50-word lexicons consisted of a high percentage of **nominals** were considered to be referential. In contrast, children whose first 50-word lexicons consisted of a high percentage of **personal-social words** and/or **function words** were considered to be expressive.

Again, these early preferences for word types used may reflect different strategies for communicating and appear to persist beyond the one-word stage. From the sample transcript, it would be reasonable to conclude that Bridget is an expressive child since 61.6% of her one-word utterances were **personal-social words** and **function words**. Overall, the best judgment from the analysis performed would be to pursue additional analysis of more diverse aspects of the semantic content of Bridget's productions. As previously stated, Nelson's data were obtained from diary accounts and represent a first 50-word lexicon, but the data from Bridget's transcript represent a single 100-utterance sampling; therefore, a comparison of the two data sets would be like comparing apples to oranges. Nelson's categories are, however, helpful in analyzing children's first 50-word lexicons and can be useful in documenting changes in one-word utterance types over time. It is because a large number of Bridget's utterances in this 100-utterance sample are longer than one word that analysis of more diverse aspects of semantic content is warranted.

Because these one-word utterance analysis procedures do not result in scores or percentages unequivocally indicating the presence of delays, these procedures (and many of those that follow) must be considered as aspects of diagnostic therapy. That is, conclusions rarely can be drawn from a single sampling of the child's productions. Samplings obtained under a variety of conditions over time, as in the course of diagnostic therapy, yield the most valuable results. This is not stated to advocate postponement of a decision, but rather to emphasize that these procedures must be considered as part of the ongoing process of hypothesis generation and testing through continuously obtaining additional data.

Comparison of Bloom's and Nelson's One-Word Utterance Types

Bloom's and Nelson's one-word utterance types are similar in some ways and different in others. Analysis of one-word utterances using Bloom's categories revealed the previously mentioned distinction between referential and relational aspects of semantic content. Bloom's **substantive words** and **naming words** categories characterize a child's use of words to refer to specific and general instances of objects, people, and events, or to *referential* aspects of semantic content. Bloom's **function words** capture the child's emerging ability to make note of the relations between objects and events. In fact, Bloom contends that a child's early two-word utterances grow out of greater explicitness in noting the relations between objects and events (e.g., "more" later becomes "more juice" or "more milk" as the context requires greater explicitness and as the child sees greater efficiency in the use of the longer utterance).

On the other hand, Nelson's categories appear to reflect a quasi-grammatical function of individual words. Nelson's categories more closely parallel a part-of-speech classification scheme beyond the individual meaning roles expressed, and they include routine forms. While more referential in nature than Bloom's scheme, Nelson's scheme may capture the transition toward two-word utterances as well as Bloom's scheme does. At the stage that a child's vocabulary includes approximately 50 words, Nelson contends that nouns, or **nominals**, account for between 50% and 65% of the words. The child's vocabulary may be considered predominately referential. Later, words for describing actions increase (Leonard, 1976). These more verb-like words parallel Nelson's **action words**. Then, words to describe attributes, locatives, and possessors of objects (Nelson's **modifiers**) increase. It is about this time that two-word utterances emerge. Consequently, the transition to two-word utterances may be predicted more accurately with Nelson's categorization scheme. Overall, when using either Bloom's or Nelson's one-word utterance types, if analysis of one-word utterances reveals approximately half or more of the utterances to be longer than one word in length, analysis of more diverse aspects of semantic content is warranted.

Analyzing the Semantic Content of One-Word and Multiword Utterances

We address two procedures to use to analyze the semantic content of one-word and multiword utterances: (1) semantic roles analysis (Retherford et al., 1981) and (2) prevalent semantic relations analysis (Brown, 1973). Both procedures are based on semantic coding of all utterances within a production transcript. The first procedure employs a set of categories delineated by Retherford et al. (1981). Analysis of the frequency of occurrence of individual semantic roles within multiterm relations yields data interpretable as characteristic of children in Brown's Stage I versus Stages II–III of linguistic development. The second procedure is based on the same semantic coding of one-word and multiword utterances but results in an analysis of frequently occurring multiterm combinations. Data are then compared to reported frequencies of occurrence of Brown's (1973) Prevalent Semantic Relations. Again, it is possible to identify combinations that are characteristic of children in Brown's Stage I versus those in Stage II–III.

Semantic Roles

The 20 semantic roles described in Table 2.1 are used to code children's utterances in Brown's (1973) Stages I and II–III. Included in this categorization scheme are semantic roles that correspond to those contained within Brown's (1973) eight Prevalent Semantic Relations, as well as categories that parallel those relations he specified as occurring with low frequency. In addition, many of the categories overlap with categories delineated by Greenfield and Smith (1976) for coding one-word utterances and by Bloom (1973) and Schlesinger (1971) for coding one-word and multiword utterances.

Detailed descriptions of nonlinguistic context, as described in Chapter 1, are crucial for determining the relational meanings expressed by children in the early stages of language acquisition. Many of the definitions in Table 2.1 rely heavily on the nonlinguistic context for successful interpretation and coding.

The first step in semantically coding one-word and multiword utterances is to become familiar with the definitions and examples of the 20 semantic roles provided in Table 2.1. Not all utterances are "codable" using these semantic roles. The content of such utterances is explained later in this chapter using four broad categories: *conversational device, communication routine, complex utterance,* and *other.*

For most utterances, the relationship between major semantic roles will be easily identifiable. In utterances longer than two semantic roles, some semantic roles are considered an expansion of one of the major roles in the semantic relation. Typically, these are expansions of the **agent** or **object** as described by Brown (1973). When a semantic role is an expansion of one of the major roles in the semantic relation, it may be helpful to set it off with parentheses to indicate this relationship. For example, the utterance "big boy jump" could be coded **(attribute) agent-action**, indicating that **agent-action** is the major semantic relation and **attribute** is an expansion of the **agent** in that relation. This is an optional coding scheme that some users may find helpful; however, we do not use it in Guide. Instead, all roles are separated by hyphens.

The occurrence of grammatical morphemes—including number, tense, modal, and auxiliary aspects of the verb system; catenative verbs; articles; plural and possessive inflections; and prepositions—are coded within the semantic category of the major semantic role. For example, "is jumping" is coded as **action**, as are "jumped," "can jump," and "jumps." An utterance containing "the doll" is coded **entity**, unless it is in relationship with an **action**, when it becomes the **agent**. In the utterance "Daddy's hat," "Daddy's" is coded **possessor**. The entire utterance "in the bed" is coded **locative**. Thus, semantic roles may encompass more than one word and must be viewed as units of meaning not directly translated by single words. Examples of the use of this convention—using one semantic role for more than one word—are provided in Example 2.3.

A few other coding conventions need to be highlighted to assist in coding. As with aspects of the auxiliary system, separable, or two-part, action verbs are coded **action**. Separable verbs that should be coded in this manner include *pick up, put away, get out, put down, put on, stand up, eat up, call up, put in, pull out, put back, turn over, sit down, fall down,* and *go back.* **Locative** is used with separable verbs only when the location is mentioned (e.g., "Mama sit down here"). Verbs typically coded **state** include *want, need, like, taste, wish, hurt, matter with, have on, smell, feel, fit,* and *hope. See* and *look* are coded **state** except when they occur at the beginning of an imperative pointing out something (e.g., "See the doggie?" meaning, "Look at the doggie"). A few of verbs that might be

TABLE 2.1.

20 Semantic Roles (and Residual Grammatical Categories)

Individual Semantic Roles

The following 15 semantic roles are used for coding semantic content of mother (adult) and child speech. Additional content may be coded more appropriately using one of the five residual grammatical categories, which follow these definitions and mother–child examples. If those codes are not appropriate, an utterance may be coded as *conversational device* or *communication routine* (described in Table 2.2, on pages 44–45), or as *complex* or *other* (see discussion in Chapter 2).

ACTION — A perceivable movement or activity engaged in by an agent (animate or inanimate).
- Mother: Can *you hit* the ball? (M addressing C)
- Child: *Sit down.* (C plops her standing bear into a sitting position)

LOCATIVE — The place where an object or action is located or toward which it moves.
- Mother: Put the flower *there.* (in response to C's query about where to set a flower)
- Child: Cookies *in bowl.* (C pulling bowl away from M)
- Child: *Doctor.* (in response to M's question of where to take a broken doll)
- Child: Jason *work.* (in response to M's question of where Jason is)

AGENT — The performer (animate or inanimate) of an action. Body parts and vehicles, when used in conjunction with action verbs, are coded *agent*.
- Mother: *I'll* push you. (C sitting in wagon)
- Child: *You* kiss bunny. (C holding stuffed bunny out to M)
- Mother: That *car* went fast.

OBJECT — A person or thing (marked by the use of a noun or pronoun) that receives the force of an action.
- Mother: Let's put away your *books.* (M and C reading books together)
- Child: Jet chases the *squirrel.* (M and C watching the dog [Jet] chasing a squirrel)

DEMONSTRATIVE — The use of demonstrative pronouns or adjectives—*this, that, these, those,* and the words *there, here,* as well as *see* and *look* when stated for the purpose of pointing out a particular referent.
- Mother: *That* big tree? (M pointing to a tree in the park)
- Child: *There* are five girls. (in response to M's query about how many girls are in C's class)
- Child: See *this?* (C holding up a picture she made)

RECURRENCE — A request for or comment on an additional instance or amount, the resumption of an event, or the reappearance of a person or an object.
- Mother: *Another* bubble. (M suggesting C blow more bubbles)
- Child: One *more* cat, Daddy. (C putting second toy cat into the toy box)

POSSESSOR — A person or thing (marked by the use of a proper noun or pronoun) that an object is associated with or to which it belongs, at least temporarily.
- Mother: Get *baby*'s blanket. (M reaching for a blanket)
- Child: *My* tower fall down. (M and C playing with blocks)
- Child: This bone is *for the dog.* (C holding up a doggie biscuit)

However, the use of the possessive pronoun *mine* in utterances like "That's mine" is unlike other possessive pronouns that don't really change in form when sentence position changes (e.g., *your* →*yours*). *My* becomes *mine;* thus the child views *mine* as a different word, not a form of *my*.z

(continues)

TABLE 2.1. (*continued*)

QUANTIFIER	A modifier that indicates amount or number of a person or an object. Prearticles and indefinite pronouns such as *a piece of, lots of, any, every*, and *each* are included.
	Mother: There sure are *a lot of* bunnies in the yard. (M referring to rabbits crossing the backyard)
	Child: *Five* toes. (C holding doll's hand and tapping its toes)
EXPERIENCER	Someone or something that undergoes a given experience or mental state. This category often implies involuntary behavior on the part of the *experiencer*, in contrast to voluntary action performed by an *agent*. When used in conjunction with state verbs, body parts and vehicles, for example, are coded *experiencer*.
	Mother: *I'd* like to see Elmo, please. (M referring to characters C is playing with)
	Child: *She* feels sick. (C hands baby doll to M)
	Child: My *finger* hurts. (C holds finger up to M to examine)
RECIPIENT	One who receives or is named as the recipient of an *object* (person or thing) from another. Often the word "to" is present.
	Dad: Can you sing "Twinkle, Twinkle" *to her*? (D and C playing with a doll)
	Child: Give *me*. (C putting stickers in a book)
BENEFICIARY	One who benefits from or is named as the beneficiary of a specified action. Often the word "for" is present.
	Dad: I put jelly on it *for you*. (D hands a piece of bread to C)
	Child: Color it *for me*. (C hands a coloring page to M)
COMITATIVE	One who accompanies or participates with an agent in carrying out a specified activity. Often the word "with" is present or implied.
	Mother: Come *with mommy*. (M standing, extending hand)
	Child: I go *mommy*. (D puts C in car seat; C stretches out arms, requesting to go with M)
CREATED OBJECT	Something created by a specific activity; for example, a song by singing, a house by building, or a picture by drawing.
	Mother: Can you make *a snake*? (M and C playing with clay)
	Child: Make *worm*. (same as above)
INSTRUMENT	Something an agent uses to carry out or complete a specified action.
	Dad: Don't color on the table *with that black pen*. (C writing on the table)
	Child: Paint *with puff paint*. (D helping C make a picture for Grandma)
STATE	A passive condition experienced by a person or object. This category often implies involuntary behavior on the part of the *experiencer*, in contrast to voluntary action performed by an *agent*.
	Mother: Would you *like* a chocolate cookie? (M and C playing with tea set)
	Child: She *feels* better. (C kisses stuffed bear and hands to M)

Residual Grammatical Categories

Five additional categories are used to code semantic content for utterances not classified as conversational devices or communication routines when none of the preceding individual semantic roles fit. (Although Retherford et al. felt it was more appropriate to label these "grammatical categories," throughout much of the discussion in text, these are included in one broad category—the 20 semantic roles—and not referred to separately as the individual semantic roles and the residual grammatical categories.)

TABLE 2.1. (continued)

ENTITY (one-term)	Any labeling of a present person or object regardless of the occurrence or nature of action being performed on or by it. To be coded as a one-term *entity*, the utterance must contain only one semantic role or grammatical category. The utterance may contain more than one word. Mother: *The Puppy.* (M and C looking at picture) Child: *Fishy.* (M and C looking in fish tank) Child: *3.* (C pointing to number on block)
ENTITY (multiterm)	The use of an appropriate label for a person or an object in the absence of any action on it (with the exception of showing, pointing, touching, or grasping); or someone or something that causes or is the stimulus to the internal state specified by a state verb; or any object or person that is modified by a possessive form. *Entity* is used to code a possession if it meets any of the preceding criteria. The code *multiterm entity* is used whenever an utterance contains more than the *entity* category. There is no substantial difference between the two categories in terms of meaning. That is, each category describes a person or an object in the absence of action on it or by it. You would not code an utterance as a *multiterm entity* if the utterance includes action. The only difference between the two categories is their occurrence in relation to other semantic roles and categories. Mother: Dirty *puppy.* (M looking at puppy footprints on floor) Child: There's *a bear.* (C pointing to toy bear)
NEGATION	The expression of any of the following meanings with regard to someone or something, or an action or state: nonexistence, rejection, cessation, denial, disappearance. Mother: I *didn't* have any eggs. (M and C playing with tea set) Child: *No* cookies. (C holding up empty bag)
ATTRIBUTE	An adjectival description of the size, shape, or quality of an object or person; also, noun adjuncts that modify nouns for a similar purpose (e.g., gingerbread man). Excluded are the semantically coded categories of *recurrence* and *quantifier*. Dad: Where's the *big* one? (D and C stacking blocks) Child: *Little* block. (same as above)
ADVERBIAL	A modifier of an action indicating time, manner, duration, distance, or frequency. (Direction or place of action is coded separately as *locative*; repetition is coded as *recurrence*.) Mother: You can color it *the next time.* (M puts away coloring book, against C's protest) Child: *Now* go. (C pushing next toy car in line)
	Also, a modifier indicating time, manner, quality, or intensity of a state, including predicate adjectives. Dad: They've got their cuddly pajamas on *today.* (D holds up dolls to show the soft pajamas) Child: I'm *full.* (C puts spoon down and looks at D)

Note. Adapted from "Semantic Roles in Mother & Child Speech: Who Tunes Into Whom?" by K. Retherford, B. Schwartz, and R. Chapman, 1981, *Journal of Child Language, 8*, pp. 583–608. © 1981 by Cambridge University Press.

EXAMPLE 2.3

SEMANTIC ROLES	
(C is pointing to picture in book) doggie jump/	**AGENT-ACTION** In this example, *doggie* is the **agent** of the **action**, *jump*.
(C is pointing to picture in book) the doggie is jumping/	**AGENT-ACTION** The semantic code for this utterance is the same as that for the preceding utterance. Articles and auxiliary verbs are not assigned a separate semantic role; they are collapsed within the major role.
(M says, "What happened?" while pointing to picture) the boy kicked the ball/	**AGENT-ACTION-OBJECT** In this example, *the boy* is the **agent** of the **action**, *kicked*, on the object, *the ball*. Again, articles are not assigned a separate semantic role.
(M says, "What happened?" while pointing to picture) that boy kick/	**DEMONSTRATIVE-AGENT-ACTION** The word *that* is a **demonstrative** indicating which **agent**, *boy*, is engaged in the **action**, *kick*.
(C reaches for wind-up rabbit) more jump/	**RECURRENCE-ACTION** In this example, *more* reflects **recurrence** of the **action**, *jump*.

considered part of the **state** verb category are coded **action** because of their relation to specific intentional verbs also coded **action**: *forget* (*remember*), *stay* (*leave*), *know* (*think*). When *being* is used as a main verb, as in "You are being silly," it is also coded **action**; otherwise forms of *be* are coded **state** (e.g., "They are funny"). The main verb *have* is coded **state** when it implies possession, but coded **action** in contexts in which an action verb synonym could be substituted (e.g., "What did you have for lunch?"). Changes in the state of an **experiencer**, where context makes the change clear, are coded **action**; the **experiencer** or **agent**, in these cases, is coded **agent**. For example, "I go night-night," as the child moves to the bedroom, is coded **agent-action-locative**. In this coding scheme, an **agent** or **experiencer** can be either animate or inanimate. Thus, "The truck hit the wall" would be coded **agent-action-object** and "The truck feels so sad" would be coded **experiencer-state-quantifier-adverbial**.

The examples in Table 2.1 can be helpful in determining the semantic role that individual words play in an utterance, but coding an entire utterance may be more difficult. Therefore, the following examples of fully coded utterances are provided for practice. Cover the right side of the page, and code the utterances on the left. Check your codings with those provided in the shaded section. The explanations should help clear up any discrepancies.

The preceding examples demonstrated the semantic roles that typically combine with the semantic role **action**. In addition, major semantic roles and expansions of major semantic roles were demonstrated. Remember that semantic roles may encompass more than one word and must be viewed as units of meaning, not directly translated by single words.

The practice utterances shown in Example 2.4 examine the use of another major semantic role, **locative**. Cover the right side of the page and code the examples.

Example 2.4 demonstrates variations in the use of the semantic role **locative**. They show how more than one word can be coded with only one semantic role. They also show how utterances with similar meaning are coded differently with the presence of an additional word(s). Now, for some practice with other semantic roles, cover the right side of Example 2.5. Then code the practice utterances.

The examples clearly point out the different relationship between major semantic relations and expansions of those major semantic roles. It is important to keep in mind the circumstances that account for a

EXAMPLE 2.4

ADDITIONAL SEMANTIC ROLES

(C drops spoon in toy cup) spoon in/	**MULTITERM ENTITY-LOCATIVE** In this example, the *spoon* is a **multiterm entity** situated *in* (**locative**) something.
(M asks, "Where is that spoon?") the spoon in the cup/	**MULTITERM ENTITY-LOCATIVE** The semantic coding for this utterance is the same as that for the preceding utterance for two reasons: First, as previously mentioned, articles are considered part of the major semantic relation. Second, *in the cup* and *in* both describe the location of the spoon and thus are coded **locative**.
(M says, "Tell me about this," pointing to picture) the spoon is in the cup/	**EXPERIENCER-STATE-LOCATIVE** Although the overall meaning of this example is similar to that of the previous two examples, one striking difference is in the use of the copula, or main verb, *is*. In this example, the semantic role **state** is used to reflect the use of the state verb. Consequently, the **entity** becomes an **experiencer**. Ultimately, this utterance translates: *the spoon* (**experiencer**) *is* in the state (**state**) of being located *in the cup* (**locative**).
(C points to spoons in a coffee pot) two spoon there/	**QUANTIFIER-MULTITERM ENTITY-LOCATIVE** *Two* (**quantifier**) indicates the number of the **multiterm entity**, *spoon*, located (**locative**) somewhere, *there*.
(C points to chair) sit down Mama/	**ACTION-MULTITERM ENTITY** In this example, the separable verb, *sit down*, is coded **action**. Note that since the location is not mentioned, the semantic role **locative** is not used.

semantic role being used as a major role in one instance and not in another. Typically, if an **attribute**, **possessor**, **recurrence**, or **demonstrative** is used alone with an **entity**, then each role is considered a major role. If, however, an action appears in the semantic relation, then the **attribute, possessor, recurrence,** or **demonstrative** becomes an expansion of the **agent** or **object**. In addition, a demonstrative form used with an action verb will always be coded **agent** or **object** to reflect the major semantic role.

There are some exceptions to these circumstances; they are demonstrated in Example 2.6. Cover the right side of the page and code the examples.

These examples demonstrate the use of semantic roles and categories that can be used in combination with **entities** or **agents** and **actions**, as well as the use of the **adverbial** category. Perhaps more importantly, the preceding practice items show the exceptions to the rule for determining when a semantic role is a major role or an expansion of a major role. In the preceding examples, each semantic role is considered to be a major role regardless of the presence of other semantic roles. **Negation** and **adverbial** are always considered to be major semantic roles, regardless of the presence of other semantic roles, as are **agent, object, experiencer, action, state**, and **locative**.

There are some additional coding categories that are always considered to be major roles, but they occur less frequently than the aforementioned categories. Example 2.7 shows semantic coding using some of these less frequently occurring semantic roles.

EXAMPLE 2.5

ADDITIONAL SEMANTIC ROLES	
(C points to picture in book) big baby/	**ATTRIBUTE-MULTITERM ENTITY** Here, *big* is an **attribute** of the **multiterm entity**, *baby*.
(C points to next picture) big baby cry/	**ATTRIBUTE-AGENT-ACTION** With the use of the **action** verb, *cry*, the baby becomes an **agent** of that **action**. In addition, now that a major semantic relation is expressed by the roles **agent** and **action** in combination, the **attribute**, *big*, becomes an expansion of the major role, **agent**.
(C pulls baby doll away from M) my baby/	**POSSESSOR-MULTITERM ENTITY** In this example, the use of the pronoun, *my*, reflects the **possessor** of the **multiterm entity**, *baby*.
(C holds up sock) this mine/	**DEMONSTRATIVE-POSSESSOR** In this example, *this* is a **demonstrative** and the pronoun, *mine*, is the **possessor**.
(C rocking baby doll in arms) my baby cry/	**POSSESSOR-AGENT-ACTION** With the use of the **action** verb, *cry*, *baby* becomes an **agent**, and the **possessor** role (for *my*) becomes an expansion of the **agent**.
(C pulls tiny doll out of bag) another baby/	**RECURRENCE-MULTITERM ENTITY** The word *another* reflects an additional instance (**recurrence**) of the **multiterm entity**, *baby*.
(C hears baby crying in another room) another baby cry/	**RECURRENCE-AGENT-ACTION** Once again, the use of the **action** verb, *cry*, changes *baby* into an **agent**, and the role of **recurrence** (for *another*) becomes an expansion of the **agent**. Recurrence typically is a major role when forms of it occur in two-term utterances in conjunction with a **multiterm entity** or an **action**. When the role of **recurrence** describes an **agent** or an **object** in a relationship with an **action**, it is not considered a major role, but an expansion of a major role.
(M says, "What should we take to the other room?") that baby/	**DEMONSTRATIVE-MULTITERM ENTITY** The demonstrative pronoun, *that*, points out a particular instance of the **multiterm entity**, *baby*.
that baby cry/	**DEMONSTRATIVE-AGENT-ACTION** Here the **demonstrative** role becomes an expansion of the **agent** with the addition of the **action**, *cry*.

Example 2.7 contains some of the infrequently occurring semantic roles. Even though those roles may not occur in every transcript, it is important to be able to recognize them when they do occur. In addition, infrequently occurring roles' changes in frequency of use over time may provide valuable diagnostic information. This is discussed in more detail in the section Interpretation of Results Obtained Using Semantic Roles Analysis.

Question forms also can be coded using the preceding semantic roles. Questions are treated like any other utterance. However, before coding the question, turn it into a statement (e.g., "What is that?" becomes "That is what"). Then, according to context, assign the semantic role of the *wh-* word in the question using the following semantic roles:

    one-term entity, multiterm entity, object, or **created object** for *what*
    action for *what doing*
    locative for *where*

EXAMPLE 2.6

ADDITIONAL SEMANTIC ROLES	
(C looks in bag where tiny dolls had been) no baby/	**NEGATION-MULTITERM ENTITY** The word *no* is an example of nonexistence, which is a type of **negation**. Here, it refers to the nonexistence of the **multiterm entity**, *baby*.
(baby in other room stops crying) no cry/	**NEGATION-ACTION** Here the word *no* refers to the lack of cessation (a type of **negation**) of the **action** *cry*.
(baby in other room stops crying) baby no cry/	**AGENT-NEGATION-ACTION** Now *baby* is the **agent** of the **action**, *cry*, but the use of the word *no* relates to the entire semantic relation. Thus, **negation** is considered a major semantic role.
(M is changing C's sister's diaper) baby wet/	**MULTITERM ENTITY-ADVERBIAL** The word *wet* describes the quality of the state the **multiterm entity**, *baby*, is in. The state verb does not have to be present to use the **adverbial** role.
(C hands doll to M) baby is wet/	**EXPERIENCER-STATE-ADVERBIAL** However, as can be seen in this example, the **state** (in this case, *is*) can be present. And when the **state** is specified (in this case using the **adverbial** *wet*), the entity (*baby*) becomes an **experiencer**.
(C runs into M's arms) run fast/	**ACTION-ADVERBIAL** The word *fast* describes the manner (**adverbial**) in which the **action**, *run*, is performed.
(M and C looking at book) I can run fast/	**AGENT-ACTION-ADVERBIAL** Now there is an **agent**, *I*, performing an **action**, *can run*, in a particular manner, *fast* (**adverbial**). Note that the modal verb *can* is coded **action** along with the main verb *run*.

    quantifier for *how many*
    adverbial for *how, how long,* and *when*
    attribute or **demonstrative** for *which*
    agent, experiencer, one-term entity, or **multiterm entity** for *who*
    attribute for *what kind of*

Keep in mind that presence of forms of the verb *to be* as a copula must be reflected in the semantic coding as **state**. Auxiliary verbs are coded with the main verb using the **action** category. Remember to check (✔) the Question column on the coding form (Semantic Roles Coding) whenever a question is coded using one of the 20 semantic roles, because the coding of the utterances may not reflect the question form. Example 2.8 demonstrates coding question forms using the semantic roles just specified.

Question forms are quite simple once you get used to thinking in terms of semantic roles and not in words. Again, remember to indicate when a question form is coded by checking (✔) the Question column on the coding form. As can be seen in the preceding examples, once the question is semantically coded, it may be difficult to tell that the original utterance was in the form of a question. In the final analysis of semantic roles and relations, it is important to be able to differentiate question forms from other utterances because some comparison data exclude question forms from analysis.

The next step is to progress through Bridget's transcript and determine the appropriate combination of semantic roles for each utterance. Record the utterance number and semantic code for each utterance on the

EXAMPLE 2.7

ADDITIONAL SEMANTIC ROLES	
(M and C are making cookies) I stir with spoon/	**AGENT-ACTION-INSTRUMENT** The pronoun, *I*, is the **agent** of the **action**, *stir*, with the **instrument**, *spoon*.
(C addressing M while the clinician, Anna, looks on) give Anna the cookies/	**ACTION-RECIPIENT-OBJECT** The **action**, *give*, refers to an **object**, *the cookies*, presented to a **recipient**, *Anna*. **Recipients** receive the object of an **action**.
(M and C are making clay cookies) the cookies are for Anna/	**EXPERIENCER-STATE-BENEFICIARY** *The cookies* (**experiencer**) are in the **state** of being, *are*, for *Anna* (**beneficiary**).
(C looking in the toy bag) there is a doggie/	**DEMONSTRATIVE-STATE-MULTITERM ENTITY** The **demonstrative** pronoun, *there*, is in the **state** of being, *is*. Although used in conjunction with the **state** verb, *is*, *doggie* is the object of the sentence rather than the subject and so is coded **multiterm entity** rather than **experiencer**.
(C crumbles clay on top of clay cookies) make chocolate-chip cookies/	**ACTION-ATTRIBUTE-CREATED OBJECT** The **action**, *make*, creates *the chocolate-chip* (**attribute**) *cookies* (**created object**).
(C turns to M, who is rocking baby) make cookies with me/	**ACTION-CREATED OBJECT-COMITATIVE** The **action**, *make*, creates the *cookies* (**created object**) and the **agent** (who is not specified) is to participate *with* the child, *me* (**comitative**).

Semantic Roles Coding form. If the utterance is a question, put a check (✔) in the Question column to differentiate it from nonquestions. For utterances that do not appear to be codable using the 20 semantic roles, record the utterance number but leave the Semantic Coding column blank. These utterances can be characterized using four additional categories—conversational devices, communication routines, complex utterances, and other—which are discussed later in the chapter. Those utterances that can be semantically coded with what has been discussed so far are shown in Form 2.4.

Typically, there are three reasons that an utterance is not semantically codable using the 20 semantic roles: (1) the utterance is a conversational device that may have been acquired as a whole unit rather than as individual roles; (2) the utterance is a communication routine that also may have been acquired as a whole unit, and semantically coding it may inflate the semantic complexity of the child's productions; or (3) the utterance is complex, requiring syntactic categories to reflect the complexity. If the utterance is still not codable, it can be coded as **other**. Identifying conversational devices and communication routines may be easier than semantically coding the utterances. The types of conversational devices and communication routines frequently occurring in child language transcripts are captured in Table 2.2.

Appropriately identifying utterances labeled as **complex** may be more difficult than identifying conversational devices and communication routines. The decision to identify an utterance as **complex** when completing the semantic analysis is based on the presence of parallel semantic roles or categories within the same utterance. That is, it is not possible to have two **agents**, **actions**, **entities**, or **objects** within the same utterance. If an utterance contains more than one of any type of major semantic role, the utterance is probably **complex**. (However, it could just be coded incorrectly.) This judgment of semantic complexity may be different than the judgment made when completing the syntactic analysis. In other words, an utterance could be classified

EXAMPLE 2.8

ADDITIONAL SEMANTIC ROLES

(clock in room buzzes; C looks up from toy) what that?/	**MULTITERM ENTITY-DEMONSTRATIVE** In this example, the word *what* is querying the semantic role of **multiterm entity**. It is querying the semantic role of a particular **entity**, *that* (**demonstrative**).
(C digs in toy box) where's the ball?/	**LOCATIVE-STATE-EXPERIENCER** The *wh-* word, *where*, is asking where (**locative**) the **experiencer**, *the ball*, *is* (**state**). The order of the words in the question was reversed to make the statement "the ball is where," so *the ball* is an **experiencer** of the **state** verb, *is*.
(C and M looking at book) what him doing?/	**AGENT-ACTION** Here the semantic role being queried is **action**. The child *is* using the *what doing* form to query the **action** of the **agent**, *him*.
(C and M looking at book) what are they doing?/	**AGENT-ACTION** Again, the semantic role being queried is **action**. The child is using the *what doing* form to get a label for the **action** *they* (**agent**) are engaged in. The auxiliary verb, *are*, is part of that **action**.
(C hears talking in the hallway) who that?/	**MULTITERM ENTITY-DEMONSTRATIVE** In this case, it is impossible to know if *who* is an **agent** or a **multiterm entity**, so the more neutral **multiterm entity** is used. A particular **entity** is being requested: *that* (**demonstrative**) entity.
(C, holding bag of marbles, looks at M) how many you got?/	**QUANTIFIER-EXPERIENCER-STATE** Here the semantic role being queried is **quantifier**. The child is using the **quantifier** to ask his mother, *you* (**experiencer**), *how many* marbles she's *got* (**state**). Because this is a question, the sentence form reverses to *you got how many* to explain why *you* is an **experiencer**.
(C putting pretend bandage on M's arm) how that feels?/	**ADVERBIAL-DEMONSTRATIVE-STATE** The child is asking for a description of the quality or intensity (**adverbial**) of his mother's **state**, *feels*, for a particular bandage, *that* (**demonstrative**) bandage.
(C and M are playing with model cars on a real track) what kinda car you driving?/	**ATTRIBUTE-OBJECT-AGENT-ACTION** The child is seeking a description, *what kinda* (**attribute**), of the *car* (**object**) that the mother, *you* (**agent**), is *driving* (**action**).

TABLE 2.2

Conversational Devices and Communication Routines

Conversational Devices

The following categories are used to code utterances and parts of utterances that are not codable using the 20 semantic roles. These categories reflect pragmatic conventions governing conversation, rather than semantic intentions.

Attention Use of an individual's name to gain attention.
  Mother: Abigail! (M calling C, who is climbing on sofa)
  Child: Mama! (M dressing C while talking to another adult)

Yes/No Response Use of affirmative (or negative) terms or tags to assert that a previous utterance or behavior is correct (or incorrect) to indicate compliance with a request (or refusal of a request) made in a previous utterance.
  Mother: Okay. (following C's request for assistance in putting puzzle together)
  Child: No. (in response to M's query if C wants a cracker)

Positive Evaluation Use of positive terms to evaluate an utterance or behavior of the other speaker.
  Mother: Right. (C manipulating puzzle, fits piece in correctly)
  Child: Very good. (M places block on top of stack and C responds)

Interjection Use of words like *um, oh*, and the like to hold a speaking turn and/or as a searching strategy for a conversational contribution.
  Mother: Oh. (following C's affirmative response to M's question of activity)
  Child: Um. (C looking at M, who has just queried C about doll's name)

Polite Form Use of terms like *please, thank you*, and the like in absence of other semantic content (e.g., "Please help me" = adverbial-action-object).
  Mother: Thank you. (C pouring M an imaginary cup of coffee)
  Child: Pretty please. (M offers imaginary plate of cookies to C)

Repetition Request Use of terms like *what, huh*, and the like to request repetition of another speaker's utterance.
  Mother: What? (C describing toy people's activities)
  Child: Hmm? (following M's question)

Accompaniment Use of *there* (in the absence of pointing or directional/locational intent), *there you go*, or *here* to accompany an action by one speaker.
  Mother: There you go. (C attempting to wrap herself in blanket, finally succeeds)
  Child: There. (C giving doll to M)

Communication Routines

The following categories are used to code utterances not codable using the 20 semantic roles (and residual grammatical categories). These communication categories are used to characterize utterances expressing typically occurring routinized forms.

Animal Utterances used to engage in routines about animal sounds and behaviors. Also use of animal sounds with no referent present. When animal sounds are used to label an animal, the residual grammatical entity category is used.
  Mother: The cow says, "Moo." (M and C playing with toy farm)
  Child: Moo. (same as above; C previously labeled toy cow appropriately)
  Child: Moo. (no referent present; C pretending to be cow)

Story/Song/Poem Utterances that consist of all or part of story text, songs, nursery rhymes, or poems.

TABLE 2.2. (*continued*)

	Mother: Where is Thumbkin? Where is Thumbkin? (M and C singing along with finger play)
	Child: Here I am. (same as above)
Counting/Alphabet	Utterances that consist of rote counting or recitation of all or part of alphabet. When context indicates counting of referents or labeling/identifying letters, the residual grammatical category **entity** (one term) is used.
	Mother: A, B, C, D. (M singing, no referent present)
	Child: One, two, three. (no referent present)
Greeting	Use of greeting and leave-taking forms reflecting adherence to routines, rather than semantic intent.
	Mother: How are you? (M and C talking on toy telephone)
	Child: Bye-bye. (C waving to M)
Say *x*	Requests for the other speaker to repeat specific information. Be sure *say* isn't being used to mean "pretend" or "suppose."
	Mother: Say I'm sorry, Eugene. (following scolding C for pulling cat's tail)
	Child: Say good morning. (C picking up doll from baby bed)
Sounds Accompanying	Noises and/or sounds used to replicate noises/sounds of vehicles or objects.
	Mother: Whoops! (toy monkey falls off trapeze)
	Child: Vroom. (C moving toy car back and forth on floor)
Name	Routine forms requesting or specifying the name of something or someone.
	Mother: What's your name? (M speaking to doll C is holding)
	Child: My name is Kiki. (C talking on telephone)

as **complex** for the semantic analysis, but the same utterance would not necessarily be assigned a stage for complex sentence development when completing the syntactic analysis. The following examples of child utterances labeled **complex** may be helpful:

doggie barked and barked/	complex
doggie bite and I cried/	complex
I want the one what's big/	complex
my shoes and pants are dirty/	complex
'cuz he jumped/	complex

When complex utterances occur in a transcript, **complex** is written on the coding line of the Semantic Roles Coding form. This permits efficient identification of the number of semantically complex utterances occurring in a transcript. Identification and analysis of semantically complex utterances is completed in the syntactic analysis of a transcript (the topic of Chapter 3) according to slightly different criteria.

Finally, utterances with ambiguous semantic content, or those that do not fit appropriately in any other category, should be coded **other**. **Other** should be reserved for peculiar utterances and used rarely, as in this example:

Mother: Okay. (M and C putting paintbrushes into jars and mixing paint)

Mother: Let's pick one color to paint with.

Child: Yeah.

(*Text continues on p. 48.*)

Guide to Analysis of Language Transcripts

FORM 2.4 Name of Child __Bridget__

SEMANTIC ROLES CODING

Utterance Number	Semantic Coding	Question
1		
2	Action	
3		
4		
5	State-Possessor-Multiterm Entity-Locative	
6	Demonstrative	✓
7	Multiterm Entity-Recurrence	✓
8	One-Term Entity	
9	One-Term Entity	
10		
11	Action-Adverbial	
12		
13	Locative	
14	Locative	
15	Agent-Action	
16	Multiterm Entity-Recurrence	✓
17	Action-Locative	
18	Demonstrative-State-Negation-Quantifier	
19	Multiterm Entity-Recurrence	✓
20	Experiencer-State-Negation-Locative	
21	Agent-Negation-Action	
22	Action-Object	
23	Locative-Experiencer-State	✓
24	Locative-Demonstrative-Experiencer-State	✓
25	One-Term Entity	

FORM 2.4

SEMANTIC ROLES CODING (continued)

Utterance Number	Semantic Coding	Question
26	Action	
27	One-Term Entity	
28	Action	
29		
30		
31	Agent-Action-Object-Adverbial	
32	Demonstrative-State-Multiterm Entity	
33	Experiencer-State-Adverbial	
34		
35	Locative-State-Recurrence-Experiencer	✓
36	Agent-Action-Object	
37		
38	Action	
39		
40	One-Term Entity	
41	One-Term Entity	
42	Attribute-Adverbial	
43	Agent-Action	
44		
45	Agent-Action-Object	
46	Action	
47		
48		
49		
50	One-Term Entity	

The form of this utterance doesn't indicate that the Recipient role is fully realized; "gimme" is often used as a one-word utterance.

Semantic Analysis

FORM 2.4

SEMANTIC ROLES CODING (continued)

Utterance Number	Semantic Coding	Question
51		
52		
53		
54		
55		
56	Agent–Action–Object	
57		
58	One-Term Entity	
59		
60	Demonstrative–State–Multiterm Entity	✓
61	Demonstrative–State–Multiterm Entity	
62	Demonstrative–Possessor	
63		
64		
65	Demonstrative–State–Possessor	
66	Multiterm Entity–Recurrence	✓
67	Recurrence	
68		
69		
70	Recurrence	✓
71		
72	Action–Object	
73	Action–Object	
74		
75	State–Adverbial	

FORM 2.4

SEMANTIC ROLES CODING (continued)

Utterance Number	Semantic Coding	Question
76		
77		
78	Negation–Multiterm Entity	
79	Negation	
80		
81	Agent–Action–Object	
82		
83	Adverbial–Locative	
84	One-Term Entity	
85		
86	Action–Possessor	
87	Action–Object	
88	Action–Object	
89	Action–Object	
90	Action–Object	
91		
92		
93	One-Term Entity	
94	One-Term Entity	
95		
96	Object–Action	✓
97	Locative–Demonstrative	
98		
99	Multiterm Entity–Locative	
100	Agent–Action	

(continues)

> Mother: Hmm. (M looking at each jar of paint)
>
> Child: What.
>
> Mother: Which color should I choose?

In this example, the child's production of "what" is not to get the type of semantic information typically obtained from a *what* question. Neither is it a request for a repetition of a previous utterance. It appears to be functioning as a request for clarification of Mom's "hmm" and therefore is more pragmatic in its function.

One more convention in coding utterances needs to be discussed. This is the convention used for utterances that have semantic content and are codable using the 20 semantic roles, but that also contain a conversational device or a conjunction. For example, in the utterance "Mommy, big truck," the child is requesting the mother's attention and commenting on a big truck. The procedure used in this case is to indicate that a conversational device (CD) was used by recording CD in parentheses prior to the semantic code for the comment. The coding for this utterance would be (CD) **attribute-multiterm entity**. The CD category is **attention**.

Communication routines (CR) rarely occur within the context of a semantically codable utterance, because the communication routine is rarely tagged onto an utterance like a conversational device is. Conversational routines tend to be embedded into an utterance and then typically end up being coded as a **created object**. For example, "One, two, three" said without counting some objects would be a counting routine. But if the child said, "I can count: one, two, three," the utterance would be coded **agent-action-created object**.

Now, from the coding form used earlier, identify the utterances that were left blank and the parts of utterances you didn't know how to code. Determine whether each is a **conversational device** or a **communication routine**, a **complex** utterance, or **other** and mark it appropriately. Then check your answers with those on Form 2.5. (Note that for learning purposes, each CD or CR coded is followed in parentheses by the type of CD or CR.) In addition, practice exercises for semantic roles analysis can be found in the *Guide Practice* web-based program.

CALCULATING THE RESULTS—SEMANTIC ROLES ANALYSIS

Following the semantic coding of utterances in the sample transcript, tally the frequency of occurrence for each role or category. Using the Total Use of 20 Semantic Roles form (found in Appendix B, online), progress utterance by utterance through the coding forms, tallying each semantic role in each utterance. For example, for the coded utterance **agent-action-object**, mark one tally in the **agent** row, one tally in the **action** row, and one tally in the **object** row. When you have tallied all utterances' roles on the coding form, count the instances of each semantic role and record that number in the # column of that row. For example, in Bridget's transcript, there were 25 instances of the **action** role, 11 **locatives**, 11 **one-term entity** roles, 11 **multiterm entity** roles, and so on.

The next step is to compute the percentage of semantic roles accounted for. To do this, add all totals in the # column and put this sum in the Total box at the bottom of the analysis form. In the sample transcript, there is a total of 129 individual roles used. Divide each individual role total by 129 to obtain the percentage of total roles accounted for. For **action**, 25 divided by 129 yields .1937; rounding this off to .194 and multiplying by 100 (to convert to a percentage) reveals that 19.4% of all semantic roles were coded **action**. Progress through the analysis form, dividing each total by the overall total and multiplying by 100 to get the percentage for each semantic role. These percentages can be added together to double-check computations. If the total is more than .3% above or below 100%, a miscalculation may have occurred. A completed Total Use of 20 Semantic Roles form is shown as Form 2.6 (on p. 51) to check against your computations.

Before results of the percentage of total utterances accounted for by each semantic role can be interpreted, the percentage of total utterances that were semantically codable needs to be computed. Using the Meaning Relationships in One-Word and Multiword Utterances form (found in Appendix B, online), progress through the coding forms and put a checkmark on the grid to indicate whether each coded utterance is one of the following: one term, two terms, three terms, four terms or longer, a conversational device, a communication routine, a complex utterance, or other. If a semantically coded utterance also contains a conversational device

(Text continues on p. 52.)

FORM 2.5   Name of Child: Bridget

SEMANTIC ROLES CODING

Utterance Number	Semantic Coding	Question
1	CR (Sounds Accompanying)	
2	Action	
3	CD (Yes/No Response)	
4	CD (Yes/No Response)	
5	State-Possessor-Multiterm Entity-Locative	
6	Demonstrative	✓
7	Multiterm Entity-Recurrence	✓
8	One-Term Entity	
9	One-Term Entity	
10	CD (Accompaniment)	
11	Action-Adverbial	
12	CD (Yes/No Response)	
13	Locative	
14	Locative	
15	(CD Attention) Agent-Action	
16	Multiterm Entity-Recurrence	✓
17	Action-Locative	
18	Demonstrative-State-Negation-Quantifier	
19	Multiterm Entity-Recurrence	✓
20	Experiencer-State-Negation-Locative	
21	Agent-Negation-Action	
22	Action-Object	
23	Locative-Experiencer-State	✓
24	Locative-Demonstrative-Experiencer-State	✓
25	One-Term Entity	

FORM 2.5

SEMANTIC ROLES CODING (continued)

Utterance Number	Semantic Coding	Question
26	Action	
27	One-Term Entity	
28	Action	
29	CD (Repetition Request)	
30	CD (Yes/No Response)	
31	Agent-Action-Object-Adverbial	
32	Demonstrative-State-Multiterm Entity	
33	(CD Yes/No Response) Experiencer-State-Adverbial	
34	CD (Yes/No Response)	
35	Locative-State-Recurrence-Experiencer	✓
36	Agent-Action-Object	
37	CD (Yes/No Response)	
38	Action	
39	CR (Sounds Accompanying)	
40	One-Term Entity	
41	One-Term Entity	
42	CD (Yes/No Response)	
43	Attribute-Adverbial	
44	Agent-Action	
45	Agent-Action-Object	
46	Action (CD Sounds Accompanying)	
47	CD (Yes/No Response)	
48	CD (Yes/No Response)	
49	CD (Yes/No Response)	
50	One-Term Entity	

(continues)

FORM 2.5

SEMANTIC ROLES CODING (continued)

Utterance Number	Semantic Coding	Question
51	CD (Yes/No Response)	
52	COMPLEX	
53	CR (Sounds Accompanying)	
54	CR (Greeting)	
55	CD (Yes/No Response)	
56	Agent-Action-Object	
57	CD (Yes/No Response)	
58	One-Term Entity	
59	CD (Repetition Request)	
60	Demonstrative-State-Multiterm Entity	✓
61	Demonstrative-State-Multiterm Entity	
62	Demonstrative-Possessor	
63	CD (Polite Form)	
64	CD (Yes/No Response)	
65	Demonstrative-State-Possessor	
66	Multiterm Entity-Recurrence	✓
67	Recurrence	
68	CD (Repetition Request)	
69	CD (Yes/No Response)	
70	Recurrence	✓
71	CD (Attention)	
72	Action-Object (CD Attention)	
73	Action-Object (CD Attention)	
74	CD (Repetition Request)	
75	State-Adverbial	

FORM 2.5

SEMANTIC ROLES CODING (continued)

Utterance Number	Semantic Coding	Question
76	CD (Yes/No Response)	
77	CD (Yes/No Response)	
78	Negation-Multiterm Entity	
79	Negation	
80	CD (Yes/No Response)	
81	Agent-Action-Object	
82	CD (Yes/No Response)	
83	Adverbial-Locative	
84	One-Term Entity	
85	CD (Yes/No Response)	
86	Action-Possessor	
87	Action-Object	
88	Action-Object	
89	Action-Object (CD Attention)	
90	Action-Object (CD Attention)	
91	CD (Repetition Request)	
92	CD (Yes/No Response)	
93	One-Term Entity	
94	One-Term Entity	
95	CD (Yes/No Response)	
96	Object-Action	✓
97	Locative-Demonstrative	
98	CR (Greeting)	
99	Multiterm Entity-Locative	
100	Agent-Action	

SEMANTIC ANALYSIS

FORM 2.6 Name of Child **Bridget**

TOTAL USE OF 20 SEMANTIC ROLES

Role	Tally	#	%
Action	‖‖‖ ‖‖‖ ‖‖‖ ‖‖‖ ‖‖‖	25	19.4
Locative	‖‖‖ ‖‖‖ ‖	11	8.5
Agent	‖‖‖ ‖‖‖‖	9	7.0
Object	‖‖‖ ‖‖‖ ‖‖	12	9.3
Demonstrative	‖‖‖ ‖‖‖‖	9	7.0
Recurrence	‖‖‖ ‖‖	7	5.4
Possessor	‖‖‖‖	4	3.1
Quantifier	‖	1	0.8
Experiencer	‖‖‖	5	3.9
Recipient		0	—
Beneficiary		0	—
Comitative		0	—
Created Object		0	—
Instrument		0	—
State	‖‖‖ ‖‖‖ ‖‖	12	9.3
Entity (one-term)	‖‖‖ ‖‖‖ ‖	11	8.5
Multiterm Entity	‖‖‖ ‖‖‖ ‖	11	8.5
Negation	‖‖‖	5	3.9
Attribute	‖	1	0.8
Adverbial	‖‖‖ ‖	6	4.7
Total		129	100.1

(CD) or a communication routine (CR), the CD or CR column is not checked. Under the 100th utterance row, total each column from the entire grid. For example, in the first 50 utterances, there were 15 one-term utterances and in the last 50 utterances, 7 one-term utterances. These sum to 22 one-term utterances. Put 22 below the 100th row in the One Term column. Tallies can be checked with those in the sample provided on Form 2.7.

Totaling the one-term, two-term, three-term, and four-term-plus tallies in the sample transcript reveals that 64 utterances were coded semantically. Put this number in the appropriate blank of the Semantic Roles Summary form (from Appendix B, online). Now divide this number by 100 total utterances. The result should be .64, and after multiplying by 100 to convert to a percentage, note that 64% of Bridget's utterances in this transcript were semantically codable. Now transfer the percentage obtained for each semantic role to the Semantic Roles Summary form. Finally, return to the meaning relationships grid and tally the number of utterances that were conversational devices, communication routines, complex utterances, and other. In Bridget's transcript, there were 30 utterances coded as conversational devices, indicating that 30% of her utterances were types of conversational devices. There were five utterances coded as communication routines, indicating that 5% of her utterances were types of communication routines. There was one instance of a complex utterance, indicating that 1% of her utterances were coded as **complex**. There were no instances of utterances coded as **other**. A completed Semantic Roles Summary form is provided as Form 2.8.

INTERPRETATION OF RESULTS—SEMANTIC ROLES ANALYSIS

Begin by examining the percentage of total utterances that could be coded using combinations of semantic roles and grammatical categories. Brown (1973) found that 70% of children's utterances in Stages I and Stages II–III of linguistic development could be semantically coded using a smaller set of semantic roles than Retherford et al.'s (1981). Based on Retherford, Schwartz, and Chapman's (1977) data, Retherford et al. (1981) found that between 64% and 85% of Stage I children's utterances were codable using the combination of semantic roles and grammatical categories described in Table 2.1. In addition, between 47% and 85% of utterances by children in Stages II and III were semantically codable. The sample analysis revealed that 64% of Bridget's utterances were semantically codable. This percentage indicates that this child's productions encode meaning relations with frequencies typical of children in Brown's Stages I and Stages II and III of linguistic development.

Next, the frequency of occurrence of individual semantic roles and residual grammatical categories should be examined. Summaries of Brown's data do not include frequency of occurrence of individual roles. Summaries of the Retherford et al. (1977) data were collected as Time 1 and Time 2. These data have been reorganized to provide a basis of comparison for results obtained from the sample transcript. Table 2.3 (on p. 55) summarizes the frequency of occurrence of each semantic role as a percentage of total roles used by the children in the Retherford et al. (1977) study. Data are presented in Table 2.3 by stage of linguistic production: Stage I = Time 1 and Stages II and III = Time 2.

As can be seen in Table 2.3, the most striking change during the early stages of linguistic production is the decrease in the frequency of occurrence of the **one-term entity** role. This, however, might be predicted on the basis of an increase in utterance length alone. In addition, substantial increases in the roles of **agent, object, demonstrative, recurrence, possessor, attribute,** and **adverbial** were noted as the children advanced to higher stages of linguistic production. Comparing results of the sample transcript to these data indicates that Bridget's use of **one-term entity** is more typical of Stages II and III than of Stage I. In addition, Bridget's use of the roles **agent, object, demonstrative, recurrence, possessor, negation,** and **adverbial** is more typical of children in Stages II and III. Overall, it can be said that this child's use of individual semantic roles in combination is typical of a child at least in Brown's Stages II and III. Because the sample size is so small for the Retherford et al. (1977) data ($N = 3$ for Stages II and III), the reader is cautioned not to overinterpret the normative data. The important change to look for in the child's use of individual semantic roles from Stage I to Stages II and III is the shift from between 30% and 7% use of **one-term entity** to between 11% and 14% use for **multiterm entity**. Obviously, this decrease in use of **one-term entity** will be accompanied by increases in use of other roles, most often in the roles of **agent, object, possessor,** and **adverbial**.

FORM 2.7 Name of Child __Bridget__

MEANING RELATIONSHIPS IN ONE-WORD AND MULTIWORD UTTERANCES

Utterance Number	One Term	Two Term	Three Term	Four Term Plus	Conversational Device	Communication Routine	Complex	Other
1								
2	✓							
3					✓✓			
4					✓✓			
5				✓				
6	✓							
7		✓						
8	✓✓							
9	✓✓							
10					✓			
11		✓						
12					✓			
13	✓✓							
14	✓✓							
15		✓✓✓						
16		✓✓						
17		✓						
18				✓				
19				✓		✓		
20								
21			✓					
22			✓					
23		✓						
24				✓				
25	✓✓✓✓							
26	✓✓✓							
27								
28								
29					✓✓			
30				✓				
31								
32			✓✓		✓			
33			✓		✓			
34				✓				
35								
36			✓					
37	✓							
38	✓✓					✓		
39					✓			
40								
41								
42		✓✓						
43								
44								
45	✓							
46								
47					✓✓✓			
48					✓✓			
49								
50	✓							

FORM 2.7

MEANING RELATIONSHIPS IN ONE-WORD AND MULTIWORD UTTERANCES (continued)

Utterance Number	One Term	Two Term	Three Term	Four Term Plus	Conversational Device	Communication Routine	Complex	Other
51								
52								
53							✓	
54								
55					✓			
56			✓					
57					✓			
58	✓							
59					✓			
60			✓✓					
61		✓						
62					✓✓			
63			✓					
64						✓✓		
65	✓							
66		✓						
67	✓							
68					✓✓			
69					✓			
70								
71		✓✓						
72		✓✓						
73		✓			✓			
74					✓✓			
75		✓						
76					✓			
77			✓					
78	✓							
79					✓			
80		✓						
81		✓✓✓						
82		✓✓						
83		✓✓						
84					✓			
85	✓							
86					✓			
87								
88								
89					✓✓			
90		✓✓			✓			
91	✓✓							
92		✓						
93		✓						
94								
95						✓		
96								
97								
98								
99								
100								
Total	22	25	11	6	30	5	1	0

FORM 2.8   Name of Child __Bridget__

SEMANTIC ROLES SUMMARY

Total Number of Semantically Coded Utterances = __64__ = __64.0__ % of Total Utterances

Percentage of Total Semantic Roles Accounted For By Each Semantic Role:

Semantic Role	%
Action =	19.4 %
Locative =	8.5 %
Agent =	7.0 %
Object =	9.3 %
Demonstrative =	7.0 %
Recurrence =	5.4 %
Possessor =	3.1 %
Quantifier =	0.8 %
Experiencer =	3.9 %
Recipient =	— %
Benefficiary =	— %
Comitative =	— %
Created Object =	— %
Instrument =	— %
State =	9.3 %
Entity (one-term) =	8.5 %
Multiterm Entity =	8.5 %
Negation =	3.9 %
Attribute =	0.8 %
Adverbial =	4.7 %

Total Number of Utterances Coded **Conversational Device** __30__ = __30.0__ % of Total Utterances

Total Number of Utterances Coded **Communication Routine** __5__ = __5.0__ % of Total Utterances

Total Number of Utterances Coded **Complex** __1__ = __1.0__ % of Total Utterances

Total Number of Utterances Coded **Other** __0__ = __0__ % of Total Utterances

TABLE 2.3

Mean Frequency of Occurrence of 20 Semantic Roles of Children in Brown's Stage I and Stages II and III

Role	Time 1 Stage I (N = 9)	Time 2 Stages II and III (N = 3)
Action	13.5	15.0
Locative	9.5	9.1
Agent	3.8	6.9
Object	2.0	5.7
Demonstrative	2.9	5.6
Recurrence	1.8	2.8
Possessor	1.1	3.9
Quantifier	1.9	1.7
Experiencer	2.4	1.5
Recipient	0.2	0.3
Beneficiary	0.1	0.2
Comitative	0.7	0.1
Created Object	0.1	0.0
Instrument	0.0	0.0
State	1.6	1.8
Entity (one-term)	30.3	6.8
Multiterm Entity	10.5	14.1
Negation	8.4	5.3
Attribute	3.0	4.1
Adverbial	1.4	2.8

Note. Computed from Retherford, Schwartz, and Chapman (1977).

Brown's Prevalent Semantic Relations

To identify Brown's (1973) Prevalent Semantic Relations, analysis will use data and theory summarized by Brown (1973) in his classic volume, *A First Language*. Brown contended that the 8 two-term prevalent semantic relations that he found to be frequently occurring in child language laid the foundation for longer utterances. The child, according to Brown, accomplished increases in utterance length by elaborating on one of the roles in some of the basic two-term semantic relations. The role that the child was likely to expand was found to be predictable. Brown's 8 two-term prevalent semantic relations are listed on the Brown's Prevalent Semantic Relations form (see Form 2.9; a blank copy can be found in Appendix B online). The roles that are in bold in five of the eight relations are the roles that the child is most likely to expand. Across the top right-three columns are the three expansion types most likely to occur in children's productions during Stages I–III. These include **demonstrative**, which Brown called nomination; **attributive**, which Brown considered to also include **recurrence**; and **possessive**. The boxes that are crossed out represent impossible expansions. For example, as shown in Form 2.9, in the two-term relation **demonstrative-entity**, **entity** is in bold print, indicating that **entity** is the role likely to be expanded. But moving across the row, the **demonstrative** box is crossed out. This is because **demonstrative-demonstrative-entity** (e.g., "that this ball") is not a likely combination. Keep in mind that Brown's **possessor-possession** would be coded **possessor-entity** using Retherford et al.'s 20 semantic roles. In addition to Brown's 8 two-term prevalent semantic relations and the expansions of those relations,

Brown suggested that some three-term relations do not represent expansions of his two-term relations. These three-term relations are listed at the bottom of Brown's Prevalent Semantic Relations form.

To complete Brown's Prevalent Semantic Relations form, progress through your Semantic Roles Coding form, identifying (a) coded utterances that coincide with Brown's two-term prevalent semantic relations, (b) expansions of two-term prevalent semantic relations, and (c) three-term prevalent semantic relations. Record the utterance number in the appropriate box for each semantic relation type. Carefully consider each coded utterance, because word order doesn't matter in the codes (e.g., **agent-action** and **action-agent** would be recorded in the same box).

Note that the first utterance on the coding forms that coincides with one of Brown's multiterm combinations is utterance #7. This is an example of **attribute-entity** even though it is listed as **multiterm entity-recurrence**. (Recall that Brown's **attribute** category includes the **recurrence** category.) In addition, keep in mind that word order is irrelevant when identifying semantic relations. So, put 7 in the Utterance Number column next to **attribute-entity**. Moving on through the coding forms, note that the next utterance that coincides with one of Brown's combinations is utterance #15. This is an example of **agent-action**, so put 15 in the Utterance Number column next to **agent-action**. Continue through the coding forms, looking for examples of Brown's two-term prevalent semantic relations, and expansions of those, and then proceed to three-term prevalent semantic relations. Once you have examined and identified all utterances as either being or not being examples of Brown's two-term, expansion of two-term, and three-term combinations, check your results with Form 2.9.

FORM 2.9   Name of Child __Bridget__

BROWN'S PREVALENT SEMANTIC RELATIONS

		Utterance Number	Demonstrative	Attributive	Possessive
Two Term	**Agent-**Action	15, 44, 100			
	Action-**Object**	22, 72, 73, 87, 88, 89, 90			
	Agent-Object		✕	✕	✕
	Demonstrative-**Entity**		✕	✕	✕
	Entity-Locative	99			
	Action-Locative	17	✕	✕	✕
	(−Entity)* **Possessor-**Possession				
	(Recurrence−)* Attribute-Entity	7, 16, 19, 66			
Three Term	Agent-Action-Object	36, 45, 56, 81			
	Agent-Action-Locative				
	Action-Object-Locative				

*Per Retherford et al. (1981)

Note. Bolded terms show the most common relations.

CALCULATING THE RESULTS—BROWN'S PREVALENT SEMANTIC RELATIONS

After identifying each example of Brown's two-term or three-term combinations, complete the Brown's Prevalent Semantic Relations Summary form. (A blank copy is provided in Appendix B, online, and a completed form is provided as Form 2.10.) Begin by counting each type of two-term and three-term relation and adding the numbers to the summary form. Then add all instances of each type of two-term relation and write the total in the Total Two-Term Utterances space. In the sample transcript, there were 16 total instances of Brown's two-term prevalent semantic relations.

Next, using the totals from the Meaning Relationships in One-Word and Multiword Utterances grid, add the totals for two-term, three-term, and four-term-plus utterances to get the total number of multiterm utterances. In the sample transcript, there were 42 multiterm utterances. Then add the one-term utterances (22) to that number to get the total number of semantically coded utterances: 64. Write these numbers on the form in the appropriate spaces. Divide the total number of instances of two-term relations by the total number of multiterm utterances and multiply by 100 to get the percentage of multiterm utterances accounted for by Brown's two-term prevalent semantic relations. In the sample transcript, 16 instances of Brown's two-term relations divided by 42 multiterm utterances yields .3809, which after multiplying by 100 indicates that 38.1% of Bridget's multiterm utterances were examples of Brown's two-term prevalent semantic relations.

Next, calculate the percentage of semantically coded utterances accounted for by Brown's two-term prevalent semantic relations. For the sample transcript, 16 was divided by 64 semantically coded utterances and then multiplied by 100 to get the percentage of semantically coded utterances accounted for by Brown's two-term prevalent semantic relations: 25%.

The next step is to count and sum all instances of each type of Brown's prevalent semantic relations' expansions and write these numbers in the blanks provided. In the sample transcript, there were zero instances of expansions. If there had been any, the total would have been divided by 42 multiterm utterances and multiplied by 100 to get the percentage of multiterm utterances accounted for by expansions of Brown's two-term prevalent semantic relations. If that had been the case, that same total would then have been divided by 64 semantically coded utterances and multiplied by 100 to get the percentage of semantically coded utterances accounted for by expansions of Brown's two-term prevalent semantic relations.

The last step is to count and sum all instances of each type of three-term prevalent semantic relation and write these numbers in the spaces provided. Then add all instances of each type and put this total in the space provided. In the sample transcript there were four examples of Brown's three-term prevalent semantic relations. Dividing this number by 42 multiterm utterances and multiplying by 100 reveals that 9.5% of Bridget's multiterm utterances were examples of Brown's three-term semantic relations. Then you would divide 4 by 64 total semantically coded utterances and multiply by 100 to get the percentage of semantically coded utterances accounted for by Brown's three-term prevalent semantic relations: 6.3%.

INTERPRETATION OF THE RESULTS—BROWN'S PREVALENT SEMANTIC RELATIONS

The first comparison in the interpretation of the summarized data is to Brown's (1973) reported frequency of occurrence of prevalent semantic relations for 12 children ranging in production abilities from Stage I to Stage II. Table 2.4 displays the mean frequency of occurrence for each of the prevalent semantic relations and each three-term combination for three children at Stage I, eight children at Early Stage II, and one child at Stage II. Data in the table represent a reorganization of individual child data presented by Brown; frequencies are reported as percentages of total multiterm utterances.

Examination of Table 2.4 reveals increases across the three stages in **action-object** and **action-locative** constructions. Decreases in **agent-action, agent-object, entity-locative,** and **attribute-entity** constructions and the total use of Brown's two-term semantic relations are present. In addition, increases in the total number of three-term semantic relations can be seen. Comparison of results obtained from analysis of Bridget's transcript and Brown's (1973) data suggests that Bridget is using constructions with frequencies most similar to Stage II. However, it cannot be determined whether this child's use of Brown's prevalent semantic relations is at a level higher than Stage II. Once again, we caution you not to overinterpret the data. Variations in situations

FORM 2.10   Name of Child __Bridget__

BROWN'S PREVALENT SEMANTIC RELATIONS SUMMARY

Two-Term Prevalent Semantic Relations   **Expansions**

__3__ **Agent**-Action   __0__ Dem   __0__ Att   __0__ Poss. = __0__

__7__ Action-**Object**   __0__ Dem   __0__ Att   __0__ Poss. = __0__

__0__ Agent-Object

__0__ Demonstrative-**Entity**   __0__ Att   __0__ Poss. = __0__

__1__ **Entity**-Locative   __0__ Dem   __0__ Att   __0__ Poss. = __0__

__1__ Action-Locative

__0__ **Possessor**-Possession   __0__ Dem   __0__ Att   = __0__

__4__ Attribute-Entity   = __0__ Total Expansions

[__16__] Total Two-Term Utterances

Three-Term Prevalent Semantic Relations

__4__ Agent-Action-Object

__0__ Agent-Action-Locative

__0__ Action-Object-Locative

[__4__] Total Three-Term Utterances

__16__ Two-Term Utterances ÷ __42__ Multiterm Utterances = __38.1__ % of Multiterm Utterances Accounted For by Brown's Two-Term Semantic Relations

__16__ Two-Term Utterances ÷ __64__ Semantically Coded Utterances = __25.0__ % of Semantically Coded Utterances Accounted For by Brown's Two-Term Semantic Relations

__0__ Total Expansions ÷ __42__ Multiterm Utterances = __0__ % of Semantically Coded Utterances Accounted For by Expansions of Brown's Prevalent Semantic Relations

__4__ Three-Term Utterances ÷ __42__ Multiterm Utterances = __9.5__ % of Multiterm Utterances Accounted For by Brown's Three-Term Semantic Relations

__4__ Three-Term Utterances ÷ __64__ Semantically Coded Utterances = __6.3__ % of Semantically Coded Utterances Accounted For by Brown's Three-Term Relations

TABLE 2.4

Mean Frequency of Occurrence of Brown's Prevalent Semantic Relations in Stages I, Early II, and II as Percentage of Total Multiterm Utterances

Codings	Stage I* (N = 3) %	Early Stage II* (N = 8) %	Stage II* (N = 1) %
Agent-action	24.0	9.4	7.0
Action-object	7.0	9.3	16.0
Agent-object	3.7	1.5	0.0
Demonstrative-entity	1.3	7.9	1.0
Entity-locative	12.7	3.9	2.0
Action-locative	2.3	3.6	5.0
Possessor-possession	9.7	7.1	11.0
Attribute-entity	7.0	5.4	5.0
TOTAL	67.7	48.1	47.0
Agent-action-object	3.7	2.9	6.0
Agent-action-locative	1.0	2.1	3.0
Agent-object-locative	0.3	1.0	0.0
TOTAL	5.0	6.0	9.0

Note. Mean frequency computed from Brown (1973).

*Based on MLUs reported by Brown; children were grouped according to stages redefined by Miller and Chapman (1981).

are likely to elicit differences in the frequency of occurrence of specific combinations. The conservative interpretation is that this child is capable of producing Brown's prevalent semantic relations with frequencies similar to children at least in Stage II. Whether this child's productions truly are more typical of children in Stage III or higher cannot be determined using this data.

It may be useful to examine the distribution of multiterm utterances into Brown's prevalent semantic relations versus other combinations. Table 2.5 displays this distribution for Stages I and II for data reported by Brown (1973). Again, the data represent a reorganization of individual child data presented by Brown.

To compare data obtained from the sample transcript to data presented in Table 2.5, one more computation is necessary. From the Meaning Relationships in One-Word and Multiword Utterances analysis grid, we can see that 42 of this child's 100 utterances were multiterm combinations of semantic roles. In addition, from the Brown's Prevalent Semantic Relations Summary, it is clear that a total of 20 utterances were Brown's two-term and three-term prevalent semantic relations (16 + 4 = 20). That means that 48% (20 ÷ 42) of this child's utterances were examples of Brown's combinations, and 52% were examples of additional combinations. This child had no examples of "uninterpretable" utterances. Now, comparing these percentages to those reported by Brown, no apparent match can be seen. This outcome may have been predicted on the basis of an extended set of coding categories. That is, when a set of coding categories containing the 20 semantic roles identified by Retherford et al. (1981) is used to code utterances and results are compared to those obtained using a coding scheme containing far fewer categories, discrepancies are to be expected.

TABLE 2.5

Mean Percent of Total Multiterm Utterances Accounted for by Brown's Prevalent Semantic Relations and Additional Combinations of Semantic Roles

Stage	Brown's prevalent semantic relations*	Additional combinations*
Stage I* ($N = 3$)	73.3	9.3
Early Stage II* ($N = 8$)	58.3	33.5
Stage II* ($N = 1$)	64.0	30.0

Note. Computed from Brown, 1973.

*Based on MLUs reported by Brown; children were grouped according to stages redefined by Miller and Chapman (1981); numbers do not total 100% because Brown had a third category called "Uninterpretable" that is not reflected in this table.

Let's compare Bridget's distribution of multiterm combinations to data reported by Retherford et al. (1977). The Retherford et al. data are summarized by percent of total semantically coded utterances rather than by percentage of total multiterm utterances. Table 2.6 displays the distribution of total semantically coded utterances into Brown's multiterm combinations versus additional combinations for children in Brown's Stages I–III. Keep in mind that the utterances in Bridget's transcript and the Retherford et al. (1977) data were coded using the 20 semantic roles previously described, and only those coinciding with Brown's categories in combination have been selected for comparison.

Bridget used similar percentages of Brown's combinations (48%) and additional combinations (52%), which is comparable to the distribution in Stage II in Table 2.6. Her percentages could also be interpreted as an indication that Bridget is using combinations characteristic of a more advanced stage of linguistic production.

Brown's own data in Table 2.5 reveal that the percentage of multiterm combinations accounted for by his eight prevalent semantic relations tends to decrease over the first three stages of linguistic production. In addition, the increase in the use of additional combinations suggests a greater attention on the part of the child to syntactic aspects of multiterm combinations. Again, overinterpretation of results is cautioned against because of the small sample size. Taken together, these results suggest that Bridget's semantic productions are at or beyond Stage II. This finding indicates that analysis of syntactic aspects of the child's productions is warranted.

Analyzing Vocabulary Diversity

The last procedure that we use to analyze semantic aspects of Bridget's productions dissects the vocabulary diversity in the language transcripts. This procedure examines referential rather than relational aspects of production in that it analyzes vocabulary only, with no attention to the use of words in combination.

The procedure that we use to analyze Bridget's vocabulary diversity in her 100-utterance language transcript is the type-token ratio described by Templin (1957). This procedure allows examination of the relationship between the total number of different words (NDW) used and the total number of words (TNW) used. For the 480 children that Templin studied, ratios of approximately 1:2 were obtained consistently for all age groups, gender groups, and socioeconomic groups, although the numbers composing these ratios varied at each level. Because of this consistency, this procedure is particularly useful in analyzing the diversity of a child's vocabulary. Further, comparison of NDW and TNW may help identify a child with a language impairment. Templin's data are applicable only to children between the ages of 3 and 8 years. However, Retherford and Hoerning (2006) and Hoerning (2007) gathered additional data from six children between the ages of 28 and 33 months.

TABLE 2.6

Mean Percent of Total Semantically Coded Utterances Accounted for by Brown's Prevalent Semantic Relations and Additional Combinations

Stage	Brown's prevalent semantic relations*	Additional combinations*
Stage I* (N = 6)	55.4	21.9
Early Stage II* (N = 3)	50.9	20.9
Stage II* (N = 2)	38.2	31.8
Stage III* (N = 1)	64.0	22.4

Note. Computed from Retherford, Schwartz, and Chapman (1977).

*Numbers do not total 100% because Retherford et al. (1977) had a third category called "Multiterm other" that is not reflected on this table.

In obtaining their language samples, Templin and Retherford and Hoerning used an adult–child interaction format, with picture books and toys as stimulus materials. Online recording of the children's spontaneous productions yielded transcripts sufficiently long to permit analysis of the middle 50 utterances. It is possible to use transcripts longer than 50 utterances; however, only 50 consecutive utterances should be used to compute the type-token ratio.

In computing the type-token ratio, each word used by the child (except repetitions) in the sample transcript is counted. In some cases, two or three words are used together as a familiar expression, and these are counted as one word (e.g., *a lot, all gone*). Figure 2.3 delineates the rules used by Templin in counting words.

Use Bridget's transcript to practice determining her TNW and NDW and computing her type-token ratio (TTR). Since the sample transcript from Bridget is 100 utterances in length, the middle 50 utterances of the transcript—utterances #26 to #75—should be used. To keep track of every word Bridget used in the middle 50 utterances, record each word on the Templin's Type-Token Ratio Analysis form. (A blank form can be found in Appendix B online.) A parts-of-speech organizational scheme was selected for efficiency only and has no bearing on the final computation. To use this organizational scheme, progress through utterances #26 to #75 of the sample transcript, recording each word in the appropriate column according to its part of speech (either alphabetically or on the basis of first occurrence). If it is difficult to determine what part of speech a particular word represents, record it anywhere; final computations are not based on correct differentiation of parts of speech. Accurate tallying of each word is crucial for the final computation. If a particular word occurs more than once, tally additional instances of the word next to the original recording of the word (e.g., "ball ⟋⟋⟋⟋ III" means the word ball occurred nine times in the transcript). When finished, compare your results with those in the completed Templin's Type-Token Ratio Analysis form for Bridget shown as Form 2.11.

The parts-of-speech organizational scheme is maintained in TTR analysis in the web-based *Guide Practice* exercises. Before conducting the TTR exercise, you may wish to practice identifying parts of speech using the Parts of Speech Analysis exercise. This practice will be helpful in completing the TTR practice and in completing the various types of structural analysis in Chapter 3.

Calculating the Results

To obtain the numbers needed for the final computation, count the NDW in each column, and put these totals in the bottom left of the columns. Transfer these totals to the spaces provided on the form. In Bridget's transcript, there were seven different nouns, 11 verbs, five adjectives, four adverbs, one preposition, five others, 12 pronouns, zero conjunctions, four negatives/affirmatives, one article, and three *wh-* words. Now add these totals and write the sum in the Total Number of Different Words space. In the sample transcript, Bridget used a total of 53 different words.

> **RULES FOR COUNTING NUMBER OF WORDS FOR TYPE-TOKEN RATIO**
>
> 1. Contractions of subject and predicate, like *it's* and *we're*, are counted as two words. Also, the contracted verb forms are counted as different words than their uncontracted forms. Thus, the word *is* in "It's a big dog" is counted as a different word than the *is* in "It is a big dog."
> 2. Contractions of the verb and the negative, such as *don't*, are counted as one word. They can go in the Verbs or Negatives/Affirmatives category, but not both.
> 3. Each part of the verbal combination is counted as a separate word. Thus, *have been playing* is counted as three words.
> 4. Semiauxiliaries are counted as only one word. Even though *wanna = want to*, count it as only one type in the Verbs category.
> 5. Hyphenated words and closed compound nouns are counted as one word. Thus, *blackboard* is one word and *fire truck* is counted as two.
> 6. Expressions that function as a unit in the child's understanding are counted as one word. Thus, *oh boy, all right*, etc. are counted as one word, while a noun like *car seat* is counted as two words.
> 7. Interjections such as *um, oh,* and *huh* are counted as one word.
> 8. Articles (*the, a, an*) count as one word.
> 9. Bound morphemes and noun and verb inflections are not counted as separate words. Thus, *cats* and *walked* are each counted as one word.
> 10. Forms of the same verb with tense and/or number differences are counted as different words. Thus, *make, makes*, and *making* are counted as three different words, not as three types of the same token.
>
> *Note.* Adapted from "Certain Language Skills in Children: Their Development and Interrelationships," by M. C. Templin, 1957, *Institute of Child Welfare Monograph Series, 26*. © 1957 by the University of Minnesota Press. © renewed 1985 by Mildred C. Templin. Adapted with permission.

FIGURE 2.3. Rules for counting number of words for type-token ratio.

Next, count each word (every instance) in the 11 categories, and write the totals the spaces provided. In the sample transcript, there were 11 total instances of nouns, 20 verbs, six adjectives, six adverbs, one preposition, five others, 21 pronouns, zero conjunctions, 13 negatives/affirmatives, three articles, and six *wh-* words. Add these totals to obtain the total number of words used. Bridget used a total of 92 words.

To complete the final computation and obtain the TTR, divide the NDW (53) by the TNW (92). The result is a TTR of .5760, which rounds to .58.

Interpreting the Results

The interpretation of the TTR is accomplished by comparing it to the normative data from Templin's analysis. Table 2.7 (on p. 65) displays the mean and standard deviation of NDW used, the mean and standard deviation of TNW used, and the resulting type-token ratio for age groups between 3 and 8 years.

Table 2.8 (on p. 65) displays the TNW, the NDW, and the resulting TTR for six children, studied by Retherford and Hoerning, who were between the ages of 28 and 33 months. Table 2.8 also displays a median and a mean for each of these measures based on the data gathered.

The data for vocabulary diversity in the language of 28- to 33-month-old children (i.e., average TNW and average NDW in the obtained language samples) were measurably different than the data available for 36- to 41-month-old children, but interestingly, the TTR values resulting from the language samples of the six 28- to 33-month-old children were similar to the TTR values reported for those children in the 36- to 41-month-old range.

Because Bridget is 28 months old, it is not appropriate to directly compare the results of her analysis to Templin's normative data, which were gathered from children 3–8 years of age. Preliminary conclusions

FORM 2.11   Name of Child **Bridget**

TEMPLIN'S TYPE-TOKEN RATIO ANALYSIS

Nouns	Verbs	Adjectives	Adverbs	Prepositions
legs	stand I	heavy	up II	to
elephant	do	another	upside down	
owie I	's IIII	pretty	better	
stroller	kick I	else I	down	
cow	gimme	good		
ball I	fall I			
Bill II	go			
	sleep			
	wake			
	take I			
	taste			

In this instance, "to" is a sign of the infinitive, but since it is almost always a preposition, list it here.

In this instance, "better" is an elliptical predicate adjective, but since it is almost always an adverb, list it here.

In this instance, "pretty" is an adverb modifying an adjective, but since "pretty" is almost always an adjective, list it here so you won't miss it if it occurs again in the transcript.

	I	I

Others

ick
boom
shhh
good night
welcome

7	11	11	20	5	6	4	6	5	5

(continues)

FORM 2.11

TEMPLIN'S TYPE-TOKEN RATIO ANALYSIS (continued)

Pronouns	Conjunctions	Negatives/Affirmatives	Articles	Wh- Words
you		yeah ︎IIII IIII	a II	huh III
it I		no		where
there II		all right		what
one		okay		
I II				
him II				
he				
this				
yours I				
here				
more				
them I				
12 21		4 13	1 3	3 6

Total Number of Different:
- Nouns ___7___
- Verbs ___11___
- Adjectives ___5___
- Adverbs ___4___
- Prepositions ___1___
- Others ___5___
- Pronouns ___12___
- Conjunctions ___-___
- Negatives/Affirmatives ___4___
- Articles ___1___
- Wh- Words ___3___

Total Number of Different Words: ___53___

Total Number of:
- Nouns ___11___
- Verbs ___20___
- Adjectives ___6___
- Adverbs ___6___
- Prepositions ___1___
- Others ___5___
- Pronouns ___21___
- Conjunctions ___-___
- Negatives/Affirmatives ___13___
- Articles ___3___
- Wh- Words ___6___

Total Number of Words: ___92___

$$\frac{\text{Total Number of Different Words}}{\text{Total Number of Words}} = \frac{53}{92} = .5760 = .58 \quad \text{Type-Token Ratio (TTR)}$$

TABLE 2.7

Vocabulary Diversity Using Templin's Data for Type-Token Ratio

Age (in years and months)	Different words		Total words		Type-token ratio
	Mean	SD	Mean	SD	Different words ÷ Total words
3-0	92.5	26.1	204.9	61.3	.45
3-5	104.8	20.4	232.9	50.8	.45
4-0	120.4	27.6	268.8	72.6	.45
4-5	127.0	23.9	270.7	65.3	.47
5-0	132.4	27.2	286.2	75.5	.46
6-0	147.0	27.6	328.0	65.9	.45
7-0	157.7	27.2	363.1	51.3	.43
8-0	166.5	29.5	378.8	80.9	.44

Note. SD = standard deviation. From "Certain Language Skills in Children: Their Development and Interrelationships," by M. C. Templin, 1957, Institute of Child Welfare Monograph Series, 26, © 1957 by the University of Minnesota Press. © renewed 2017 by Mildred C. Templin. Reprinted with permission.

TABLE 2.8

Vocabulary Diversity of Children Ages 28 Months to 33 Months

Age (in months)	TNW	NDW	TTR
28	143	66	.46
30	120	60	.50
31	117	50	.43
33	153	59	.39
33	155	69	.45
33	152	69	.45
Median	147.5	63	.45
Mean	140	62.2	.45

Note. TNW = total number of words; NDW = number of different words; TTR = type-token ratio. Computed from Retherford and Hoerning (2006) and Hoerning (2007).

about Bridget's vocabulary diversity can be reached by comparing her total number of words (TNW), number of different words (NDW), and type-token ratio (TTR) to the data gathered by Retherford and Hoerning. However, consider the small number of subjects in this study, and note that comparisons to the data obtained should be made with caution. Regardless, the data provide beginning information about the vocabulary diversity of children under the age of 3.

Comparison of Bridget's TTR of .58 to the TTRs obtained by Retherford and Hoerning reveals that Bridget's TTR is higher. This suggests that the child's vocabulary in the sample transcript is more diverse than would be expected for the TNW used. TTRs greater than .50 indicate the use of more different words than is typical for the TNW. Is this an asset or a deficit? That is difficult to say. TTRs significantly below .50 may reflect a lack of diversity and may potentially indicate language-specific deficiency (Miller, 1981).

Although type-token ratios were intended to be used only as a type of normative data, valuable information can be gained by comparing NDW and TNW to the means obtained by Templin. Reduced NDWs and TNWs have been implicated as potential indicators of a language disorder (Klee, 1992; Miller, 1991; Miller, Andriacchi, & Nockerts, 2015; Watkins, Kelly, Harbers, & Hollis, 1995). Bridget's sample transcript contained 53 different words and 92 total words. This can be compared to the mean of 62.2 different words and 140 total words for the 28- to 33-month-old children studied by Retherford and Hoerning. Bridget's NDW is slightly lower than the mean demonstrated by this group, while her TNW used is substantially lower. Because mean and standard deviation data for these subjects are not available, it is not possible to make a clear-cut determination about the significance of these differences. However, given that Bridget's NDW was relatively close to the mean NDW observed by Retherfod and Hoerning and her TTR was higher than the mean TTR of these subjects, it is likely that her vocabulary is reasonably diverse for her age.

Interpretation of TNW and NDW for children between the ages of 3 and 8 years of age is more straightforward. Because Templin's data include both a mean and standard deviation for TNW and NDW at each age, differences in vocabulary diversity can be measured more precisely. Take, for example, a 4-year-old whose results indicate that he used 80 different words and 175 total words. His TTR would be .45, the exact TTR reported by Templin. However, again, it is important to look at the results more closely. Templin's data indicate that the mean NDW used by 4-year-old children was 120.4 with a standard deviation of 27.6 and the mean TNW used by 4-year-old children was 268.8 with a standard deviation of 72.6. Therefore, a child who used fewer than 92.8 NDW and 196.2 TNW might be at risk for a language delay or disorder.

Some researchers have questioned using TTR to measure vocabulary diversity, noting that TTR is affected by sample size: As the sample length increases, TTR decreases because fewer different words are used as words and words are repeated (Miller, Andriacchi, & Nockerts, 2015). Other researchers suggest that NDW may be a more accurate measure for predicting language impairment (Klee, 1992; Miller, Andriacchi, & Nockerts, 2015; Watkins, Kelly, Harbers, & Hollis, 1995). Klee and Watkins and colleagues showed that number of different words (NDW) differentiated preschool children with specific language impairment (SLI) from same-age peers with typical language acquisition. Miller, Andriacchi, and Nockerts (2015) pointed out that NDW increases with age for children between 3 and 13, but TTR remains stable for this age group per Templin's (1957) data, further suggesting that TTR may not be a diagnostic indicator. Scott and Windsor (2000) also found evidence that TNW is an indicator for language impairment, but this research examined the spoken and written work of school-age children. In any event, results must be considered in greater detail before drawing a conclusion.

Pavelko and Owens (2017) documented typically developing children's growth in total number of words (TNW), clauses per sentence (CPS), and words per sentence (WPS) for children ages 3 to 8 years of age. As mentioned previously, reduction in the number of different words (NDW) and the total number of words (TNW) have been described as potential indicators of a language impairment, particularly for children in this age range. Pavelko and Owens' data are presented in Table 2.9. Although this data does not apply to Bridget, who is age 28 months, the data may be pertinent for other comparisons (including for Sara [Appendix E] who is 4 years 10 months), to determine whether a child's language performance is within or outside of what is typically expected.

Pavelko and Owens data are based on a 50-utterance sample using a conversational context. Their data show a significant progression by age for measures of MLU, WPS, and CPS. Note, however, that their MLU measures are not included in *Guide* because Pavelko and Owens altered Brown's rules for counting morphemes and calculating MLU, and comparison to other data we present in Chapter 3 of *Guide* would be inaccurate.

Implications for Intervention

After the selected semantic analysis procedures have been completed, an examination of the results is necessary to develop intervention goals. Data obtained from each of the analyses can lead to development of appropriate intervention goals as long as the results are considered in light of what is known about typical language acquisition. The sequence of accomplishments in typical language acquisition can be used as a basis for providing opportunities for the child to use new vocabulary expressing individual semantic roles and/or

TABLE 2.9

Means (*M*) and Standard Deviations (*SD*s) for TNW, WPS, and CPS by Age

Language sampling analysis metric		Age category						
		3-0 to 3-5 *N* = 20	3-6 to 3-11 *N* = 40	4-0 to 4-5 *N* = 45	4-6 to 4-11 *N* = 55	5-0 to 5-11 *N* = 54	6-0 to 6-11 *N* = 33	7-0 to 7-11 *N* = 23
TNW	*M*	192.30	244.05	261.40	278.71	299.81	337.73	364.52
	SD	61.22	58.07	69.98	60.14	61.46	72.50	54.24
WPS	*M*	5.27	6.24	6.48	6.97	7.33	8.05	8.61
	SD	1.39	1.17	1.37	1.26	1.21	1.42	1.14
CPS	*M*	1.09	1.15	1.19	1.21	1.29	1.36	1.39
	SD	.13	.11	.13	.11	.13	.14	.14

Note. From "Sampling Utterances and Grammatical Analysis Revised (SUGAR): New Normative Values for Language Sample Analysis Measures," by S. L. Pavelko and R. E. Owens, 2017, *Language, Speech, and Hearing Services in Schools, 48*, pp. 197–215. © 2017 by S. L. Pavelko and R. E. Owens. Reprinted with permission.

semantic relationships. Clinical experience has shown that the forms likely to emerge next in the acquisition sequence are predictable; consequently, opportunities for emergence can be provided. The suggestions delineated here are general considerations for intervention, not hard-and-fast rules.

When children at the one-word utterance stage are identified by percentages of one-word utterances exceeding 50% of total utterances and the use of categories within Bloom's (1973) or Nelson's (1973) one-word utterance types are documented, opportunities for developing additional vocabulary within Bloom's or Nelson's utterance types can be provided. That does not mean that a specific set of vocabulary words is taught. It does mean that the child can be provided with repeated exposure to vocabulary that falls within Bloom's or Nelson's categories. Early in the one-word stage, the categories that the child is most likely to produce include **substantive** and **naming words** for Bloom's categories, and **nominals**, **modifiers**, and/or **personal-social words** for Nelson's categories. Later, children add **function words** for Bloom's categories and **action words** for Nelson's categories. Sufficient opportunities for children to acquire the new vocabulary types must be provided during intervention activities. The specific vocabulary representing these one-word utterance types should be determined by the child's interests and his or her regular activities.

When limited use of semantic roles has been identified for a particular child using Retherford et al.'s (1981) coding scheme, opportunities for encoding more diverse roles must be ensured. Typically, goals and objectives related to semantic role use are combined with goals and objectives developed as a result of Brown's prevalent semantic relations analysis. Clinical experience has shown that semantic roles encoding familiar objects and persons precede the production of verb relations, such as **agent-action** and **action-object**. Appropriate objectives would include targeting object and person relations (**demonstrative-entity**, **attribute-entity**, **entity-locative**, **possessor-possession**) for the child early in the two-word period, and verb relations (**agent-action**, **action-object**, **action-locative**) for the child late in the two-word period. Three-term relations can be targeted next, as can the semantic roles identified by Retherford et al. as infrequently occurring, since they are likely to occur in three-term and expanded forms. Again, specific vocabulary should not be taught; opportunities for using targeted semantic relations within structured activities should be provided.

Targeting semantic relations may be of particular importance for children with a diagnosis of autism spectrum disorder (ASD). A large majority of verbal children with a diagnosis of ASD will go through a period of echolalia prior to transitioning to a rule-governed, generative language system (Wetherby & Woods, 2006; Woods & Wetherby, 2003). It is common for children with ASD to produce utterances of considerable length and syntactic complexity, yet, at the same time, not comprehend the individual meaning behind the words in those utterances. Because the utterances are learned as a whole echolalic chunk, these children may not spontaneously generate even the simplest two-term semantic relations. As a result, their expressive communication may be limited to those utterances they can memorize and repeat. Therefore, analysis of semantic relations becomes an essential part of designing an intervention plan for children on the autism spectrum; such analysis may reveal a significant lack of semantic relations diversity. Of equal importance is intervention that systematically targets spontaneous, creative generation of a variety of semantic relations across contexts and communication partners.

Results obtained from analyzing vocabulary diversity can be used to develop goals and objectives for increasing vocabulary. TTRs, NDWs, and/or TNWs that are found to be 1 standard deviation below the norms provided suggest a lack of vocabulary diversity. Further examination of the completed TTR form may also reveal a pattern of semantic use. For example, children with SLI may have specific difficulty with verb acquisition (Oetting, 1999). Children with ASD may rely on ambiguous pronouns, such as *this* and *that*, instead of using specific nouns, and they may have a specific difficulty using conceptual words, such as adjectives, adverbs, or prepositions. These patterns may be revealed through a completed TTR and could point to potential targets for intervention. Intervention should focus on increasing vocabulary, typically within developmentally appropriate semantic fields (e.g., noun categories, such as vehicles, plants, animals; verb categories, such as cooking, play, school; temporal terms; polar adjectives). In this area, specific vocabulary can be taught, but the focus should be on developmentally appropriate semantic fields.

Overall, analysis of both referential aspects of semantic production and relational aspects of semantic production provides results that can be used to develop intervention goals and objectives. As the discussions in the following chapters demonstrate, results obtained from semantic analysis can be combined with results obtained from syntactic and pragmatic analyses to develop comprehensive goals and objectives for intervention.

CHAPTER 3
Syntactic ANALYSIS

Introduction

Analyzing syntactic aspects of language transcripts will help identify children beyond the one-word stage who have delays in language production. In addition, examining the developmental level of a variety of syntactic structures is essential to appropriately determine intervention goals and objectives. The syntactic analysis procedures described in this chapter are compatible with the semantic analysis procedures described in the previous chapter. However, these syntactic procedures are more appropriate for children whose language abilities have advanced beyond the one-word stage. It would be appropriate to analyze the semantic aspects of a child's language production using the multiterm procedures from Chapter 2 and then analyze the syntactic aspects using the procedures in Chapter 3. Information obtained from analysis procedures could then be combined to diagnose language production delays and develop intervention goals and objectives.

In addition to the procedures described in *Guide*, there are several other procedures available for analyzing syntactic aspects of language production: Lee's (1974) Developmental Sentence Scoring (DSS) and Lee's (1966) Developmental Sentence Types (DST); Crystal, Fletcher, and Garman's (1976, 1991) *Language Assessment, Remediation, and Screening Procedure* (LARSP); and Miller's (1981) Assigning Structural Stage (ASS), among others. Although the procedures described in *Guide to Analysis of Language Transcripts* do not differ demonstrably from those procedures developed by Miller (1981), the directions and interpretations are more explicit, and forms for analysis are provided. The intent is not to duplicate procedures or to offer alternative procedures, but to provide experience both in determining the syntactic level of language production and in interpreting results obtained from such analysis. The experience gained here will be beneficial in using any of the aforementioned procedures, since all procedures are based on the analysis of documented aspects of syntactic production.

These procedures involve identifying a variety of syntactic structures and then documenting the developmental level of each structure. The most typical stage and the most advanced stage for each structure will be assigned so that results can be compared to normative data in order to determine the presence or absence of syntactic delays. Once a delay has been documented, the stage assignments form the basis of decision rules for determining intervention goals and objectives.

Analyzing Mean Length of Utterance in Morphemes

The procedure that we use to analyze utterance length is based on procedures described by Brown (1973) to examine the structural changes in children's productions on the basis of increases in utterance length. Brown documented changes in structural complexity concomitant with increases in utterance length as determined by meaning units—or morphemes. The rules for assigning morphemes to utterances have been presented in the literature (Bloom & Lahey, 1978; Brown, 1973; Miller, 1981; Owens, 1992; Owens & Pavelko, 2015; Paul & Norbury, 2012) and appear fairly straightforward. Some inconsistencies in assigning morphemes do exist however. In addition, problems periodically arise from analysis of utterances produced by children with language delays or language disorders because their utterances may not follow a normal developmental sequence. Here, a modification of Brown's rules is used for assigning morphemes, and examples of utterances

RULES FOR ASSIGNING MORPHEMES TO UTTERANCES

1. Select a portion of the transcript that appears to be representative of the range of the child's abilities. Assign morphemes to 100 consecutive utterances, since selecting individual utterances for assigning morphemes can inflate the resulting MLU. However, be aware of transcripts with a high number of responses to yes/no questions, which can deflate the resulting MLU.

2. Assign morphemes only to utterances that are completely intelligible. Following the rules for numbering utterances in a transcript (see Chapter 1), only assign morphemes to utterances that are numbered. Do not number or assign morphemes to any repeated, partially intelligible, unintelligible, or interrupted utterances.

3. Only assign morphemes to repetitions in the most complete form within an utterance as a result of stuttering or false starts (e.g., given the utterance "my dad dad is big," count only "my dad is big"). Occasionally, a child repeats a word for emphasis or part of a phrase for clarification. In these cases, count all words (e.g., given the utterance "my dad is big, big," count all words if one of the repeated words [*big*] has more emphasis than the first).

4. Do not assign morphemes to fillers (e.g., *um, well, oh*) or to singsong repetitions (*teetot, teetot*), or to sounds accompanying utterances (e.g., *beep beep*). However, do assign morphemes to short words like *hi, yeah,* and *no*.

5. Treat compound words (e.g., *ice cream, pocketbook, high school*) and closely related words like *all gone* as single words, even though they consist of two or more free morphemes. Likewise, assign one morpheme to indefinite and reflexive compound pronouns (e.g., *anything, somebody, nothing, everyone, herself*). The reason for this is because children do not appear to have use of each constituent morpheme within these compounds; therefore, treat them like single words.

6. Treat proper nouns (e.g., *Japanese, Mr. Smith*) and ritualized reduplications (e.g., *choo-choo, night-night, quack-quack*) as single words. If the child produces an utterance containing "choo-choo train" and there is evidence of the use of *train* separate from *choo-choo*, assign *choo-choo* and *train* one morpheme each.

7. Assign only one morpheme to diminutive forms of words (e.g., *doggie, mommy, Billy, funny*). The reason for this is that children use many diminutive forms as the only form of the word produced, either because they do not have productive control over the suffix or because adults often use only the diminutive form of words when speaking with children.

8. Assign one morpheme to auxiliary verbs (e.g., *will, have, may*).

9. Assign only one morpheme to catenative forms, even though they represent two to three morphemes in the expanded form (e.g., *gonna = going to; wanna = want to; hafta = have to*).

10. Assign one morpheme to all inflectional affixes (i.e., plural -*s*, singular and plural possessive -*s*, present third-person singular -*s*, regular past tense -*ed*, past participle -*ed* and -*en*, present participle -*ing*, comparative -*er*, and superlative -*est*). (This is in addition to the morpheme[s] assigned to the word onto which the form is inflected.) An incorrect use of an inflection should not be counted as a separate morpheme. For example, *rided* would receive only one morpheme.

11. Inflections marked on gerunds and predicate adjectives are not counted as verb-tense inflections (e.g., *jogging* is fun; I am *bored*). Assign only one morpheme to the entire word.

12. Assign only one morpheme to irregular past-tense and past-participle forms (e.g., *rode, swum*). The reason for this is that children do not appear to have derived these from the present-tense form. (An incorrect use of an inflection added to an irregular past-tense or past-participle form should not be counted as a separate morpheme. For example, *swummed* would receive only one morpheme.)

13. Assign two morphemes to negative contractions (e.g., *can't, don't, won't*) only if there is evidence within the transcript that the child uses each part of the contraction (e.g., *do* and *not*) separately. If the child does not use each part of the contraction separately, assign only one morpheme to the negative contraction. The reason for this is because until the child uses each part separately, the child does not appear to have productive control over the contraction.

14. Assign two morphemes to all nonnegative contractions (e.g., *I'm, he's, they've, you'll, she'll, they're*).

15. Common derivational affixes should be assigned their own morphemes. Common affixes include *re-, un-, -ly,* and *-en*. Do not assign morphemes to such affixes as *al-* in *already* or *a-* in *around*.

Note. Adapted from Brown, R. (1973). *A First Language: The Early stages.* Cambridge, MA: Harvard University Press.

FIGURE 3.1. Rules for assigning morphemes to utterances.

produced by children with language delays and language disorders is provided. Figure 3.1 summarizes the rules for assigning morphemes to utterances that have been used with the sample transcript from Chapter 1.

For practice, try to determine the number of morphemes in a few utterances in Example 3.1, before turning to the sample transcript. As was done in the previous chapter, cover the right side of the page, determine the number of morphemes in the utterance, and then check your values with those provided in the shaded

EXAMPLE 3.1

MORPHEME ASSIGNMENT	
(C points to picture in photo album) there Daddy/	MORPHEMES = 2 In this utterance, each word is assigned one morpheme.
(C puts baby doll in crib and covers her) go night-night/	MORPHEMES = 2 The word *night-night* is assigned only one morpheme. This is because it is assumed that *night-night* functions as a single concept for the child.
(C places empty juice cup on table) allgone juice/	MORPHEMES = 2 Again, a word like *allgone* functions as a single word for most children and in most cases is written as one word in the transcript.
(C points to picture in picture book) two doggies/	MORPHEMES = 3 The use of the plural inflection accounts for the addition of one morpheme. Remember, the diminutive form receives only one morpheme.
(C pulls circus train out of box) big choo-choo train/	MORPHEMES = 2 OR 3 Without any additional utterances, only two morphemes can be assigned to this utterance. If there is evidence that the child uses the word *train* separate from *choo-choo*, three morphemes could be assigned to this utterance. Two morphemes are never assigned to *choo-choo*.
(C picks up monkey that fell off bar) he fell down/	MORPHEMES = 3 No credit is given for past tense of irregular verbs, since children appear not to have derived these from the present tense form.
(C watches baby brother eating raisins) he likes raisins/	MORPHEMES = 5 The use of the third-person singular present tense receives a morpheme, as does the plural *-s*.
(C shakes his head and says) I don't like raisins/	MORPHEMES = 5 OR 6 The negative contraction *don't* is assigned two morphemes only if there is evidence that each piece of the uncontracted form (*do* and *not*) is used separately or together elsewhere in the transcript
(C kicks ball, then turns to M) I kicked the ball/	MORPHEMES = 5 The regular past tense *-ed* receives a morpheme. Evidence of use in the uninflected form is not needed.
(M and C are racing cars around track) he's gonna catch me/	MORPHEMES = 5 Since *he's* is a nonnegative contraction, it receives two morphemes. The catenative form of *going to* (*gonna*) receives only one morpheme. Brown indicated that catenatives were assigned two morphemes in older children, but for consistency in these analyses, one morpheme will always be assigned to catenatives.

(continues)

EXAMPLE 3.1 (*continued*)

(M says to crying C, "Did she hurt you?") yeah she hit me/	**MORPHEMES = 4** With no boundary marker indicating a pause between *yeah* and the rest of this utterance, one morpheme is assigned to each word in this utterance. If there had been a pause between *yeah* and the rest of the utterance, it would have been segmented into two utterances.
(C pulls large stuffed dog from surprise box) oh that's a big doggie/	**MORPHEMES = 5** The filler *oh* does not receive a morpheme in the count. The diminutive form of *dog* (*doggie*) receives one morpheme only. The contractible copula is a nonnegative contraction, so *that's* is assigned two morphemes.
(C sets dog next to middle-size dog) that is a big doggie/	**MORPHEMES = 5** In this utterance, the uncontracted form of the copula is used. This does not change the morpheme count, but the example is provided to demonstrate a pragmatic convention of "uncontracting" the copulas used for emphasis
(C puts handful of popcorn in mouth) I am eating popcorn/	**MORPHEMES = 5** The present progressive form of *eat* receives a morpheme, so that *eating* receives a total of two morphemes. The compound word *popcorn* receives only one morpheme.
(C is explaining why he was late) she couldn't find her pocketbook/	**MORPHEMES = 5 OR 6** *Couldn't* is assigned two morphemes only if there is evidence that each piece of the uncontracted form (*could* and *not*) is used separately or together elsewhere in the transcript. The compound word *pocketbook* receives only one morpheme.
(C is relating story to M) she didn't say hi/	**MORPHEMES = 4 OR 5** *Didn't* is assigned two morphemes only if there is evidence that each piece of the contracted form (*did* and *not*) is used separately or together elsewhere in the transcript. Greeting terms are not treated as fillers and are assigned one or more morphemes.
(C points to arm) he hitted me/	**MORPHEMES = 3** Assigning a morpheme to incorrect use of the regular past tense -*ed* inflates the MLU. Thus, no morpheme is assigned. However, valuable information is obtained if attempts by the child to mark past tense are noted.
(C holds up picture) look it Mommy/	**MORPHEMES = 2 OR 3** In most cases, the child's use of *look it* (*lookit*) functions as one word. Thus, only one morpheme is assigned. If there is evidence that the child uses *look* and *it* independently of one another, then each is counted as a separate morpheme. The use of *Mommy* as an attention-getter does receive a morpheme.

EXAMPLE 3.1 (*continued*)

(C points to picture in book) that's a silly one/	**MORPHEMES = 5** The contractible copula and the pronoun onto which it is contracted each are assigned a morpheme. The adjective, *silly*, is assigned only one morpheme.
(C hands cars to M) Mommy do it/	**MORPHEMES = 2 OR 3** The use of *do it* also typically functions as one word. If there is evidence that the child uses *do* and *it* independently of one another, then each is counted as a separate morpheme.
(C pours milk from pitcher) I didn't spilled it/	**MORPHEMES = 4 OR 5** In this utterance, the child is attempting to mark the past tense but has not realized that the rule for marking the past tense is to mark it on the auxiliary verb. Therefore, the child has marked past tense on both the main verb *spill* and the auxiliary *did*. Counting double-marking of past tense in auxiliary and main verb inflates the MLU, so the past tense *-ed* on *spilled* is not counted. The rule for assigning morphemes to negative contractions holds here as in previous examples, resulting in four or five total morphemes.
(M asks, "And who knocked the cart over?") the man the man the big man/	**MORPHEMES = 3** The use of false starts in an utterance is disregarded. Count only the most complete form.
(C pulls truck away from other child) that's my big my big truck/	**MORPHEMES = 5** Again, false starts, even if they occur within an utterance, are disregarded. Count only the most complete form.
(C continues arguing with other child) that's my new one my new truck/	**MORPHEMES = 8** This utterance is different from the previous two in that the repetition is not considered a false start but a clarification of an unclear sentence constituent. The child apparently decided that the listener might not know what *one* referred to and therefore provided additional information. This is not considered a false start and, as a result, each word in the repetition receives a morpheme.

section. The explanations should help clear up any questions. Also, the *Guide Practice* web-based practice site has additional exercises you may wish to complete.

With that practice, assigning morphemes to the utterances in Bridget's transcript should be easier. In addition, a completed syntactic analysis of a transcript obtained from a conversation with an older child, Sara, is included (in Appendix E) to provide experience in making some of the more difficult judgments. Using the transcript of Bridget (from Chapter 1) and a blank Structural Stage Analysis form (located in Appendix C, online), record the number of morphemes for each utterance in the Number of Morphemes column. When the number of morphemes for all of the child's utterances has been recorded, add the morphemes for each utterance to obtain the total number of morphemes. To obtain the mean length of utterance (MLU) in morphemes, divide this total by the total number of utterances (in Bridget's case, 100). Note: If any utterance is not assigned one or more morphemes, the total number of utterances may be less than 100 (e.g., if an utterance is a filler, it would not be assigned a morpheme and therefore would reduce the total number of utterances). For Bridget's transcript, compare your morpheme assignments, the total morpheme calculation, and the resulting MLU in morphemes with those in Form 3.1.

Guide to Analysis of Language Transcripts

FORM 3.1   Name of Child: **Bridget**

STRUCTURAL STAGE ANALYSIS

Utterance Number	Number of Morphemes	Negation	Yes/No Question	Wh- Question	Noun Phrase	Verb Phrase	Complex Sentence
1	1						
2	2						
3	1						
4	1						
5	4						
6	1						
7	2						
8	1						
9	1						
10	3						
11	1						
12	1						
13	1						
14	1						
15	4						
16	2						
17	4						
18	4						
19	2						
20	4						
21	2						
22	3						
23	3						
24	4						
25	2						
26	2						
27	2						
28	2						
29	1						
30	5						
31	4						
32	4						
33	4						
34	1						
35	4						
36	3						
37	1						
38	1						
39	1						
40	1						
41	1						
42	2						
43	2						
44	3						
45	3						
46	3						
47	1						
48	1						
49	1						
50	2						
Subtotal 1	**105**						

Note: "It" and "do" appear separately as part of other utterances.

FORM 3.1

STRUCTURAL STAGE ANALYSIS (continued)

Utterance Number	Number of Morphemes	Negation	Yes/No Question	Wh- Question	Noun Phrase	Verb Phrase	Complex Sentence
51	1						
52	3						
53	1						
54	1						
55	1						
56	4						
57	1						
58	1						
59	1						
60	4						
61	4						
62	3						
63	1						
64	4						
65	1						
66	2						
67	1						
68	1						
69	1						
70	1						
71	1						
72	3						
73	3						
74	1						
75	2						
76	1						
77	1						
78	3						
79	1						
80	1						
81	5						
82	1						
83	3						
84	1						
85	1						
86	2						
87	3						
88	3						
89	3						
90	3						
91	1						
92	1						
93	1						
94	1						
95	1						
96	3						
97	3						
98	1						
99	2						
100	2						
Subtotal 2	**95**						

Based on possessive "s" morpheme added to possessive pronoun.

Note that in the preceding utterance, she elaborates the directive, so it makes sense to give credit for both morphemes in "look it" in these utterances.

[105] + [95] = 200
No. of Morphemes (Subtotal 1)   No. of Morphemes (Subtotal 2)   Total No. of Morphemes

Total No. of Morphemes / Total No. of Utterances = [200 / 100] = 2.00 MLU

For Bridget's transcript, you should have obtained an MLU of 2.00 morphemes. This value provides very little information without additional analyses. One mechanism for analyzing this MLU is to compare it to data provided by Miller and Chapman (1981) on the predicted MLU ranges for 123 children. Table 3.1 summarizes the predicted MLUs, MLU ranges, and standard deviations for the children in their study.

The following computation permits evaluation of the MLU obtained from Bridget's transcript (in Chapter 1) or for any obtained MLU:

$$\frac{\text{obtained MLU} - \text{predicted MLU}}{\text{predicted } SD} = SD \text{ below the mean for CA}$$

$$\frac{2.00 - 2.23}{.510} = -.45 \; SD \text{ below the mean for 27 months}$$

Although Bridget is 28 months of age, the values for 27-month-olds are used. The MLU for the sample transcript fell .45 standard deviations below the mean for children 27 months of age. This MLU clearly reflects utterances that would be considered within normal limits in terms of mean length of morpheme. But this is a cursory analysis. Therefore, the next step is to examine variations in utterance length by completing a length distribution analysis, which can add to the interpretation of the obtained MLU. After you analyze variations in utterance length and identify grammatical morphemes, you will fill in the remaining columns of the Structural Stage Analysis form.

TABLE 3.1

Predicted MLU Ranges and Linguistic Stages of Children Within 1 Predicted Standard Deviation of the Mean

Age ± 1 mo.	Predicted MLU[a]	Predicted SD[b]	Predicted (Middle ±1 SD 68%)	Brown's Stages within 1 SD of predicted MLU						
				EI	LI	III	EIV	LIV/ EIV	LV	Post V
18	1.31	.325	.99–1.64	X	X					
21	1.62	.386	1.23–2.01	X	X	X				
24	1.92	.448	1.47–2.37	X	X	X				
27	2.23	.510	1.72–2.74		X	X				
30	2.54	.571	1.97–3.11		X	X	X			
33	2.85	.633	2.22–3.48			X	X			
36	3.16	.694	2.47–3.85			X	X	X		
39	3.47	.756	2.71–4.23				X	X	X	
42	3.78	.817	2.96–4.60				X	X	X	X
45	4.09	.879	3.21–4.97				X	X	X	X
48	4.40	.940	3.46–5.34				X	X	X	X
51	4.71	1.002	3.71–5.71					X	X	X
54	5.02	1.064	3.96–6.08					X	X	X
57	5.32	1.125	4.20–6.45						X	X
60	5.63	1.187	4.44–6.82						X	X

[a]MLU is predicted from the equation MLU = −.548 + .103 (AGE). [b]SD is predicted from the equation SD MLU = −.0446 + .0205 (AGE).

Note. From "The Relation Between Age and Mean Length of Utterance in Morphemes," by J. F. Miller and R. S. Chapman, 1981, *Journal of Speech and Hearing Research, 24*(2), p. 158. © 1981 by the American Speech-Language-Hearing Association. Reprinted with permission.

Guide to Analysis of Language Transcripts

Analyzing Variations in Utterance Length

In this analysis procedure, the utterances in Bridget's transcript are tallied by length in morphemes. This allows you to examine the distribution of utterances by length and to determine the range of utterance lengths within this transcript. Using the partially completed Structural Stage Analysis form and a blank Length Distribution Analysis form (found in Appendix C, online), progress utterance by utterance through the Number of Morphemes column of the Structural Stage Analysis form. Mark each utterance in the Tally column on the Length Distribution Analysis form in the row next to the number of morphemes that each utterance contains. For example, in the sample transcript, utterance #1 contains one morpheme, so mark a tally next to the box indicating one morpheme length. Utterance #2 contains two morphemes, so mark a tally next to the box indicating two morpheme lengths. Proceed through the Structural Stage Analysis form until all 100 utterances have been tallied. Then count the tallies in each row and record that number in the Total column for the corresponding row. Check your tallies and totals with those in the Length Distribution Analysis Form 3.2.

FORM 3.2   Name of Child __Bridget__

LENGTH DISTRIBUTION ANALYSIS

Length in Morphemes	Tally	Total
1																																											51
2															16
3																17
4														14
5				2
6		0
7		0
8		0
9		0
10		0
11		0
12		0
13		0
14		0
15		0

(Annotation pointing to the "51" total: "This appears inconsistent with Bloom's and Nelson's One-Word Utterance Types analyses in Chapter 2 in which 52 one-word utterances were counted, but note that utterance #27, "legs," is a one-word utterance with two morphemes.")

Upper Bound Length = __5__ morpheme(s)

Lower Bound Length = __1__ morpheme(s)

Totals obtained should be: 51 utterances one morpheme in length, 16 utterances two morphemes in length, 17 utterances three morphemes in length, 14 utterances four morphemes in length, and the two longest utterances were five morphemes in length. Upper bound length and lower bound length are reported at the bottom of the Length Distribution Analysis form; they provide analysis of variability in utterance length. To determine the upper bound length, check the Total column for the longest utterance in morphemes. In the sample transcript, there were two utterances that were five morphemes in length. Thus, in this transcript, the upper bound length, or the longest utterance, was five morphemes. Put 5 in the blank next to "Upper Bound Length." To determine the lower bound length, check the Total column for the shortest utterance in morphemes. In this sample, there were 51 utterances that were one morpheme in length. Thus, the lower bound length, or the shortest utterance, was one morpheme. Put 1 in the blank next to "Lower Bound Length."

This analysis may not appear to provide information substantially different from the MLU in morphemes. But, in fact, it does. A length distribution analysis is necessary for interpretation of an obtained MLU. The analysis may confirm the obtained MLU by indicating that there is appropriate variation in length of utterance around the mean length. Brown (1973) has provided expected upper bound lengths significantly higher than the target MLU for each of his five stages. His target values were data sampling points for each stage. He used these values to compare children's productions at each stage. These target values are not to be interpreted as midpoints or boundaries for stages. Table 3.2 summarizes the target values and the upper bound length for each stage of Brown's five stages of linguistic development.

As can be seen in Table 3.2, the upper bound length for each stage is substantially longer than the mean might indicate. Completing a length distribution analysis provides insight into the variation in length of utterances that a particular child is capable of producing. The obtained MLU can be validated by completing a length distribution analysis. The MLU of 2.00 morphemes from the sample transcript, which is midway between Stage I and Stage II in Table 3.2, implies that this child should produce utterances five to seven morphemes in length. This child produces utterances five morphemes in length, the upper bound length for Stage I. Are we to conclude that Bridget is incapable of producing utterances as long as her MLU would predict? That would be too strong a conclusion. The conservative conclusion would be that for this particular sample, Bridget produced utterances that did not vary around the mean as much as would be expected for her MLU.

The length distribution analysis also can confirm sample representativeness. Had Bridget produced a great number of responses to yes/no questions, as observed directly by a preponderance of yes/no responses in the sample transcript, a lower MLU would have been obtained and the length distribution analysis would have revealed restricted length variation. Such a finding would suggest a need for obtaining another sample of this child's language under more natural interactional conditions. In contrast, a very high MLU with little variation in length around the mean may be the result of obtaining a sample under narrative or storytelling conditions. Obtaining another sample under conversational conditions or using another part of the transcript would be recommended in this case as well.

TABLE 3.2

Target MLU in Morphemes and Upper Bound Lengths for Each Stage

Stage	MLU	Upper bound length
I	1.75	5
II	2.25	7
III	2.75	9
IV	3.50	11
V	4.00	13

Note. From *A First Language: The Early Stages* (p. 56), by R. Brown, 1973, Cambridge, MA: Harvard University Press. © 1973 by the President and Fellows of Harvard College. Reprinted with permission.

Reductions in variation in utterance length also may be indicative of additional problems beyond sample representativeness. A child with utterances clustering closely around the mean may have a specific deficit in production abilities. For example, children with apraxia-like behaviors or speech motor control problems tend to produce utterances resulting in low MLUs and minimal variation in utterance length around the mean. Children who are learning language in a very rote manner tend to produce utterances resulting in MLUs of varying lengths but with minimal variation around the mean. Children with autism-like behaviors present profiles such as this. Chapman (1981) provides an excellent discussion on the importance of completing a length distribution analysis and the implications of its results. The appropriate interpretation of the length distribution results for the sample transcript would be that this sample seems reasonably representative and that there may be a restriction in the amount of variation in utterance length around the obtained mean length. There also may be concern in regard to the large number of one-morpheme utterances (51). This may have brought the MLU down, resulting in a less-than-typical profile of variability about the mean.

Analyzing Use of Grammatical Morphemes

The next analysis procedure that we use results in a stage assignment reflecting mastery of grammatical morphemes. The stage assignments are based on data reported by de Villiers and de Villiers (1973) and indicate the stage at which each of the 14 grammatical morphemes studied by Brown (1973) is used correctly in 90% of the utterances where a particular grammatical morpheme is necessary (i.e., obligatory context). Brown designated 90% correct use in obligatory contexts as mastery level. Using this 90% criterion, de Villiers and de Villiers reported the stage at which each of the 14 grammatical morphemes typically is *mastered*. Table 3.3 summarizes the development for a variety of linguistic structures throughout Brown's stages of linguistic production, including grammatical morphemes. The fourth column indicates the stage at which each of the 14 grammatical morphemes is used in 90% of obligatory contexts. The other structures in Table 3.3 are reported at their *emergence level* and are discussed individually in the following six sections describing the analysis procedures for each structure. It may be useful to print the table at this time (available for convenient printing from the *Guide Practice* web-based program), instead of having to flip back and forth as each analysis procedure is discussed.

To determine mastery of the 14 grammatical morphemes in Bridget's transcript, we identify the obligatory contexts for and the use of each grammatical morpheme. Instances of correct use of the grammatical morphemes are easier to identify than instances of obligatory contexts in which the grammatical morphemes are not used. With practice, it should be possible to identify each obligatory context with ease.

Before beginning the grammatical morphemes analysis, examine the practice utterances provided in Example 3.2. Reviewing these provides experience both in identifying the 14 grammatical morphemes and in determining obligatory contexts when the grammatical morphemes are not used. Again, cover the shaded side of the page, identify the use of and/or the obligatory contexts for each of the 14 grammatical morphemes, and then check your results with those provided in the shaded section. The explanations offered should help clear up any discrepancies.

For additional practice, you may wish to complete the web-based exercises in *Guide Practice* at this time. Then return to Bridget's transcript, and examine each utterance for the use of and/or the obligatory context for each grammatical morpheme. Remember, there may be more than one instance of the use of and/or the obligatory context for any grammatical morpheme in each utterance. Using a blank Grammatical Morphemes Analysis form (available in Appendix C, online), record the utterance number for each obligatory context for the 14 grammatical morphemes in the Obligatory Context column. If the grammatical morpheme was used correctly in the obligatory context, record the utterance number in the Use column, too. It may be easier to consider each of the 14 grammatical morphemes individually as you examine each utterance for the obligatory context for and/or the use of a particular grammatical morpheme. This means that it will be necessary to go through the transcript 14 times. It is possible to examine each utterance once for the obligatory context for and/or the use of all 14 grammatical morphemes; however, it is more likely that some will be missed that way.

(Text continues on p. 83.)

TABLE 3.3

Production Characteristics of Linguistic Development Organized by Brown's Stages

Stage	MLU	Age (months)	Grammatical morphemes	Negation	Yes/No questions	Wh- questions	Complex sentences	Stage	Noun phrase elaborations[d]	Verb phrase elaborations[d]
Early I	1.01–1.49	19–22[a] 16–26[b]	Occasional use	*no* as single-word utterance (but not as a negative response to a yes/no question)	Marked with rising intonation	*what* + *this/that*	None used	I[d]	NP = (M) + N[e] Elaborated NPs occur only alone	Main Verb: uninflected; occasional use of *-ing* Auxiliary: not used Copula: not used Verb + Particles: occasional use Verb + Particles: occasional use
Late I / Early II	1.50–1.99	23–26 18–31	Occasional use	*no* + noun or verb *not* + noun or verb		*what* + NP or VP *where* + NP or VP				
II	2.00–2.49	27–30 21–35	1. Present progressive of verb *-ing*[c] 2. Regular plural *-s* 3. Preposition *in*				Semiauxiliary appears: *gonna, gotta, wanna, hafta*	II[d]	NP same as Stage I Object NP elaboration appears: V + NP	Main Verb: occasionally marked Auxiliary: 1. Semiauxiliary appears 2. Use of present progressive *-ing* without auxiliary Copula: appears without tense/number inflection
III	2.50–2.99	31–34 24–41	4. Preposition *on* 5. Possessive *-s*	NP + (negative) + VP		Wh- word + sentence *why, who,* and *how* questions appear	Object NP complement; full sentence takes the place of object of the verb	III[d]	NP = ((demonstrative) (article)) + (M) + N Subject NP elaboration appears: NP + V	Main Verb: 1. Obligatory 2. Overgeneralization of regular past *-ed* Auxiliary: Present tense forms appear: *can, will, be, do*
Early IV	3.00–3.49	35–38 28–45		NP + auxiliary + (negative) + VP NP + copula + (negative) + VP	Inversion of auxiliary verb and subject noun	Inconsistent auxiliary inversion *when* questions appear	Simple infinitive phrases appear Simple *wh-* clauses appear Conjoined sentences with conjunction *and*			

(continues)

TABLE 3.3 (continued)

Stage	MLU	Age (months)	Grammatical morphemes	Negation	Yes/No questions	Wh-questions	Complex sentences	Noun phrase elaborations[d]	Verb phrase elaborations[d]
Late IV/ Early V	3.50–3.99	39–42 31–50	No others mastered	No change	No change	No change	Multiple embeddings Conjoined and embedded clauses in the same sentence	NP = ((demonstrative) (article)) + (M) ((possessive) + (adjective)) + N Subject NP is obligatory; noun or pronoun always appears in subject position	Main Verb: regular past -ed (double marking of main verb and auxiliary for past in negative sentences) Auxiliary: 1. Past modals appear, including *could, would, should, must, might* 2. *be* + present progressive -*ing* appears Verb Phrase: semi-auxiliary complements take NP
Late V	4.00–4.49	43–46 37–52	6. Regular past tense of verb -*ed* 7. Irregular past tense of verb 8. Regular third-person singular present tense -*s* 9. Definite and indefinite articles 10. Contractible copula	Past tense modals and *be* in contracted and uncontracted form		See Grammatical Morphemes column (6–14)	Relative clauses appear Infinitive phrases with subjects different from that of main sentence Conjunction *if* used	NP = same as Stage IV Number agreement between subject and predicate verb phrase continues to be a problem beyond Stage V	See Grammatical Morphemes column (6–10)
V+	4.50–4.99	47–50 41–59	11. Contractible auxiliary 12. Uncontractible copula 13. Uncontractible auxiliary 14. Irregular third-person singular present tense		No data		Gerund phrases appear *Wh*-infinitive phrases appear Unmarked infinitive phrases appear Conjunction *because* used		See Grammatical Morphemes column (11–14) Main Verb/Auxiliary 1. Past tense *be* appears as main verb and auxiliary 2. Infrequent use of present perfect tense with auxiliary marked
V++	5.00–5.99	51–67 43–67	No data	No data	No data	No data	Conjunctions *when, but,* and *so* appear		

Note. N = Noun, NP = Noun Phrase, V = Verb, VP = Verb Phrase, M = Modifier.
[a]Predicted age range. [b]Age range within 1 *SD* of predicted values. [c]Based on 90% use in obligatory contexts, except stages EI–LI/EII. [d]Stages I, II, and III have been used to describe developments within only noun phrase elaboration and verb phrase elaboration based on sources of these data. [e]The following are definitions of sentence notations:

= means is expanded or elaborated as described
(x) the item within the parentheses is optional
((x) (y)) either one of the items in the brackets must occur

S = NP + VP
VP = V + NP

EXAMPLE 3.2

GRAMMATICAL MORPHEMES	
(C points to picture in book) two puppies/	This is an example of the correct use of the regular plural -s. Therefore, there is an obligatory context for and a correct use of a regular plural -s grammatical morpheme.
(C pulls second tiny doll from bag) two baby/	In this utterance, there is an obligatory context for the regular plural -s, but the child has not used the plural inflection.
(C points to box in corner) puppy in box/	This is an example of an obligatory context for and a correct use of the preposition in. Determining the obligatory context for many of the grammatical morphemes, especially prepositions, requires that the transcript include detailed description of the nonlinguistic context. This utterance also contains an obligatory context for articles preceding the nouns, but the articles are not used. In addition, this utterance contains an obligatory context for the contractible copula (is in [the] box), and, again, that grammatical morpheme is not used.
(C hears baby crying in another room) baby cry/	If the context notes indicate that the child is describing an ongoing activity, this utterance can be considered an obligatory context for the present progressive tense of the verb (-ing). Obviously, it was not used in this utterance. In addition, there is an obligatory context for the contractible auxiliary without use. There also is questionable obligatory context for an article without use. The reason this would be considered questionable is that many times children use the word baby as a proper name, and an article would not be required.
(C points to puppy still in box) puppy there/	The context notes for this utterance indicate that the child was pointing out one of the puppies still in the box. Therefore, this would be an obligatory context for the preposition, in. In addition, there is an obligatory context for an article (a or the) and a contractible copula (a/the puppy is [in] there).
(C hands M's hat to clinician) mommy hat/	Again, from the context notes, it can be seen that the child is talking about his mother's hat. Thus, there is an obligatory context for the possessive -s without use of that grammatical morpheme.
(clinician asks, "Where's your owie?" and C holds out hand) on finger/	This utterance contains an obligatory context for and a correct use of the preposition, on.
(C dances doll across toy piano keys) Mommy singing/	This is an instance of an obligatory context for and a correct use of the present progressive tense of the verb (-ing). This utterance also contains an obligatory context for the contractible auxiliary, but the auxiliary is not used. Note that the auxiliary does not have to be present to give the child credit for correct use of -ing.
(C hands book to M) Daddy's book/	This utterance contains an obligatory context for and a correct use of the possessive -s.

(continues)

EXAMPLE 3.2 (*continued*)

(C knocks doll off barn) she falled down/	This utterance contains an obligatory context for the irregular past tense of the verb. However, the child's use is of the regular form, and thus there is incorrect use of the irregular past. This is simply an obligatory context for the irregular past.
(puppy knocks C down) puppy jumped on me/	This utterance contains an obligatory context for and the correct use of the regular past tense of the verb. It also contains an obligatory context for and a correct use of the preposition, *on*. In addition, it contains an obligatory context for an article.
(C points to puppy) that a puppy!/	This utterance contains an obligatory context for the contractible copula, but the copula is not used. In addition, there is an obligatory context for and a correct use of the article, *a*.
(C points to one of the puppies) he barks/	This is an example of an obligatory context for and a correct use of the regular third-person singular present tense of the verb. The regular form is easy to identify by looking for the use of proper names or singular pronouns. These are often followed by the regular third-person singular present tense of the verb.
(C points to another puppy) that's my puppy/	This utterance contains an obligatory context for and a correct use of the contractible copula. The possessive pronoun, *my*, does not require use of the possessive -*s* grammatical morpheme, and therefore this utterance does not contain an obligatory context for the possessive -*s*.
(C scoops raisins into a pile) these are my ones/	This utterance contains obligatory contexts for and correct use of two grammatical morphemes: the uncontractible copula (*are* [plural form]) and the regular plural -*s*.
(M says, "You need to hurry," as C puts toys in bag) I'm hurrying/	This utterance, too, contains obligatory contexts for and correct use of two grammatical morphemes: the contractible auxiliary (*am*) and the present progressive tense of the verb (-*ing*).
(C makes doll jump up and down) him jumping/	This utterance contains an obligatory context for the contractible auxiliary without the correct use. It also contains an obligatory context for and a correct use of the present progressive tense of the verb.
(M says, "Who's ready for ice cream?") I am/	This utterance is in response to a question, and in this elliptical form, the copula is uncontractible (*I'm* cannot be said as a response). Thus, this is an obligatory context for and a correct use of the uncontractible copula.
(M says, "Who's making all that noise?") he is/	This utterance is also in response to a question, and again, as a response, *he's* isn't possible. The preceding utterance makes this an obligatory context for and a correct use of the uncontractible auxiliary.
(C shows M a new toy) do you like it↑/	This utterance contains no obligatory contexts. *Do* is an auxiliary and not a form of the verb *to be*, which is what Brown studied in the contractible and uncontractible forms.

EXAMPLE 3.2 (*continued*)

(C walks dolls away from toy piano) they were singing/	This utterance contains an obligatory context for and a correct use of the present progressive tense (*-ing*) of the verb. In addition, since using the contracted form of the auxiliary eliminates the tense information (*They are singing* and *They were singing* both contract to *They're singing*), this is an example of an uncontractible auxiliary. De Villiers and de Villiers (1978) indicated that uncontractible forms typically are syllabic, as in this example. The previous two examples are uncontractible in the elliptical form.
(C points to puppy climbing out of box) he does that every time/	This is an example of an obligatory context for and a correct use of the irregular third-person singular present tense of the verb.

Once all the obligatory contexts for and uses of the 14 grammatical morphemes have been identified, add the number of uses of each grammatical morpheme and divide this total by the total number of obligatory contexts for that grammatical morpheme. Multiply this number by 100 to get the percentage of use in obligatory contexts for a specific grammatical morpheme. Put this number in the % Correct Use in Obligatory Contexts column. Check your results with those in Form 3.3.

As can be seen from the completed Grammatical Morphemes Analysis form, several grammatical morphemes were not present in the sample transcript, nor were the obligatory contexts present. For these missing grammatical morphemes, no statement can be made regarding mastery. In addition, several of the grammatical morphemes occurred so infrequently that the resulting percentages are questionable. Both of these problems point to the need for obtaining samples that are relatively lengthy. As discussed in Chapter 1, a sample of 100 utterances is the absolute minimum length.

So what conclusions can we draw from the grammatical morphemes analysis of Bridget's transcript? First, in spite of few instances of each, this child apparently has mastered the regular plural *-s*, the preposition *in*, and the possessive *-s*. In addition, the contractible copula appears to have been mastered. We are more confident of Bridget's mastery of this last grammatical morpheme because there were eight instances of correct use. It can also be concluded that five grammatical morphemes do not appear to have been mastered: the regular past tense *-ed* (with 33% correct use in obligatory contexts), the irregular past tense of the verb (with 43% correct use in obligatory contexts), indefinite and definite articles (with 35% correct use in obligatory contexts), the contractible auxiliary (with 50% correct use in obligatory contexts), and the uncontractible copula (with 50% correct use in obligatory contexts). In addition, one obligatory context was noted for each of two grammatical morphemes (the preposition *on* and the regular third-person singular present tense *-s*). Only one obligatory context for each occurred, with no use, which yields 0% correct use for these two grammatical morphemes. No conclusions can be drawn for the grammatical morphemes *-ing*, uncontractible auxiliary, and irregular third-person singular present tense. Stages are assigned according to mastery of grammatical morphemes, which we discuss in the Summary and Interpretation section near the end of the chapter.

Analyzing the Complexity of Negation

Negation analysis results in a stage assignment reflecting negation's structural complexity within a transcript. The stage assignments are based on data reported by Klima and Bellugi (1966); Chapman (1978, as cited in Miller, 1981); and Chapman, Paul, and Wanska (1981). Changes in the child's ability to incorporate negative elements into an utterance typically occur with increases in utterance length. The fifth column in Table 3.3 indicates the changes in structural complexity of negation and the stage at which those changes emerge. Keep in mind that the stage assignments reflect *emergence* of a new way of producing negation and not *mastery* of this new form. In addition, note that changes do not occur at every stage.

FORM 3.3   Name of Child **Bridget**

GRAMMATICAL MORPHEMES ANALYSIS

Grammatical Morpheme	Obligatory Context	Use	% Correct Use in Obligatory Contexts
1. *-ing*	—	—	—
2. plural *-s*	27, 78, 81	27, 78, 81	100
3. *in*	17, 97	17, 97	100
4. *on*	13	—	0
5. possessive *-s*	62, 65	62, 65	100
6. regular past tense *-ed*	36, 45, 96	96	33
7. irregular past tense	2, 5, 44, 46, 56, 81, 86	51, 81, 86	43
8. regular third-person singular present tense *-s*	75	—	0
9. articles *a, an, the*	8, 9, 13, 17, 25, 27, 32, 40, 41, 50, 58, 60, 61, 81, 84, 93, 94	17, 25, 32, 60, 61, 81	35
10. contractible copula	18, 20, 32, 33, 35, 60, 61, 65	18, 20, 32, 33, 35, 60, 61, 65	100
11. contractible auxiliary	21, 24	21	50
12. uncontractible copula	23, 62	23	50
13. uncontractible auxiliary	—	—	—
14. irregular third-person singular present tense	—	—	—

To determine the stage that characterizes a child's level of negation, analyze each utterance within the child's transcript for developmental complexity. The first step is to identify negative elements within the transcript. Identifying negative elements is easier than identifying some syntactic structures because there are a limited number of ways in which negation can be incorporated into an utterance at these developmental levels. These include the use of *no* as a single-word utterance (except in response to a question) or adding *no* to a noun or verb, as well as the use of *not* in contracted and uncontracted forms in various sentence positions. After identifying utterances with negation, determine the stage that best characterizes each negative element. This second step may be more difficult. To increase your ability to make such judgments, use the practice utterances provided in Example 3.3. Cover the right side of the page, compare the utterance to the descriptions provided in the fifth column of Table 3.3, assign a stage, and then check your results with those provided. The explanations in the shaded section should help clear up any questions. You may wish to turn to *Guide Practice* web-based exercises for additional practice.

The practice you just completed should help you identify negative elements and assign stages to the developmental complexity of each. Now, return to the sample transcript and examine each utterance for the presence of negative elements. If there is no negative element in the utterance, mark a dash (—) for that utterance in the Negation column on the Structural Stage Analysis form used earlier to record the number of morphemes for each of Bridget's utterances. When you identify an utterance with a negative element, compare that utterance to the descriptions of increases in complexity provided in the fifth column of Table 3.3 to determine the stage that best characterizes the complexity of the negative element within the utterance. Then record the stage number for that utterance in the Negation column on the Structural Stage Analysis form. When each utterance has been examined for the presence of negative elements and stage assignments have been recorded, compare your results with those provided on Form 3.4 (on p. 88).

Bridget's transcript contained four negative utterances, ranging in complexity from Late Stage I/Early Stage II– Stage II to Early IV–Late Stage IV/Early Stage V. Utterances #3 and #33 pose some problems and therefore are not included in the total of the four negative utterances. Utterance #3 is simply a negative response to the mother's question; therefore, it is not included in the total of negative utterances. Utterance #33 includes a negative response to the mother's question, "Do you want to put him up there?" The child responds, "No [I don't want to put him up there because] it's heavy." The utterance is not a negative utterance in terms of the presence of negative elements incorporated into the utterance structure. It is a negative response that is elliptical in relation to the mother's utterance and is a clarification of that negative response. Therefore, it is not appropriate to include it in the total of negative utterances.

The stage assignments for individual utterances recorded on the Structural Stage Analysis form are used to complete the Production Characteristics Summary form, which we address in the Summary and Interpretation section at the end of the chapter. Before tallying these instances of negation on the summary form, the complexity of five other syntactic structures should be analyzed. The tallying of stage assignments for individual utterances allows for examination of the most frequently occurring stage for negation as well as the most advanced stage. These data can only be interpreted in relation to stage assignments for other structures.

Analyzing the Complexity of Yes/No Questions

Analyzing the complexity of yes/no questions yields a stage assignment reflecting that complexity. Such analysis is done in the same manner as we used for grammatical morphemes and negation. The developmental sequence of changes in complexity and stage assignments is based on data reported by Klima and Bellugi (1966) and Chapman et al. (1981). The sixth column in Table 3.3 summarizes the sequence of developmental changes for yes/no questions. As with negation, stage assignments reflect appearance of changes in producing yes/no questions and not mastery of the changes. And like the preceding syntactic structure, changes in complexity of yes/no questions do not occur at every stage.

Before identifying the yes/no questions and determining the developmental complexity of each question in Bridget's transcript, turn to Example 3.4 (on p. 89). The practice-example utterances have been selected to demonstrate some of the problems that are frequently encountered when describing the developmental complexity of yes/no questions. The practice gained in assigning stages to these utterances will be helpful when such analysis is performed on the sample transcript. Cover the right side of the page, compare the utterance to the descriptions of developmental changes in Table 3.3, and assign a stage. Then check your results with those in the shaded section. The explanations provided should help clear up any questions.

(Text continues on p. 90.)

EXAMPLE 3.3

NEGATION	
(M and C are playing with a circus set; M says, "Do you want me to put him in the wagon?") no/	**NO STAGE ASSIGNED** This is not an example of *no* as a negative sentence. It is *no* as a single-word response to a yes/no question, so a stage is not assigned. A transcript that contains many responses to yes/no questions will erroneously report the stage for negation. A transcript such as this would be rejected on the basis of a lack of representativeness prior to beginning analysis of structural complexity.
(C pushes M's hand away as she tries to wipe his mouth) no/	**EARLY STAGE I (EI)** The use of *no* as a single-word utterance is the earliest type of negative sentence. Assigning Early Stage I to this utterance in a transcript with utterances considerably longer than one word may distort the assignment of an overall stage for negation, but it represents the accurate stage assignment.
(C hits doll with a teddy bear, then looks at M and says) no hit/	**LATE STAGE I/EARLY STAGE II–STAGE II (LI/EII–II)** This utterance is an example of a *no* + verb sentence form. This form is characteristic of Late Stage I/Early Stage II, but it continues to be used through Stage II.
(C pulls on M's arm) not go/	**LATE STAGE I/EARLY STAGE II–STAGE II (LI/EII–II)** This utterance is an example of a *not* + verb sentence form, also characteristic of Late Stage I/Early Stage II through Stage II.
(as M leaves room, C shakes head and looks at M) me no go/	**STAGE III (III)** This utterance is an example of a negative sentence in the form NP + negative + VP, with the negative element integrated into the sentence. This form emerges in Stage III.
(C puts girl doll in car) Daddy not go/	**STAGE III (III)** This is another example with the negative element integrated into the sentence: NP + negative + VP. In this case, the negative element is *not* instead of *no*. This utterance and the preceding one are characteristic of the same stage.
(C opens box of people and animals) there aren't any kikis here/	**EARLY STAGE IV–LATE STAGE IV/EARLY STAGE V (EIV–LIV/EV)** This utterance is an example of the verb, *be*, in the plural present tense negative contracted form. This form (NP + auxiliary + negative + VP) appears in Early Stage IV, at the same time as auxiliary elements in contracted and uncontracted forms.
(C picks up a toy dog and shakes her head) not a kiki/	**LATE STAGE I/EARLY STAGE II–STAGE II (LI/EII–II)** This utterance is an example of *not* + noun with an article included. As discussed in the third example, assigning Late Stage I/Early Stage II to the utterance appears to underestimate the child's abilities to produce negative structures. Therefore, the best stage assignment that can be made is to assign the range of stages.

EXAMPLE 3.3 (*continued*)

(puppy jumps on clinician and C looks at her) he no bite you/	**STAGE III (III)** This utterance contains a negative element integrated within the sentence between the NP and the VP (NP + negative + VP).
(C's baby brother is babbling and C says to M) he isn't silly/	**EARLY STAGE IV–LATE STAGE IV/EARLY STAGE V (EIV–LIV/EV)** This negative sentence contains the present tense of the verb, *be*, in the negative contracted form. It is typical of examples provided in the literature for Early Stage IV (NP + copula + negative).
(M holds up dirty socks) those aren't mine/	**LATE STAGE V (LV)** This utterance contains the plural form of the verb, *be*, in the form of a negative contraction.
(M says from other room, "Did you find your hat?") it wasn't there/	**LATE STAGE V (LV)** This utterance contains a negative contraction of the past-tense form of the verb, *be*.
(C turns cup upside down on table) no juice/	**LATE STAGE I/EARLY STAGE II–STAGE II (LI/EII–II)** This utterance is an example of the *no* + noun form of negation. It is characteristic of Late Stage I/Early Stage II, but the range of stages is recorded.
(C pushes blue crayon away) I don't want that one/	**EARLY STAGE IV–LATE STAGE IV/EARLY STAGE V (EIV–LIV/EV)** This utterance contains an auxiliary ("the dummy *do*," an auxiliary form used to negate the sentence) in the negative contracted form, which appears in Early Stage IV (NP + auxiliary + negative + VP).
(clinician drops box of little bears and begins to pick them up) you shouldn't do that/	**LATE STAGE V (LV)** This utterance contains the modal auxiliary verb, *should*, in the past-tense and negative contracted form. Past-tense modals in contracted and uncontracted form appear in negative sentences at this stage.
(C turns puzzle piece around and around) this one doesn't fit/	**EARLY STAGE IV–LATE STAGE IV/EARLY STAGE V (EIV–LIV/EV)** Again, there is an auxiliary, *does*, in the negative contracted form.
(C hugs teddy bear after pulling it out of box) I couldn't find him/	**LATE STAGE V (LV)** This utterance contains the past-tense modal auxiliary, *could*, in the negative contracted form.

Guide to Analysis of Language Transcripts

FORM 3.4

STRUCTURAL STAGE ANALYSIS

Name of Child: **Bridget**

Utterance Number	Number of Morphemes	Negation	Yes/No Question	Wh- Question	Noun Phrase	Verb Phrase	Complex Sentence
1	1						
2	2						
3	1	|					
4	4						
5	1						
6	2						
7	1						
8	1						
9	1						
10	3						
11	3						
12	1						
13	1						
14	4						
15	2						
16	4						
17	4	EIV-LIV/EV					
18	2						
19	4						
20	4	EIV-LIV/EV					
21	2						
22	3	EIV-LIV/EV					
23	4						
24	2						
25	2						
26	2						
27	2						
28	1						
29	3						
30	5						
31	4						
32	4						
33	4	|					
34	4						
35	3						
36	1						
37	1						
38	1						
39	1						
40	1						
41	1						
42	2						
43	2						
44	3						
45	3						
46	1						
47	1						
48	1						
49	1						
50	1						
Subtotal 1	**105**						

Annotation (row 3): response to yes/no question

Annotation (row 33): response to yes/no question plus explanation

FORM 3.1

STRUCTURAL STAGE ANALYSIS (continued)

Utterance Number	Number of Morphemes	Negation	Yes/No Question	Wh- Question	Noun Phrase	Verb Phrase	Complex Sentence
51	1						
52	3						
53	1						
54	1						
55	1						
56	4						
57	1						
58	1						
59	1						
60	4						
61	4						
62	3						
63	1						
64	1						
65	4						
66	2						
67	1						
68	1						
69	1						
70	1						
71	1						
72	3						
73	3						
74	1						
75	2						
76	1						
77	1						
78	3						
79	1						
80	5						
81	1						
82	3						
83	1						
84	1						
85	2						
86	3						
87	1						
88	1						
89	3						
90	3						
91	1						
92	1						
93	1						
94	1						
95	1						
96	3						
97	1						
98	1						
99	2						
100	2						
Subtotal 2	**95**						

Annotation (row 62): Based on possessive "s" morpheme added to possessive pronoun.

Annotation (rows 89–90): Note that in the preceding utterance, she elaborates the directive, so it makes sense to give credit for both morphemes in "look it" in these utterances.

No. of Morphemes (Subtotal 1) [105] + No. of Morphemes (Subtotal 2) [95] = Total No. of Morphemes 200

Total No. of Morphemes / Total No. of Utterances = [200 / 100] = 2.00 MLU

EXAMPLE 3.4

YES/NO QUESTIONS	
(C picks up an apple) ball↑/	**EARLY STAGE I–STAGE III (EI–III)** Yes/No questions are marked only with rising intonation during these four stages. It is impossible to differentiate among these stages in the child's productions, so the best way to assign a stage is to assign a range. When this information is put together with other stage assignments, the adequacy of the child's productions can be determined.
(C shows cow to M) see↑/	**EARLY STAGE I–STAGE III (EI–III)** This yes/no question is of the same form as the previous one, and the four stages cannot be differentiated at this point.
(C turns empty cookie box upside down) more↑/	**EARLY STAGE I–STAGE III (EI–III)** Again, this is a yes/no question marked only with rising intonation, and, as in the preceding two examples, these four stages cannot be differentiated
(C hands empty cup to M) more juice↑/	**EARLY STAGE I–STAGE III (EI–III)** Although this utterance is longer than the preceding three, it is of the same form. Therefore, these four stages cannot be differentiated.
(C talking to toy monkey) do like monkeys↑/	**EARLY STAGE I–STAGE III (EI–III)** This utterance contains the "dummy do." But the subject noun phrase is omitted. It would be inappropriate to assign Early Stage IV–Late Stage V, so we must assign Early Stage I–Stage III.
(C hands puzzle piece to M) da no go↑/	**EARLY STAGE I–STAGE III (EI–III)** Again, this is a yes/no question marked only with rising intonation. No differentiation of stages is possible.
(C picks up doll from doll bed) baby wet↑/	**EARLY STAGE I–STAGE III (EI–III)** This is one more example of a yes/no question marked only with rising intonation.
(C turns to M as she leaves the room) am I gonna go↑/	**EARLY STAGE IV–LATE STAGE V (EIV–LV)** Finally, this is an example of a yes/no question with inversion of the auxiliary and the subject noun. This form emerges in Early Stage IV.
(C looks on as M dumps cookie out of box) is that the only one↑/	**EARLY STAGE IV–LATE STAGE V (EIV–LV)** This also is an example of a yes/no question with the inversion necessary to form a question. In this utterance, the main verb, be, is inverted. The ability to invert all or part of the verb phrase with the noun phrase appears in Early Stage IV.
(C picks up last cupcake) can I eat this one↑/	**EARLY STAGE IV–LATE STAGE V (EIV–LV)** This yes/no question also contains auxiliary inversion. Although assigning the same stage to the last three utterances seems to distort the apparent differences in complexity, it appears to be the best alternative. The differences in complexity will be captured in the verb phrase analysis.
(C hands wind-up toy to M) will you fix this↑/	**EARLY STAGE IV–LATE STAGE V (EIV–LV)** This yes/no question is of the same auxiliary inversion form. The obviously higher level of complexity will be credited to the child in the verb phrase analysis.

These practice utterances should have clarified the two ways in which children construct yes/no questions. Although other changes in complexity are apparent within yes/no questions, such changes reflect changes in structures other than the formation of the question. You may wish to turn to *Guide Practice* web-based exercises for additional practice.

Now, return to the sample transcript. To determine the stage that characterizes Bridget's level of yes/no question production, examine each yes/no question in the sample transcript for developmental complexity. First, identify the yes/no questions and then examine the ways in which they were formed. Examine each utterance for the presence of rising intonation or verb-phrase inversion. To determine the stage that describes each individual yes/no question, compare each question to the descriptions provided in Table 3.3. Progress through the transcript, recording a dash (—) for each utterance that is not a type of yes/no question in the Yes/No Question column on the Structural Stage Analysis form used earlier. If the utterance is a type of yes/no question, compare that utterance to the descriptions provided in the sixth column of Table 3.3 to find which stage best describes the complexity of that question. Then record the stage number or range of stages for that utterance in the Yes/No Question column on the Structural Stage Analysis form. After each yes/no question in the sample transcript has been analyzed, compare your results with those in the partially completed Structural Stage Analysis, Form 3.5.

Three utterances should have been identified as types of yes/no questions in the sample transcript. Each of these yes/no questions was formed using rising intonation, and thus each was typical of Early Stage I–Stage III. Although these utterances appear to be a minimal amount of data for analyzing the developmental level of yes/no questions, it is not uncommon to find that only a small percentage of the utterances are question forms. These instances of yes/no questions should be tallied on the Production Characteristics Summary form after the complexity of four other syntactic structures (*wh-* questions, noun phrases, verb phrases, and complex sentences) has been analyzed. Final interpretation of the level of complexity of yes/no questions can be made only after the developmental level of all other syntactic structures has been analyzed and summarized.

Analyzing the Complexity of *Wh-* Questions

Analysis of the developmental level of *wh-* questions results in a stage assignment reflecting the complexity of the questions. Unlike the preceding analyses, the analysis of *wh-* questions considers two aspects of the structure to be analyzed. The first consideration in determining the developmental level of a *wh-* question is the type of *wh-* question. For example, *what* questions appear early in the developmental sequence, and *when* questions appear much later. A stage is assigned to a particular *wh-* question according to which type of *wh-* question it is. The second consideration is the form of the question. For example, "*what* + NP"-question forms occur early in the developmental sequence, while questions with auxiliary inversion occur considerably later in the sequence. The form of the question and the type of *wh-* word are used to refine the judgments about stage assignment. For example, a *what* question with auxiliary inversion is assigned a higher stage than a *what* question without auxiliary inversion.

Both aspects of the *wh-* question are considered in assigning a stage to each utterance. The changes in type and form of the *wh-* questions are summarized in the seventh column of Table 3.3. The stage assignments are based on data reported by Klima and Bellugi (1966); Ervin-Tripp (1970); Tyack and Ingram (1977); and Chapman et al. (1981). Changes in type and form reflect the appearance of these changes and not mastery of the changes.

To determine the stage that characterizes the child's level of *wh-* question development, analyze each *wh-* question within the sample transcript for type and form. To improve your ability to identify changes in type and form, complete the practice utterances in Example 3.5. Cover the right side of the page, make the stage assignment, and then check your assignments with those provided in the shaded section.

This practice should be helpful in assigning stages on the basis of both the type and the form of the *wh-* question. Now return to the sample transcript and determine the stage that best characterizes the type and form of each *wh-* question. Progress through the transcript and record a dash (—) for each utterance that is not a *wh-* question and the appropriate stage for each *wh-* question in the *Wh-* Question column on the Structural

(Text continues on p. 93.)

FORM 3.5 Name of Child __Bridget__

STRUCTURAL STAGE ANALYSIS

Utterance Number	Number of Morphemes	Negation	Yes/No Question	Wh- Question	Noun Phrase	Verb Phrase	Complex Sentence
1	1	—	—				
2	2	—	—				
3	1	—	—				
4	1	—	—				
5	4	—	EI–III				
6	1	—	—				
7	2	—	—				
8	1	—	—				
9	1	—	—				
10	1	—	—				
11	3	—	—				
12	1	—	—				
13	1	—	—				
14	1	—	—				
15	4	—	—				
16	2	—	—				
17	4	—	—				
18	4	EIV–LIV/EV	—				
19	2	—	—				
20	4	—	—				
21	4	EIV–LIV/EV	—				
22	2	—	—				
23	3	EIV–LIV/EV	—				
24	4	—	—				
25	2	—	—				
26	2	—	—				
27	2	—	—				
28	2	—	—				
29	1	—	—				
30	5	—	—				
31	4	—	—				
32	4	—	—				
33	4	—	—				
34	1	—	—				
35	4	—	—				
36	3	—	—				
37	1	—	—				
38	1	—	—				
39	1	—	—				
40	1	—	—				
41	1	—	—				
42	1	—	—				
43	2	—	—				
44	2	—	—				
45	3	—	—				
46	3	—	—				
47	1	—	—				
48	1	—	—				
49	1	—	—				
50	1	—	—				
Subtotal 1	**105**						

FORM 3.5

STRUCTURAL STAGE ANALYSIS (continued)

Utterance Number	Number of Morphemes	Negation	Yes/No Question	Wh- Question	Noun Phrase	Verb Phrase	Complex Sentence
51	1	—	—				
52	3	—	—				
53	1	—	—				
54	1	—	—				
55	1	—	—				
56	4	—	—				
57	1	—	—				
58	1	—	—				
59	1	—	—				
60	4	—	EI–III				
61	4	—	—				
62	3	—	—				
63	1	—	—				
64	1	—	—				
65	4	—	—				
66	2	—	—				
67	1	—	—				
68	1	—	—				
69	1	—	—				
70	1	—	EI–III				
71	1	—	—				
72	3	—	—				
73	3	—	—				
74	1	—	—				
75	2	—	—				
76	1	—	—				
77	1	—	—				
78	3	LI/EII–II	—				
79	1	—	—				
80	1	—	—				
81	5	—	—				
82	1	—	—				
83	3	—	—				
84	1	—	—				
85	1	—	—				
86	2	—	—				
87	3	—	—				
88	3	—	—				
89	1	—	—				
90	3	—	—				
91	1	—	—				
92	1	—	—				
93	1	—	—				
94	1	—	—				
95	1	—	—				
96	3	—	—				
97	3	—	—				
98	1	—	—				
99	2	—	—				
100	2	—	—				
Subtotal 2	**95**						

[105] + [95] = 200
No. of Morphemes (Subtotal 1) + No. of Morphemes (Subtotal 2) = Total No. of Morphemes

$$\frac{\text{Total No. of Morphemes}}{\text{Total No. of Utterances}} = \left[\frac{200}{100}\right] = 2.00 \text{ MLU}$$

EXAMPLE 3.5

WH- QUESTIONS

(M tells C to pick up toys quickly) what?/	**NO STAGE ASSIGNED** This child is simply asking for a repetition of the statement or has learned to say *what* as a stalling technique. Repetition requests are not coded as *wh-* questions.
(C points to doughnut and looks at M) wazit?/ [what this?]	**EARLY STAGE I (EI)** This probably is the most basic type of *wh-* question in that it functions as a generic question type. It is a *what* question type and is in the form of a reduced *what* + *this*.
(clock makes noise and C looks to M) what that?/	**EARLY STAGE I (EI)** This question is characteristic of the same stage as the preceding example, even though it is more complex (*what* + *that*).
(C holds up small plastic animal) what this one?/	**LATE STAGE I/EARLY STAGE II–STAGE II (LI/EII–II)** Although this is the same type of question as the preceding two (*what*), it is in a more complex form: *what* + NP. Consequently, it is assigned a more advanced stage range.
(C hears voices outside door and asks M) where Daddy?/	**LATE STAGE I/EARLY STAGE II–STAGE II (LI/EII–II)** This question is of a different type (*where*) than the preceding questions, but it is in the same form: *where* + NP. Thus, it is assigned the same stage.
(C is drawing with marking pens) where the green one is?/	**STAGE III (III)** This question is the same type of question as the preceding one (*where*), but it is in a more complex form: *wh-* word + sentence. This form emerges in Stage III.
(C is digging through toy box) where's the big one?/	**EARLY STAGE IV–LATE V (EIV–LV)** Again, this is a *where* question, but this one reflects inversion of the verb and noun phrase. This form emerges in Early Stage IV.
(clinician enters room and adjusts remote control camera) what him doing?/	**LATE STAGE I/EARLY STAGE II–STAGE II (LI/EII–II)** This is an example of a simple *what doing* question (*what* + VP) that emerges in Late Stage I/Early Stage II and does not change in form through Stage II.
(C watching as M leaves the room) where going?/	**LATE STAGE I/EARLY STAGE II–STAGE II (LI/EII–II)** This is a *where* + VP question form that emerges in Late Stage I/Early Stage II and does not change in form through Stage II.
(clinician enters room to adjust camera) who that is?/	**STAGE III (III)** The *who* question type emerges in Stage III, and the form of this particular *who* question is typical of Stage III (*wh-* word + sentence).
(someone shouts in hallway) who is that?/	**EARLY STAGE IV–LATE V (EIV–LV)** This *who* question shows evidence of inversion of the verb and noun phrase. So even though it is a Stage III question type, it is in the Early Stage IV form.

EXAMPLE 3.5 (*continued*)

(C pushes puppy away) why him bite me?/	STAGE III (III) This type of question emerges in Stage III, and it is in the Stage III form (no inversion).
(C fitting blocks together) how this one go?/	STAGE III (III) This is another question type to emerge in Stage III, and the noninverted form continues.
(C looks at clinician) when is my mom coming?/	EARLY STAGE IV–LATE V (EIV–LV) *When* questions emerge in Early Stage IV, so the assignment is simple on those grounds. But notice that this utterance also contains an example of auxiliary inversion, which also emerges at this stage. Consequently, it is assigned Early Stage IV on the basis of type and form.

Stage Analysis form used earlier. When a dash or a stage has been recorded for all 100 utterances, compare your results with those in Form 3.6.

The sample transcript contained eight *wh-* questions ranging in complexity from Late Stage I/Early Stage II–Stage II to Late Stage V. These *wh-* questions should be recorded on the Production Characteristics Summary form.

Before moving on to the analysis of other structures, one type of *wh-* question not included in the total needs to be examined. Five questions might have been assigned Early Stage I. All of these were a type of *what* question, and all were in the form of "huh?" Although these are *what* questions, and the only information to use when assigning a stage to them is the type, tallying these in Early Stage I may distort the child's level of *wh-* question development. These *what* questions are different from other Early Stage I *what* questions in that they are not querying a specific semantic role. Typically, children use Early Stage I *what* questions to query the label of an object. The five *what* questions in this transcript appear to have been used to request repetition of the mother's utterance, not to obtain the label for an object. This use of *what?* or *huh?* serves a pragmatic function, not a semantic one. Analysis of the syntactic form of these questions underestimates the child's syntactic abilities. Therefore, these five questions should be eliminated from the syntactic analysis. They are considered in the next chapter when we examine pragmatic aspects of this child's productions.

Thus, the total number of *wh-* questions is eight. But one more type of *wh-* question should be reexamined. Utterances #7, #16, #19, and #66 are all examples of a routine form for this child (i.e., "What else?"). She appears to use this form in various places in conversation when she wants to move on to play with and talk about other toys. If she had used the fully elaborated form, "What else is in the box?" or "What else should we do?" Early Stage IV would be the more appropriate assignment. Given the abbreviated form of her utterances, Late Stage I/Early Stage II–Stage II was judged to be the best stage assignment. Before the developmental level of *wh-* questions in this child's productions can be interpreted, the complexity of three more syntactic structures must be analyzed. Only after all aspects of syntactic production have been analyzed can each structure be appropriately interpreted.

Analyzing the Complexity of Noun Phrases

Analysis of the complexity of the noun phrase results in a stage assignment; stage assignments reflect the type and amount of elaboration of the noun phrase as well as the position of the noun phrase within the utterance. Stage assignments are based on data reported by Brown and Bellugi (1964), Cazden (1968), Ingram (1972), de Villiers and de Villiers (1973), Brown (1973), and Chapman (1978, as cited in Miller, 1981). Increases in complexity of the noun phrase occur with increases in utterance length, but the increases in complexity of the noun phrase are not simply increases in length. The tenth column for Stages I, II, III of Table 3.3 and the ninth column for subsequent stages summarize the changes in the noun phrase with increases in utterance

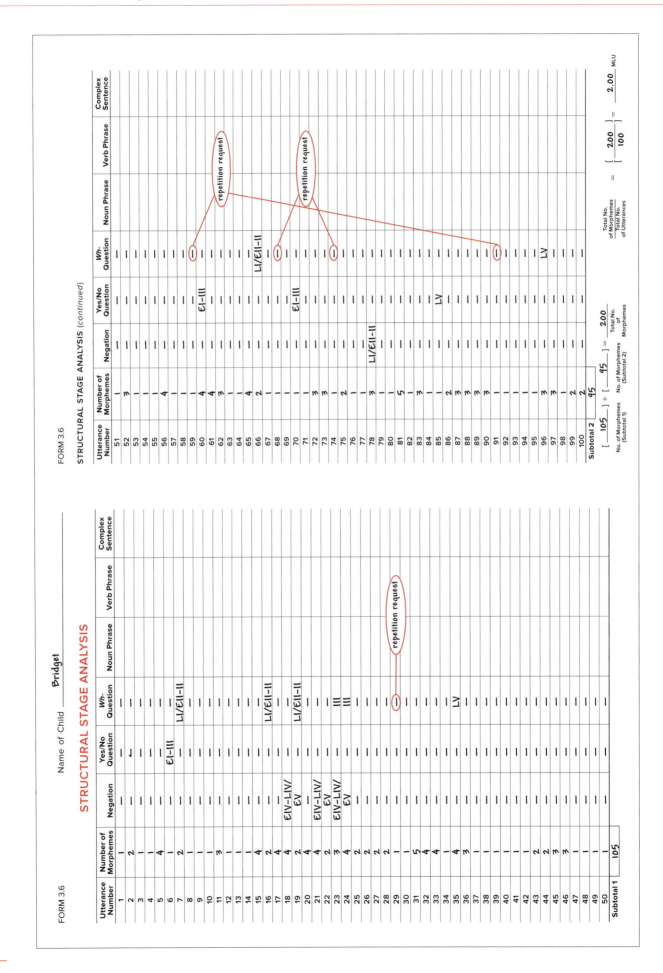

length. The summaries reflect the emergence of new ways to increase the complexity of the noun phrase and not mastery of the forms.

Judgments about the developmental complexity of the noun phrase are more difficult to make than those for some of the preceding structures, partly because the vast majority of utterances contain a noun phrase. In addition, there is greater variability in the specificity of the noun phrase. Pragmatic requirements are such that not all utterances containing a noun phrase are in the most complex form that the child is capable of producing. In addition, many utterances contain only a noun phrase because the child is responding to a question from the other speaker or clarifying a previous utterance. Assignment of a stage to these utterances may underestimate the child's abilities. For these reasons, a greater number of practice utterances are given in Example 3.6 to provide experience in making these more difficult judgments. Cover the right side of the page, compare the noun phrases within the utterances to the descriptions provided in the Noun Phrase column of Table 3.3, and assign a stage. Note: The complexity of noun phrases has broader stages for Stages I, II, and III per Brown (1973). For this reason, the broad Stages I, II, and III, are indicated in the ninth column in Table 3.3. Once you have assigned stages, check your judgments with those provided in the shaded section. The explanations should help clarify differences. You may also wish to turn to *Guide Practice* web-based exercises for additional practice.

Now, with the experience gained from the practice utterances, return to the sample transcript and examine each utterance for the presence of one or more noun phrases. If there is no noun phrase in the utterance, mark a dash (—) for that utterance in the Noun Phrase column on the Structural Stage Analysis form used earlier. When an utterance that contains a noun phrase is identified, compare that noun phrase to the descriptions of noun phrases in the tenth column of Table 3.3 to determine the stage that best characterizes the complexity of the noun phrase or phrases in the utterance. Then record the stage number for that utterance in the Noun Phrase column on the Structural Stage Analysis form. When each utterance has been examined for the presence of noun phrases and stage assignments have been recorded, compare your results with those in Form 3.7 (on p. 99).

Forty-six utterances containing noun phrases should have been identified. The noun phrases in this transcript ranged in complexity from Stage I–Stage II to Late Stage IV/Early Stage V. These utterances should be tallied on the Production Characteristics Summary form after the complexities of two more syntactic structures have been analyzed.

Analyzing the Complexity of Verb Phrases

The stage assignments that are made for verb phrase development are based on data reported by Klima and Bellugi (1966), Cazden (1968), Brown (1973), de Villiers and de Villiers (1973), and Chapman et al. (1981). The eleventh column of Table 3.3 summarizes the changes in complexity of the verb phrase and the stage at which those changes emerge. Changes in complexity of verb phrases overlap with developments in other structures more than some of the other structures analyzed. Most notably, increases in complexity of the verb phrase coincide with advances in the development of grammatical morphemes. Final interpretation of the developmental complexity of the verb phrase will depend on the child's mastery of grammatical morphemes.

To determine the stage that best characterizes the child's level of verb phrase development, examine each utterance for the presence of a verb phrase. Then compare each verb phrase to the developments summarized in the eleventh column for Stages I, II, and III of Table 3.3 and the tenth column for subsequent stages and assign a stage to the verb phrase in that utterance. Like the judgments made in analyzing noun phrase development, judgments about verb phrases are more difficult to make than with some of the other syntactic structures. Therefore, a greater number of practice utterances are provided in Example 3.7 (on p. 100) for verb phrases than for some of the other structures. Cover the right side of the page, compare the utterance to the developments described in Table 3.3, and assign a stage. Then check your stage assignments with those provided in the shaded section. The explanations provided should help clear up any questions. You may also wish to turn to *Guide Practice* web-based exercises for additional practice.

(Text continues on p. 98.)

EXAMPLE 3.6

NOUN PHRASE	
(C reaches for box of cookies) more cookie/	**STAGE I–STAGE II (I–II)** This utterance is an example of an elaborated noun phrase that includes an optional modifier (M) *more*: NP = (M) + N. Because the noun phrase does not change in form from Stage I to Stage II, the range of stages is used.
(C points to picture in book) kitty/	**STAGE I–STAGE II (I–II)** Because the modifier is optional in Stage I and the form of the noun phrase does not change in Stage II, the stage range is the best assignment.
(C points to another picture in book) pretty kitty/	**STAGE I–STAGE II (I–II)** This utterance includes the optional modifier that typifies the form of the elaborated noun phrase in Stages I and II. This is an example of NP = (M) + N, with the elaborated NP occurring alone. The stage range is the best assignment.
(C reaches for box of crackers on counter) want more cracker/	**STAGE II (II)** This utterance contains an elaborated noun phrase; the type of elaboration is specified in Stage II. The object noun phrase emerges in Stage II; the NP only occurs in the object position: NP = VP + NP.
(C sees clinician roll ball to M) that ball/	**STAGE III (III)** This utterance is also an example of an elaborated noun phrase, but it includes an optional demonstrative form, that, which emerges in Stage III.
(C points to picture in book) that a baby/	**STAGE III (III)** This utterance contains an elaborated noun phrase with two optional forms; a demonstrative, *that*; and an article, *a*. It is presumed that the demonstrative represents a subject noun phrase and the article plus noun represents the object noun phrase. The verb is omitted. Utterances of this type and form emerge in Stage III: NP = {(demonstrative) (article)} + (M) + N. Consequently, Stage III is assigned to this utterance.
(C pulls tiny doll from bag) that a tiny baby/	**STAGE III (III)** This utterance contains an article, *a*, plus a modifier, *tiny*, plus a noun in the object noun phrase position. The demonstrative form, *that*, is in the subject noun phrase position. Noun phrases in this form appear in Stage III.
(C points to bus with toy kittens in it) that alotta kitties/	**STAGE III (III)** The use of *alotta* in this utterance represents an article and the optional modifier in a noun phrase. The demonstrative form, *that*, is in the subject noun phrase position. A verb is not necessary to assign Stage III.
(C points to juice box) orange juice/	**STAGE I–STAGE II (I–II)** Noun phrase elaboration occurs only alone with no verb present.
(C takes juice glass from M) drink juice/	**STAGE II (II)** This utterance has a noun phrase with no elaboration, but the presence of the verb, *drink*, places the noun phrase in Stage II: NP = VP + NP.

EXAMPLE 3.6 (*continued*)

(C puts cup to doll's mouth) drink orange juice/	**STAGE II (II)** This utterance has a noun phrase in the object position with elaboration. The presence of the verb, *drink*, places the noun phrase in Stage II: NP = VP + NP.
(C holds puppy out to clinician) kiss the puppy/	**STAGE III (III)** Although this utterance contains a verb, the constituent that is the most significant is the object noun phrase, *the puppy*. This noun phrase comprises an article plus a noun. This form is characteristic of Stage III.
(C pushes puppy away) hit that naughty puppy/	**STAGE III (III)** The noun phrase in this utterance is in the object position. It contains a demonstrative, *that*, and a modifier, *naughty*, before the noun, *puppy*. Noun phrases of this type are characteristic of Stage III: NP = {(demonstrative) (article)} + (M) + N.
(puppy jumps out of box) that puppy jump/	**STAGE III (III)** The noun phrase in this utterance is in the subject position. Subject noun phrases appear in Stage III. This is the best cue for stage assignment. But the form of this noun phrase also is consistent with Stage III in that there is a demonstrative, *that*, with the noun. No modifier is present, but the modifier is optional at this stage.
(C pushes puppy away) that puppy licked my face/	**LATE STAGE IV/EARLY STAGE V (LIV/EV)** There are two noun phrases in this utterance: a subject noun phrase, *that puppy*, and an object noun phrase, *my face*. The presence of a subject noun phrase suggests at least Stage III. However, the possessive pronoun, *my*, in the object noun phrase of a NP + VP complete utterance indicates Late Stage IV/Early Stage V. The possessive is one of the optional constituents in Late Stage IV/Early Stage V.
(M asks, "Where should we put the sprinkles?") on that cookie/	**STAGE III (III)** The noun phrase in this utterance contains a demonstrative, *that*, and a noun, *cookie*, in the object position. Noun phrases of this type and in this position are characteristic of Stage III.
(C points to cookie on plate) I want that cookie/	**LATE STAGE IV/EARLY STAGE V (LIV/EV)** There are two noun phrases in this utterance: a subject noun phrase, I, and an object noun phrase, *that cookie*. The object noun phrase is in Stage III form (demonstrative plus noun). The subject noun phrase is in the form of a pronoun, but stage assignment is more difficult. To assign Late Stage IV, the subject noun phrase is obligatory where pragmatically appropriate, and a noun or a pronoun appears in the subject position. Because it was necessary for the child to include the subject noun phrase in his utterance due to pragmatic convention, and he did, Late Stage IV/Early Stage V is assigned.

(*continues*)

EXAMPLE 3.6 (*continued*)

(M points to picture in book and says, "What is that?") a baby crying/	**STAGE III (III)** The noun phrase, *a baby*, in this utterance is in the subject position and consists of an article plus a noun. Both of these are indicative of Stage III: NP = NP + VP.
(C shows finger to clinician) hurt my little finger/	**LATE STAGE IV/EARLY STAGE V (LIV/EV)** Although there is only one noun phrase and it is in the object position, the presence of the possessive pronoun, *my*, with the adjective, *little*, makes this noun phrase typical of Late Stage IV/Early Stage V.
(C pushes puppy away) he eated my cookie/	**LATE STAGE IV/EARLY STAGE V (LIV/EV)** The two noun phrases in this utterance are indicative of Late Stage IV/Early Stage V. The subject noun phrase pronoun, *he*, and the object noun phrase containing the possessive pronoun, *my*, confirm Late Stage IV/Early Stage V.
(C reaches for cookie on plate) eat my big cookie/	**LATE STAGE IV/EARLY STAGE V (LIV/EV)** This utterance contains only an object noun phrase, which could result in a lower stage assignment. But this noun phrase contains a possessive pronoun and an adjective preceding the noun. Noun phrases with these constituents are characteristic of Late Stage IV/Early Stage V.
(C points to box in corner) lotta doggies goes in there/	**LATE STAGE IV/EARLY STAGE V (LIV/EV)** The most significant thing to note in this utterance is the lack of number agreement between the subject and the verb. Although this lack of number agreement continues to be a problem beyond Stage V, the presence of a subject noun phrase, *lotta doggies*, and an object noun phrase, *in there*, indicates at least Late Stage IV/Early Stage V: NP + VP + NP. And with no further data on which to base a judgment, Late Stage IV/Early Stage V is assigned. This would indicate that assigning a stage higher than Late Stage IV/Early Stage V is not probable when analyzing noun phrases.

Return to the sample transcript and examine each utterance for the presence of a verb phrase. As with the preceding structures, if there is no verb phrase in the utterance, mark a dash (—) for that utterance in the Verb Phrase column on the Structural Stage Analysis form used earlier. For those utterances that do contain a verb phrase, record the stage number for the verb phrase's complexity in that utterance in the Verb Phrase column on the form. When each utterance has been examined for the presence of a verb phrase and stage assignments have been recorded, compare your results with those in the sample on Form 3.8 (on p. 104).

The sample transcript contained 39 utterances with verb phrases. The verb phrases in the utterances in the sample transcript ranged in complexity from Stages I–II to Late Stage V. These verb phrases should be tallied on the Production Characteristics Summary form after the complexity of one more syntactic structure is analyzed.

Analyzing the Complexity of Complex Sentences

The last aspect of syntactic development that we analyze is the complex sentence. The frequency of occurrence of complex sentences is very low in transcripts obtained from children within Brown's stages of linguistic

(Text continues on p. 103.)

SYNTACTIC ANALYSIS

FORM 3.7 Name of Child __Bridget__

STRUCTURAL STAGE ANALYSIS

Utterance Number	Number of Morphemes	Negation	Yes/No Question	Wh-Question	Noun Phrase	Verb Phrase	Complex Sentence
1	1	—	—	—	—		
2	2	—	—	—	—		
3	1	—	—	—	—		
4	1	—	—	—	—		
5	4	—	—	—	LIV/EV		
6	1	—	—	—	—		
7	2	—	EI-III	—	I-II		
8	1	—	—	LI/EII-II	I-II		
9	1	—	—	—	—		
10	1	—	—	—	—		
11	3	—	—	—	—		
12	1	—	—	—	—		
13	1	—	—	—	I-II		
14	4	—	—	—	LIV/EV		
15	4	—	—	LI/EII-II	—		
16	2	—	—	—	III		
17	4	—	—	LI/EII-II	III		
18	4	EIV-LIV/EV	—	—	—		
19	2	—	—	—	—		
20	4	EIV-LIV/EV	—	—	LIV/EV		
21	4	—	—	—	LIV/EV		
22	2	EIV-LIV/EV	—	—	III		
23	3	—	—	III	LIV/EV		
24	4	EV	—	III	III		
25	2	—	—	—	III		
26	2	—	—	—	I-II		
27	2	—	—	—	—		
28	2	—	—	—	—		
29	1	—	—	—	—		
30	1	—	—	—	LIV/EV		
31	5	—	—	—	III		
32	4	—	—	—	LIV/EV		
33	4	—	—	—	LIV/EV		
34	1	—	—	LV	—		
35	4	—	—	—	LIV/EV		
36	3	—	—	—	LIV/EV		
37	1	—	—	—	III		
38	1	—	—	—	—	—	
39	1	—	—	—	I-II		
40	1	—	—	—	I-II		
41	1	—	—	—	—		
42	2	—	—	—	—		
43	2	—	—	—	LIV/EV		
44	2	—	—	—	LIV/EV		
45	3	—	—	—	—		
46	3	—	—	—	—		
47	1	—	—	—	—		
48	1	—	—	—	I-II		
49	1						
50	1						
Subtotal 1	105						

based on its abbreviated form, only VP was assigned (note pointing to utterance 38)

FORM 3.7
STRUCTURAL STAGE ANALYSIS (continued)

Utterance Number	Number of Morphemes	Negation	Yes/No Question	Wh-Question	Noun Phrase	Verb Phrase	Complex Sentence
51	1	—	—	—	—		
52	3	—	—	—	—		
53	1	—	—	—	—		
54	1	—	—	—	—		
55	4	—	—	—	LIV/EV		
56	1	—	—	—	—		
57	1	—	—	—	I-II		
58	1	—	—	—	—		
59	4	—	EI-III	—	III		
60	4	—	—	—	III		
61	4	—	—	—	III		
62	3	—	—	—	—		
63	1	—	—	—	—		
64	1	—	—	—	III		
65	4	—	—	—	—		
66	2	—	—	LI/EII-II	—		
67	1	—	—	—	—		
68	1	—	—	—	—		
69	1	—	—	—	—		
70	1	—	EI-III	—	I-II		
71	3	—	—	—	II		
72	3	—	—	—	II		
73	1	—	—	—	—		
74	2	—	—	—	I-II		
75	1	—	—	—	—		
76	3	—	—	—	I-II		
77	1	—	—	—	—		
78	LI/EII-II	—	—	—	—		
79	1	—	—	—	—		
80	5	—	—	—	LIV/EV		
81	3	—	—	—	I-II		
82	1	—	—	—	—		
83	1	—	—	—	—		
84	2	—	—	—	I-II		
85	3	—	—	—	II		
86	3	—	—	—	II		
87	3	—	—	—	II		
88	1	—	—	—	—		
89	1	—	—	—	—		
90	1	—	—	—	I-II		
91	1	—	—	—	I-II		
92	3	—	—	LV	—		
93	3	—	—	—	III		
94	1	—	—	—	—		
95	2	—	—	—	I-II		
96	1	—	—	—	—		
97	2	—	—	—	LIV/EV		
98							
99							
100							
Subtotal 2	95						

[105] + [95] = 200
No. of Morphemes (Subtotal 1) + No. of Morphemes (Subtotal 2) = Total No. of Morphemes

Total No. of Morphemes / Total No. of Utterances = [200 / 100] = 2.00 MLU

EXAMPLE 3.7

VERB PHRASE	
(C falls down and looks at M) fall down/	**STAGE I–STAGE II (I–II)** This utterance contains a verb plus a particle. Verb phrases of this form are used occasionally in Stage I but do not change in form through Stage II. The best stage assignment is the range of stages.
(puppy jumps out of box) puppy jump/	**STAGE I–STAGE II (I–II)** This utterance contains a noun phrase and a verb phrase, with the verb phrase containing a main verb in an uninflected form. This form of the verb is consistent with Stage I through Stage II. The presence of the noun phrase has no bearing on the stage assignment.
(C curls up in doll bed, then sits up) I is sleeping/	**STAGE III (III)** The verb phrase in this utterance contains a main verb in the present progressive tense. The auxiliary, *is*, is included, and even though it is in an incorrect form for first person, the inclusion of the auxiliary requires the assignment of Stage III.
(M and C looking at picture book) he could hug you/	**LATE STAGE IV/EARLY STAGE V (LIV–EV)** The most significant thing to note for stage assignment is the presence of the modal auxiliary, *could*. This type of auxiliary is characteristic of Late Stage IV/Early Stage V.
(C points to picture in book) baby cry/	**STAGE I–STAGE II (I–II)** The verb phrase in this utterance is in an uninflected form. Thus, the most appropriate stage assignment is Stage I–Stage II.
(C responding to M, who asked what the baby drank) the baby drank milk/	**STAGE LV** The main verb, *drank*, is an irregular past tense verb form. This grammatical morpheme is mastered in Stage LV.
(another child is crying in the hall) baby crying/	**STAGE I–STAGE II (I–II)** The reason for the difficulty in assigning a stage to this utterance is that the present progressive *-ing* is used occasionally in Stage I and more consistently in Stage II. The auxiliary is not used in either stage. The best solution is to assign the range of stages.
(puppy crawls in clinician's lap) her gonna bite/	**STAGE II (II)** The use of the semiauxiliary, *gonna*, in this verb phrase indicates Stage II. The only time Stage II would be assigned as opposed to the range of Stage I–Stage II is when the semiauxiliary or the copula is included without other information that could influence a higher stage assignment.
(C points to one of the puppies) she can jump/	**STAGE III (III)** This utterance contains an obligatory main verb. The presence of the present tense auxiliary, *can*, preceding the verb in this verb phrase also indicates Stage III.
(puppy puts front paws up on edge of box) puppy'll jump/	**STAGE III (III)** This utterance contains an obligatory main verb. The verb phrase in this utterance also contains an auxiliary, *will*, but in this utterance it is in the contracted form.

EXAMPLE 3.7 (continued)

(puppy chases heels of clinician) she's gonna bite you/	**LATE STAGE IV/EARLY STAGE V (LIV/EV)** The verb phrase in this utterance contains the auxiliary, *is*, the semiauxiliary, *gonna*, and the main verb, *bite*. But the most important thing to note is that the semiauxiliary complement, *gonna bite*, takes a noun phrase. Verb phrases of this type appear in Late Stage IV/Early Stage V.
(clinician picks up puppy) she bites/	**LATE STAGE V (LV)** The verb phrase in this utterance only contains a main verb. But the main verb includes correct number agreement in the use of regular third-person singular present tense. This is the eighth grammatical morpheme and it is mastered in Late Stage V. The consistent use of this grammatical morpheme results in the assignment of Late Stage V.
(C gestures toward puppy in box) she was a naughty puppy/	**STAGE V+ (V+)** The verb phrase in this utterance consists of the copula, the verb *be*, as a main verb. It is in the past tense, a form that emerges in Stage V+. In addition, it is an uncontractible copula, which, as a grammatical morpheme, is mastered in Stage V+.
(C pulls toys out of toy box) is big!/	**STAGE II (II)** This utterance also contains a copula, *is*, but without tense or number inflection. The copula appears in this form in Stage II.
(as clinician leaves the room, C turns to M) she eated my cookie/	**STAGE III (III)** The main verb in this utterance is an irregular verb, but the child has marked the past tense of the verb by using the regular past tense *-ed* inflection. Overgeneralization of the past tense *-ed* voccurs in Stage III.
(C relating story to M) she was jumping on the couch/	**STAGE V+ (V+)** The verb phrase in this utterance contains the past tense form of the verb, *be*, as an auxiliary. This form appears in Stage V+.
(C and M playing with cars and toy gas station) you need gas↑/	**STAGE III (III)** This utterance contains an uninflected main verb, and no auxiliary verbs are present. The main verb is obligatory to hold this utterance together. The main verb becomes obligatory in Stage III.
(C makes horse bump car and says to M) horsie bumped the car/	**LATE STAGE V (LV)** The main verb in this utterance includes the regular past tense *-ed* inflection used correctly. Although Stage III is assigned for incorrect or overgeneralized use and Late Stage IV/Early Stage V is assigned for double-marking, Late Stage V is assigned for correct use. This is due to the fact that the *-ed* inflection is mastered in Late Stage V as a grammatical morpheme.
(C relating story to M) he should go night-night/	**LATE STAGE IV/EARLY STAGE V (LIV/EV)** This utterance contains a past tense modal auxiliary in the verb phrase. Modals of this type appear in Late Stage IV/Early Stage V.

(continues)

EXAMPLE 3.7 (continued)

(clinician puts cookie toppings on table) I have eaten those kind/	**STAGE V+ (V+)** The verb phrase in this utterance is in the present perfect tense, and the child has correctly marked the tense on the auxiliary verb. This is a relatively infrequently occurring form in adult conversation, and it is reported to be marked correctly only after reaching Stage V+.
(C referring to puppy) I might get one/	**LATE STAGE IV/EARLY STAGE V (LIV/EV)** The presence of the modal auxiliary in the verb phrase is the best cue for stage assignment. Modals of this type appear in Late Stage IV/Early Stage V.
(clinician enters room and C points to mat) I was jumping on that/	**STAGE V+ (V+)** This utterance contains the past-tense form of the verb, *be*, as an auxiliary verb. The verb *be* emerges in past-tense form in Stage V+.
(C makes toy dog eat a treat then says to M) the doggie ate the treat/	**LATE STAGE V (LV)** The main verb in this utterance includes the irregular past tense, *ate*, used correctly. Late Stage V is assigned for correct use. This is because the irregular past tense of the verb is mastered in Late Stage V as a grammatical morpheme.
(C points to a puppy in the story) puppy do eat/	**STAGE III (III)** This utterance contains an obligatory main verb. The presence of the present tense auxiliary, *do*, preceding the main verb in this verb phrase indicates Stage III.
(C talking about what she just ate) eat cookie/	**STAGE I–STAGE II (I–II)** This utterance contains an uninflected main verb without an auxiliary or copula. Verb phrases of this form are common in Stage I but do not change in form through Stage II. The best stage assignment is the range of stages.
(C responding to M asking what C is doing) I am eating cookies/	**LATE STAGE IV/EARLY STAGE V–V+ (LIV/EV–V+)** The presence of *be* + the present progressive, *am eating*, is a cue for stage assignment. This type of verb phrase appears in Late Stage IV/Early Stage V but is not mastered until Stage V+. This verb form is also a contractible auxiliary that is mastered in Stage V+. Thus, a range of stages is assigned.
(C indicating she wants to draw) I wanna make a picture/	**LATE STAGE IV/EARLY STAGE V (LIV/EV)** This utterance contains a noun phrase that is a complement of the infinitive within the semiauxiliary. Semiauxiliary noun phrase complements emerge in Late Stage IV/Early Stage V.
(C indicating what the wolf in the story needs to do) He must blow on the house/	**LATE STAGE IV/EARLY STAGE V (LIV/EV)** The presence of the past-tense modal auxiliary, *must*, in the verb phrase is the best cue for stage assignment. Modals of this type appear in Late Stage IV/Early Stage V.
(C pretending toy monkey is hungry) he is hungry/	**LATE STAGE V (LV)** In this utterance, the contractible form of *be*, the copula, is the main verb form and is a grammatical morpheme that is mastered in Late Stage V. Note that the contractible copula does not need to be contracted to count as a contractible form.

EXAMPLE 3.7 (continued)

(C points to a girl in a picture) she is sleeping/	**STAGE V+ (V+)** In this utterance, the form of *be* is an auxiliary and *sleeping* is the main verb. This is an example of a contractible auxiliary, a grammatical morpheme that is mastered in Stage V+. Note that the contractible auxiliary does not need to be contracted to count as a contractible form.
(C talking about where her friends had been) they were swimming/	**STAGE V+ (V+)** In this utterance, the auxiliary form of *be* is uncontractible because *they were* cannot be reduced further. This grammatical morpheme, the uncontractible auxiliary, is mastered in Stage V+.
(C indicating she hasn't changed her shirt) I did not changed my shirt/	**LATE STAGE IV/EARLY STAGE V (LIV/EV)** In this negative sentence, the child uses the regular past tense *-ed* but double-marks past tense by also including the auxiliary, *did*. This main verb form emerges in Late Stage IV/Early Stage V.

production. At the upper end of Brown's stages, typically fewer than 20% of the child's utterances are complex (Paul, 1981). And in the early stages, complex sentences are rarely used.

The stage assignments for complex sentence development are based on data provided by Limber (1973) and Paul (1981). The data reported by Paul provide stage assignments on the basis of the stage at which 50% of the children in her sample used the structure and the stage at which 90% used the structure. The data summarized in the eighth column of Table 3.3 reflect the stage at which 50% of the children used the structure. The decision was made that data on complex sentence development will be at the *emergence* level rather than the *mastery* level, because this plan was followed for data on all other structures except grammatical morphemes.

First identify the complex sentences in the transcript. This may be more difficult than making the stage assignments. Some practice in doing this was gained in the preceding chapter on semantic analysis, where a few utterances were provided as examples of complex sentences. However, the practice provided here will be more extensive and will include explanations for stage assignments.

There are two main reasons that an utterance is considered syntactically complex. First, the utterance is considered complex if it contains two or more sentences within the utterance that are connected by conjunctions. These usually take the form of two or more full-sentence propositions connected by *and, but, so, or, because, before*, or *after*. Second, according to Paul (1981) an utterance is considered complex if it contains a dependent clause (i.e., a sentence-like segment that contains a main verb). These dependent clauses are embedded within the sentence and take a variety of forms, including infinitive phrases, *wh-* clauses, relative clauses, full propositional complements, and gerunds.

Although the identification of complex sentence types becomes easier with practice, some practice utterances will be helpful before returning to the sample transcript. In Example 3.8, cover the right side of the page, compare each utterance with the descriptions provided in the eighth column of Table 3.3, and assign a stage. Then check your assignments with those provided in the shaded section. The explanations given should help clear up any discrepancies. Also turn to *Guide Practice* web-based exercises for additional practice.

These examples should be helpful in identifying complex sentences within the sample transcript. In addition, the explanations of why each is considered complex should help in making stage assignments. Now, return to the sample transcript and examine each utterance to determine whether it is an example of a complex sentence. If an utterance is not a complex sentence, mark a dash (—) in the Complex Sentence column on the Structural Stage Analysis form used earlier. If an utterance is complex, compare it to the descriptions in the eighth column of Table 3.3 and assign a stage to the utterance. After each utterance has been examined to

(Text continues on p. 106.)

Guide to Analysis of Language Transcripts

FORM 3.8
STRUCTURAL STAGE ANALYSIS

Name of Child: **Bridget**

Utterance Number	Number of Morphemes	Negation	Yes/No Question	Wh- Question	Noun Phrase	Verb Phrase	Complex Sentence
1	1	—	—	—	—	—	
2	2	—	—	—	—	I-II	
3	1	—	—	—	—	—	
4	1	—	—	—	LIV/EV	III	
5	4	—	EI-III	—	—	I-II	
6	1	—	—	—	—	—	
7	2	—	—	—	I-II	—	
8	1	—	—	—	I-II	—	
9	1	—	—	—	—	—	
10	3	—	—	—	—	I-II	
11	1	—	—	—	—	—	
12	1	—	—	—	I-II	—	
13	4	—	—	LI/EII-II	—	III	
14	1	—	—	—	LIV/EV	III	
15	4	—	—	—	—	III	
16	2	—	—	—	—	—	
17	4	—	—	LI/EII-II	III	III	
18	4	EIV-LIV/EV	—	—	III	LV	
19	2	—	—	—	—	—	
20	4	EIV-LIV/EV	—	—	LIV/EV	LV	
21	4	—	—	—	LIV/EV	III	
22	2	—	—	—	III	III	
23	3	EIV-LIV/EV	—	—	—	LV	
24	4	—	—	III	III	III	
25	2	—	—	—	III	—	
26	2	—	—	—	—	I-II	
27	2	—	—	—	—	—	
28	2	—	—	—	—	I-II	
29	1	—	—	—	—	—	
30	5	—	—	—	LIV/EV	III	
31	4	—	—	—	III	LV	
32	4	—	—	—	LIV/EV	III	
33	4	—	—	LV	LIV/EV	LV	
34	1	—	—	—	III	III	
35	4	—	—	—	LIV/EV	LV	
36	3	—	—	—	LIV/EV	III	
37	1	—	—	—	—	—	
38	1	—	—	—	—	I-II	(I-III) *No inflection on main verb, but obligatory*
39	1	—	—	—	I-II	—	
40	1	—	—	—	I-II	—	
41	1	—	—	—	—	I-II	
42	2	—	—	—	III	III	
43	2	—	—	—	LIV/EV	III	
44	3	—	—	—	LIV/EV	III	
45	3	—	—	—	—	—	
46	1	—	—	—	—	I-II	
47	1	—	—	—	—	—	
48	1	—	—	—	—	—	
49	1	—	—	—	—	—	
50	1	—	—	—	—	—	
Subtotal 1	**105**						

FORM 3.8
STRUCTURAL STAGE ANALYSIS (continued)

Utterance Number	Number of Morphemes	Negation	Yes/No Question	Wh- Question	Noun Phrase	Verb Phrase	Complex Sentence
51	1	—	—	—	—	—	
52	3	—	—	—	—	III	
53	1	—	—	—	—	I	
54	1	—	—	—	—	—	
55	1	—	—	—	—	III	
56	4	—	—	—	LIV/EV	I	
57	1	—	—	—	—	—	
58	1	—	—	—	I-II	I	
59	1	—	—	—	—	—	
60	4	—	EI-III	—	III	LV	
61	4	—	—	—	III	LV	
62	3	—	—	—	III	—	
63	1	—	—	—	—	—	
64	1	—	—	—	—	—	
65	4	—	—	—	—	LV	
66	2	—	—	LI/EII-II	III	—	
67	1	—	—	—	—	—	
68	1	—	—	—	—	—	
69	1	—	EI-III	—	—	—	
70	1	—	—	—	—	—	
71	3	—	—	—	I-II	I-II	
72	3	—	—	—	—	I-II	
73	1	—	—	—	—	—	
74	1	—	—	—	—	I-II	
75	2	—	—	—	—	—	
76	1	—	—	—	—	—	
77	1	—	—	—	—	—	
78	3	LI/EII-II	—	—	—	—	
79	1	—	—	—	—	—	
80	5	—	—	—	LIV/EV	LV	
81	3	—	—	—	—	—	
82	1	—	—	—	—	—	
83	1	—	—	—	I-II	—	
84	1	—	—	—	—	—	
85	2	—	—	—	III	LV	
86	3	—	—	—	III	III	
87	1	—	—	—	—	III	
88	3	—	—	—	III	III	
89	3	—	—	—	III	III	
90	3	—	—	—	III	—	
91	1	—	—	—	—	—	
92	1	—	—	—	—	—	
93	1	—	—	—	I-II	I-II	
94	1	—	—	—	I-II	—	
95	1	—	—	LV	—	LV	
96	3	—	—	—	III	—	
97	1	—	—	—	—	—	
98	1	—	—	—	—	—	
99	2	—	—	—	LIV/EV	LIV/EV	
100	2	—	—	—	LIV/EV	III	
Subtotal 2	**95**						

No. of Morphemes (Subtotal 1) [105] + No. of Morphemes (Subtotal 2) [95] = 200 Total No. of Morphemes

Total No. of Morphemes / Total No. of Utterances = [200] / [100] = 2.00 MLU

EXAMPLE 3.8

COMPLEX SENTENCES	
(C relating event to clinician) doggie barked and barked/	**EARLY STAGE IV (EIV)** This utterance contains the conjunction *and*. It is conjoining the two sentences *the doggie barked* and *the doggie barked*.
(C continuing story) doggie bite and I cried/	**EARLY STAGE IV (EIV)** This utterance also contains the conjunction *and*. In this example, the two utterances that are conjoined are more obvious.
(C points to cookie on plate) I want the one what's big/	**LATE STAGE V (LV)** This utterance contains a relative clause, *what's big*, but the child has used a *wh-* word to introduce the clause. Even though the form is incorrect, Late Stage V is assigned. The relative clause modifies the noun, *one*.
(C brushes flour off pants) my shoes and pants are dirty	**EARLY STAGE IV (EIV)** This utterance is an example of another type of conjoined complex utterance. The two sentences that are conjoined are *my shoes are dirty* and *my pants are dirty*.
(C pulls on door) I want to go/	**EARLY STAGE IV (EIV)** This utterance contains a simple infinitive phrase. To assign this stage, the child must use the full infinitive, not the catenative form (*wanna*) or a reduction (*go* for *to go*).
(C picks up plastic animal) pretend he's a monster/	**STAGE III (III)** This utterance contains an object noun phrase complement. The complement *he's a monster* is a full sentence and may or may not be introduced by the word *that*.
(C looking for M to drive up) I gotta go when Mom comes/	**STAGE V++ (V++)** This utterance contains the conjunction *when*, which appears at Stage V++.
(C pulls plastic animal out of bag) I know what that is/	**EARLY STAGE IV (EIV)** This example contains a simple *wh-* clause. The sentence *that is* is linked to the main sentence with a *wh-* word.
(C holds up doll dress) this is for her to wear/	**LATE STAGE V (LV)** This utterance contains an infinitive phrase with a subject different than the subject of the main verb.
(C gestures to cupcakes on rack) the ones what have hats on are mine/	**LATE STAGE V (LV)** This utterance contains a relative clause, *what have hats on*. The relative clause modifies the noun *ones*. Again, the relative clause introducer does not have to be correct to give the child credit for use of the relative clause.
(M asks, "Why did you do that?" after C eats handful of cookie dough) I felt like eating it/	**STAGE V+ (V+)** This utterance contains a gerund clause, *eating it*. Gerunds are verbs acting as nouns and include a verb plus *-ing* used within a noun clause. Gerunds appear in Stage V+.

(*continues*)

EXAMPLE 3.8 (*continued*)

(C picks up marking pen) help me draw/	**STAGE V+ (V+)** This utterance contains an unmarked infinitive phrase. These are usually introduced by one of the following: *let, help, watch, make, need, see, hear,* and *feel*. This utterance implies "Help me to draw."
(C opens game box) I'll show you how to do it/	**STAGE V+ (V+)** This utterance contains a *wh-* infinitive phrase. These are marked with both a *wh-* word and *to*. (Recall that *how* is considered a *wh-* word.)
(C starts to search toy box) I think I know where it is/	**LATE STAGE IV/EARLY STAGE V (LIV/EV)** This is an example of multiple embedding. It contains an embedded clause, *where it is*, that is embedded within another clause, *I know*, that is embedded within the main sentence, *I think*.
(C grabbing for backpack to leave) I hafta go home/	**STAGE II (II)** This example contains the semiauxiliary *hafta*, which emerges in Stage II.
(C holds up cookie) I have a cookie if I eat dinner/	**LATE STAGE V (LV)** This complex utterance contains the conjunction *if*. This type of complex sentence emerges in Late Stage V.
(M asks, "Why did you color on the wall?") I colored because wanted to/	**STAGE V+ (V+)** This utterance contains the conjunction *because*. This type of complex sentence emerges in Stage V.
(C picks up a game) this is the one that I like/	**LATE STAGE V (LV)** This utterance contains a relative clause, *that I like*, introduced by the relative pronoun *that*. The relative clause modifies the noun *one*. This form emerges in Late Stage V.

determine whether it is complex and each stage assignment has been recorded, compare your results to those on Form 3.9.

The sample transcript contained only one utterance that was an example of a complex sentence. This complex sentence should be tallied on the Production Characteristics Summary form. With practice, transcripts can be scanned for examples of complex sentences very quickly, since very few complex sentences occur in transcripts of children within Brown's stages of linguistic production. Also, identifying complex sentences is easier to do after a verb phrase analysis has been completed. Judgments about the verb phrase typically illuminate the clause structure of the utterance, so the decision about whether the utterance is a complex sentence is made during verb phrase analysis. You may want to turn to *Guide Practice* web-based exercises for additional practice in identifying various types of complex sentences.

When all the boxes on the Structural Stage Analysis form have been filled in, you must analyze the data obtained from dissecting the preceding seven syntactic structures. The analysis of these data should be combined with the MLU data and length distribution analysis to provide an interpretation of the structural complexity of this child's productions.

Summary and Interpretation

To summarize the analysis of syntactic structures, transfer the results from the breakdown of each structure to the Production Characteristics Summary form (found in Appendix C, online). This tally form displays the range of the child's performance for each syntactic structure and the relationship between each performance. The visual display can be helpful in understanding the assignment of the Most Typical Stage and the Most Advanced Stage for each structure (on the Data Summary and Interpretation form).

FORM 3.9 Name of Child __Bridget__

STRUCTURAL STAGE ANALYSIS

Utterance Number	Number of Morphemes	Negation	Yes/No Question	Wh- Question	Noun Phrase	Verb Phrase	Complex Sentence
1	1	–	–	–	–	I–II	–
2	2	–	–	–	–	–	–
3	1	–	–	–	–	–	–
4	1	–	–	–	–	–	–
5	4	–	–	–	LIV/EV	III	–
6	1	–	EI–III	–	–	I–II	–
7	2	–	–	LI/EII–II	I–II	–	–
8	1	–	–	–	I–II	–	–
9	1	–	–	–	–	–	–
10	1	–	–	–	–	–	–
11	3	–	–	–	–	I–II	–
12	1	–	–	–	–	–	–
13	1	–	–	–	I–II	–	–
14	1	–	–	–	–	–	–
15	4	–	–	LI/EII–II	LIV/EV	III	–
16	2	–	–	–	III	III	–
17	4	–	–	–	III	LV	–
18	4	EIV–LIV/EV	–	–	–	–	–
19	2	–	–	LI/EII–II	–	–	–
20	4	EIV–LIV/EV	–	–	LIV/EV	LV	–
21	4	–	–	–	LIV/EV	III	–
22	2	EIV–LIV/EV	–	–	III	III	–
23	3	EIV–LIV/EV	–	III	LIV/EV	LV	–
24	4	–	–	III	III	III	–
25	2	–	–	–	–	–	–
26	2	–	–	–	–	I–II	–
27	2	–	–	–	I–II	–	–
28	2	–	–	–	–	I–II	–
29	1	–	–	–	–	–	–
30	5	–	–	–	LIV/EV	III	–
31	4	–	–	–	III	LV	–
32	4	–	–	–	LIV/EV	LV	–
33	4	–	–	–	–	LV	–
34	1	–	LV	–	–	–	–
35	4	–	–	–	LIV/EV	LV	–
36	3	–	–	–	LIV/EV	III	–
37	1	–	–	–	–	–	–
38	1	–	–	–	–	I–III	–
39	1	–	–	–	–	–	–
40	1	–	–	–	I–II	–	–
41	1	–	–	–	I–II	–	–
42	1	–	–	–	–	–	–
43	2	–	–	–	LIV/EV	III	–
44	2	–	–	–	LIV/EV	III	–
45	3	–	–	–	–	I–II	–
46	3	–	–	–	–	–	–
47	1	–	–	–	–	–	–
48	1	–	–	–	–	–	–
49	1	–	–	–	I–II	–	–
50	1	–	–	–	–	–	–
Subtotal 1	105						

FORM 3.9

STRUCTURAL STAGE ANALYSIS (continued)

Utterance Number	Number of Morphemes	Negation	Yes/No Question	Wh- Question	Noun Phrase	Verb Phrase	Complex Sentence
51	1	–	–	–	–	–	EIV
52	3	–	–	–	–	III	–
53	1	–	–	–	–	–	–
54	1	–	–	–	–	–	–
55	1	–	–	–	–	–	–
56	4	–	–	–	LIV/EV	III	–
57	1	–	–	–	–	–	–
58	1	–	–	–	I–II	–	–
59	1	–	–	–	–	–	–
60	4	–	EI–III	–	III	LV	–
61	4	–	–	–	III	LV	–
62	3	–	–	–	III	–	–
63	1	–	–	–	–	–	–
64	1	–	–	–	–	LV	–
65	4	–	–	–	III	–	–
66	2	–	–	LI/EII–II	–	–	–
67	1	–	–	–	–	–	–
68	1	–	–	–	–	–	–
69	1	–	–	–	–	–	–
70	1	–	EI–III	–	–	–	–
71	1	–	–	–	I–II	I–II	–
72	3	–	–	–	II	I–II	–
73	3	–	–	–	II	–	–
74	1	–	–	–	–	–	–
75	2	–	–	–	–	I–II	–
76	1	–	–	–	–	–	–
77	1	–	–	–	–	–	–
78	3	LI/EII–II	–	–	–	–	–
79	1	–	–	–	I–II	–	–
80	1	–	–	–	–	–	–
81	5	–	–	–	LIV/EV	LV	–
82	3	–	–	–	I–II	–	–
83	3	–	–	–	–	–	–
84	1	–	–	–	–	–	–
85	1	–	–	–	–	LV	–
86	2	–	–	–	II	LV	–
87	3	–	–	–	II	III	–
88	3	–	–	–	II	III	–
89	3	–	–	–	II	III	–
90	3	–	–	–	II	III	–
91	1	–	–	–	–	–	–
92	1	–	–	–	I–II	–	–
93	1	–	–	–	I–II	–	–
94	1	–	–	–	I–II	–	–
95	1	–	–	–	–	–	–
96	3	–	–	LV	–	LIV/EV	–
97	3	–	–	–	III	–	–
98	1	–	–	–	–	–	–
99	2	–	–	–	I–II	–	–
100	2	–	–	–	LIV/EV	III	–
Subtotal 2	95						

[105] + [95] = 200 Total No. of Morphemes

Total No. of Morphemes / Total No. of Utterances = [200] / [100] = 2.00 MLU

The first step in summarizing the data is to transfer the percent-use computations for each grammatical morpheme from the Grammatical Morphemes Analysis form into the appropriate stage box on the Production Characteristics Summary form. The percent use for the present progressive tense of the verb -ing is entered next to the number 1 in the box for Stage II under the Grammatical Morphemes column. Since there were no instances of the present progressive tense (i.e., present tense progressive aspect) in the sample transcript, put a dash (—) next to #1. The percent use for the regular plural -s is recorded next to number 2 in the same box. In the sample transcript, 100% correct use of the regular plural -s in obligatory contexts was obtained, so record 100% next to number 2. Now proceed through the Grammatical Morphemes Analysis form and enter the remaining percentages for grammatical morpheme use next to the appropriate numbers on the summary form. If there are no instances of a particular grammatical morpheme in the transcript and no obligatory contexts for that grammatical morpheme, put a dash (—) next to the number for that grammatical morpheme. If there are no instances of use but some number of obligatory contexts for a particular grammatical morpheme, put a zero next to the number for that grammatical morpheme. This notation differentiates those grammatical morphemes that were not used in the obligatory contexts from those grammatical morphemes for which no data was obtained.

The next step in summarizing analysis data is to tally the occurrences of each stage for each syntactic structure analyzed. Referring to the Structural Stage Analysis form, record the stage number assigned to each instance of negation onto the Production Characteristics Summary form. If a particular utterance was assigned a range of stages (e.g., *no* + noun = Late Stage I/Early Stage II–Stage II), be certain to record that range on the summary form. When all negations have been accounted for, tally the stage number assigned to each yes/no question on the summary form. Again, record a range of stages if that is the notation on the Structural Stage Analysis form. Next, tally the stage number assigned to each *wh-* question on the summary form. Then tally the stage number assigned to each noun phrase and the stage number assigned to each verb phrase. Finally, tally the stage number assigned to each complex sentence. Remember that for some structures, a tally is entered only at one particular stage. For other structures, a range of stages is tallied. This is indicated by drawing a vertical line through as many boxes as necessary and then marking the tally in the top left of the box at the end of that line.

Once a stage has been tallied for each instance of each structure, check your tallies with those in the sample summary form, Form 3.10. The summary form provides a visual display to compare the developmental complexity of the structures analyzed for this particular child. Initial examination of this visual display reveals a great deal of variability in the developmental complexity of the structures analyzed for this child. Although this may seem inappropriate, considerable variation in the developmental complexity of a particular structure and across structures is expected. In fact, the developmental level of a particular structure may vary as much as two stages on either side of the most frequently occurring level of that structure (Miller, 1981). This variability is the result of the ongoing nature of linguistic development. Most children do not master a single form of a particular structure (e.g., subject noun phrase elaboration) before going on to work on the production of another form of that structure (e.g., subject noun phrase pronouns). Rather, the child works on the production of a variety of forms at the same time, and a sampling of the child's production abilities at a single point in time will reveal many forms to be at a particular level of complexity, with some instances of more advanced forms and some instances of less advanced forms. Also, not all the forms at earlier stages are incorrect (e.g., use of regular plural -s); rather, their continued use would be expected. This adds variability as children advance through stages of linguistic production. Ironically, minimal variability, as opposed to considerable variability, may be indicative of a problem in language production (Miller, 1981).

This expected variability does make the interpretation of the data difficult. For this reason, interpretation is based on two stage assignments for each syntactic structure. First, a stage number should be assigned for each syntactic structure on the basis of the most frequently occurring stage for that structure. This means that the summary form needs to be examined and the number of instances of a particular stage for each structure needs to be counted. The stage with the greatest number of tallies is considered to be the most frequently occurring stage, reflecting the child's typical performance for that structure. It is labeled the Most Typical Stage. Second, a stage number should be assigned for the Most Advanced Stage each structure. The highest stage

FORM 3.10 Name of Child __Bridget__

PRODUCTION CHARACTERISTICS SUMMARY

Stage	Grammatical Morphemes	Negation	Yes/No Questions	Wh- Questions	Complex Sentences	Stage	Noun Phrase	Verb Phrase
Early I			↓	↓		I	↓	↓
Late I/ Early II		↓				II	↓ llll ⊬⊬⊬ ⊬⊬⊬ — ⊬⊬⊬ ll	↓ ⊬⊬⊬ llll
II	1. — 2. 100% 3. 100%	l		llll		III	⊬⊬⊬ ⊬⊬⊬ l	↓ ⊬⊬⊬ ⊬⊬⊬ — ⊬⊬⊬ ll
III	4. 0% 5. 100%		lll	ll		✕	✕	✕
Early IV		↓			l			
Late IV/ Early V		↓ lll					⊬⊬⊬ llll ⊬⊬⊬	l
Late V	6. 33% 7. 43% 8. 0% 9. 35% 10. 100%			ll				⊬⊬⊬ ⊬⊬⊬ l
V+	11. 50% 12. 50% 13. — 14. —							
V++								

number for each structure should be identified regardless of the frequency of occurrence. This stage reflects the forms the child is in the process of acquiring.

Finally, these two stage assignments for each structure (Most Typical Stage and Most Advanced Stage) are compared to each other, to the obtained MLU, and to the child's chronological age for interpretation. Like the variability expected for an individual structure, the stage assignments are expected to vary as much as two stages on either side of the MLU stage assignment (Miller, 1981). Again, since variability is expected, minimal variability may indicate a problem in syntactic aspects of language production.

Transfer the data obtained to the Data Summary and Interpretation form (found in Appendix C, online). First, record the MLU obtained from the morphemic analysis. An MLU of 2.00 morphemes was obtained for the 100-utterance sample transcript, so record 2.00 in the blank for MLU on the Data Summary and Interpretation form. Next, by comparing this to Table 3.3, it can be seen that this MLU is within the range of MLUs for Stage II (2.00–2.49 morphemes). Record Stage II in the next blank, indicating the stage assigned on the basis of MLU. This stage assignment is considered a pivot point to which other structures will be compared. It is helpful also to complete the variability about the mean on the Data Summary and Interpretation form using the formula from page 75 and the values from Table 3.1. The MLU for this child was 45 standard deviations below the expected mean.

Now record the upper and lower bound lengths obtained from the length distribution analysis. The upper bound length of five morphemes raises concerns about variations in utterance length for the obtained MLU.

Next, the Most Typical Stage and the Most Advanced Stage are determined for each structure analyzed. The stage assignments for grammatical morphemes are the most difficult to make because these stage assignments are not based on the frequency of occurrence of a stage. These assignments are based on the percentages compiled for each grammatical morpheme. Consider the Most Typical Stage first. Looking at the Production Characteristics Summary form, note that of the three grammatical morphemes in Stage II, this child used two at the mastery level. No data were obtained on the remaining grammatical morpheme for this stage. For Stage III grammatical morphemes, this child used one at the mastery level. The remaining grammatical morpheme for this stage was assigned a 0% use, which is different from no data, as previously discussed. For Late Stage V, percentages ranging from 0% to 100% use in obligatory contexts were obtained. In Stage V+, 50% use for two grammatical morphemes was obtained, and no data on the remaining two grammatical morphemes were available. To assign the Most Typical Stage, the stage that reflects consistent use of the grammatical morphemes of that stage at the mastery level must be determined. Because 0% use was obtained for the preposition *on*, grammatical morpheme #4 in Stage III, that stage cannot be assigned. Thus, record Stage II in the Grammatical Morphemes blank for the Most Typical Stage. If data on grammatical morpheme #4 had indicated greater than 90% correct use, Stage III would have been assigned as the Most Typical Stage.

To assign the Most Advanced Stage for grammatical morphemes, examine the Production Characteristics Summary form for the stage that reflects more than 0% use for any of the grammatical morphemes in that stage. In the sample transcript, Bridget used grammatical morphemes #11 and #12 in 50% of the obligatory contexts. Thus, Stage V+ is assigned as the Most Advanced Stage. If no data or 0% use had been obtained for grammatical morphemes #11 and #12, Late Stage V would have been assigned as the Most Advanced Stage. But since this child is beginning to use the contractible auxiliary and the uncontractible copula (grammatical morphemes #11 and #12) in some of the obligatory contexts, Stage V+ can be considered the Most Advanced Stage for grammatical morphemes. Record this stage as the Most Advanced Stage for grammatical morphemes on the Data Summary and Interpretation form.

Determining the Most Typical Stage and the Most Advanced Stage for the remaining structures in the sample transcript is considerably easier than it was for grammatical morphemes. Beginning with negation, there were four negative structures tallied on the Production Characteristics Summary form: one at the Late Stage I/Early Stage II–Stage II level and three at the Early Stage IV–Late Stage IV/Early V level. The stage with the greatest number of tallies is Early Stage IV–Late Stage IV/Early V. Record this stage number as the Most Typical Stage for negation. The Most Advanced Stage for negation is the same. Record Early Stage IV–Late Stage IV/Early V as the Most Advanced Stage for negation on the Data Summary and Interpretation form.

Turning to yes/no questions, there were three yes/no questions tallied on the Production Characteristics Summary form and all of them were typical of Early Stage I to Stage III. Thus, Early Stage I–Stage III is assigned as the Most Typical Stage and as the Most Advanced Stage. Record this in the appropriate blanks on the Data Summary and Interpretation form.

For *wh-* questions, there were four questions tallied at Late Stage I/Early Stage II–Stage II, two at Stage III, and two at Late Stage V. The Most Typical Stage is Late Stage I/Early Stage II–Stage II and the Most Advanced Stage is Late Stage V. Record these in the appropriate blanks on the Data Summary and Interpretation Form.

For noun phrase, the Production Characteristics Summary form reveals 14 utterances in which the noun phrase was typical of Stage I–Stage II, seven utterances at Stage II, 11 utterances in which the noun phrase was typical of Stage III, and 14 utterances in which the noun phrase was typical of Late Stage IV/Early Stage V. The most frequently assigned stage happens to be two stages: Stage I–Stage II and Stage LIV/EV. Record these stages under the Most Typical Stage. The Most Advanced Stage was Late Stage IV/Early Stage V. Record this in the blank for noun phrase on the Data Summary and Interpretation form.

For verb phrase elaboration, there were nine utterances in which the verb phrase was typical of Stage I–Stage II, one utterance in which the verb phrase was typical of Stage I–Stage III, 17 utterances in which the verb phrase was typical of Stage III, one utterance in which the verb phrase was typical of Late Stage IV/Early Stage V, and 11 utterances in which the verb phrase was typical of Late Stage V. The most frequently assigned stage was Stage III, of which there were 17 instances. Record Stage III as the Most Typical Stage for verb phrase elaboration on the Data Summary and Interpretation form. The Most Advanced Stage for verb phrase was Late Stage V, with 11 instances, so record this as the Most Advanced Stage for verb phrase elaboration on the summary form.

Finally, when examining complex sentences, note that only one complex sentence was in the sample transcript—an example of an Early Stage IV complex sentence. Thus, Early Stage IV is assigned as the Most Typical Stage and the Most Advanced Stage for complex sentences. Record this on the Data Summary and Interpretation form.

Now check your stage assignments and your determination of Most Typical Stage and Most Advanced Stage for each of the syntactic structures with those in the sample provided on Form 3.11. As previously mentioned, final interpretation is based on three comparisons: (1) the Most Typical Stage to MLU stage; (2) the Most Typical Stage to the Most Advanced Stage; and (3) MLU stage to the child's chronological age.

Comparison of Most Typical Stage to MLU Stage

When comparing the Most Typical Stage for each of the syntactic structures analyzed to the stage determined by the obtained MLU, considerable variability is expected. The MLU stage is the same as the stage assigned as the Most Typical Stage for grammatical morphemes. The Most Typical Stage for negation is two stages above the MLU stage. For yes/no questions, the MLU stage is the midpoint in the range of stages assigned as the Most Typical Stage. For *wh-* questions, the MLU stage is within the range of stages assigned as the Most Typical Stage. For noun phrase, the MLU stage is consistent with Stage I–II but below the range of stages assigned as the Most Typical Stage if Stage LIV–EV is considered. The Most Typical Stage for verb phrase is one stage higher than the MLU stage. Finally, the Most Typical Stage for complex sentences is two stages above the MLU stage.

So, what is the conclusion from this first set of comparisons? For five of the structures analyzed, the variability present would be expected on the basis of the obtained MLU. But the Most Typical Stage for three of the structures appears to be higher than would be expected on the basis of MLU: The Most Typical Stage for negation, noun phrase possibly, and complex sentences is two stages above the stage for MLU. One explanation could be that the sample is not representative and contains many elliptical utterances, resulting in an artificially low MLU. Another explanation could be that the child's MLU is lagging behind the child's abilities in formulating negative utterances and complex sentences, implying a length constraint. In other words, for some reason, physiological or cognitive, this child is unable to produce utterances as long as the complexity of those utterances would suggest. But the Most Typical Stage for negation and complex sentences was assigned on the basis of a total of four utterances. Concluding a length constraint on the basis of so few utterances

FORM 3.11   Name of Child __Bridget__

DATA SUMMARY AND INTERPRETATION

Mean Length of Utterance in Morphemes (MLU)

_____2.00_____ morphemes

Structural Stage by MLU: Stage ____II____

Upper Bound Length: ____5____ morpheme(s)

Lower Bound Length: ____1____ morpheme(s)

*CA=28 mos.
use 27 mos. figures
2.00-2.23 = -.45
.510*

	Most Typical Stage	Most Advanced Stage
Grammatical Morphemes:	Stage II	Stage V+
Negation:	Stage EIV–LIV/EV	Stage EIV–LIV/EV
Yes/No Questions:	Stage EI–III	Stage EI–III
Wh- Questions:	Stage LI/EII–II	Stage LV
Noun Phrase:	Stage I–II, LIV/EV	Stage LIV/EV
Verb Phrase:	Stage III	Stage LV
Complex Sentences:	Stage EIV	Stage EIV

Comments: __Most Typical Stage assignments are consistent with or higher than the stage by MLU; largest gap is between MLU and stages of Negation, Noun Phrase, and Complex Sentences. There are gaps between Most Typical Stage and Most Advanced Stage for all structures except Negation, Yes/No Questions, Noun Phrase, and Complex Sentences. Structural Stage by MLU is within normal limits for CA.__

would be inappropriate. Should a problem in terms of the length of utterance be suspected with this amount of data? Here is where the next set of comparisons enters the picture.

Comparison of Most Typical Stage to Most Advanced Stage

Results of the sample analysis reveal a difference of four stages between the Most Typical Stage and the Most Advanced Stage for grammatical morphemes. The Most Typical Stage for negation was the same as the Most

Advanced Stage. For yes/no questions, the Most Typical Stage was the same as the Most Advanced Stage. For *wh-* questions, the Most Typical Stage was three stages lower than the Most Advanced Stage. The Most Typical Stage for noun phrase elaboration was consistent with the Most Advanced Stage if you consider the greater of the two Most Typical Stages. For verb phrase elaboration, the Most Typical Stage was also two stages below the Most Advanced Stage. Finally, the Most Typical Stage for complex sentences was the same as the Most Advanced Stage.

Returning to the question from the previous section, there is a reasonable gap between the Most Typical Stage and the Most Advanced Stage for three of the seven structures analyzed. This suggests that this child is exploring more sophisticated means of producing *wh-* questions and verb phrases and as well as ways of consistently marking grammatical morphemes in obligatory contexts. For negation and yes/no questions, her production appears to have plateaued. Such plateaus are common in normal language acquisition (Miller, 1981). The variability observed is typical as the child works on more sophisticated accomplishments for some structures while she plateaus in her production in other areas. And with only one complex utterance in the sample, it is impossible to have anything other than no gap for complex sentences. The lack of a gap between the Most Typical Stage and the Most Advanced Stage for negation, yes/no questions, noun phrase, and complex sentences is not reason for concern for this particular child. The gap between the Most Typical Stage and the Most Advanced Stage is only one of the things examined in interpreting the summary information. If no gap is observed between the Most Typical Stage and the Most Advanced Stage for most of the structures analyzed, there may be reason for concern about the child's advancements in form for the production of some structures. This is discussed in greater detail in the Implications for Intervention section of this chapter.

Overall, it should be concluded that the transcript obtained from Bridget evidences a reasonable amount of variability in the developmental level of the structures analyzed. The Most Typical Stage for the seven structures analyzed are at levels appropriate for the MLU stage, and the relationship between the Most Typical Stage and the Most Advanced Stage reflects plateauing for some structures and acquisition of more sophisticated forms than typical performance for other structures. One final comparison is necessary.

Comparison of MLU Stage to Child's Chronological Age

Final interpretation of the analysis data requires comparison of the MLU stage to the child's chronological age. Regardless of the relationship between the Most Typical Stage and the MLU stage and the relationship between the Most Typical Stage and the Most Advanced Stage, this final comparison is crucial. When the child's age is higher than the age range for the MLU stage as reported by Miller and Chapman (1981), it might be concluded that a delay in production exists. When the child's age falls within the age range for the MLU stage, it can be assumed that the length of the child's utterances is appropriate for his or her age. And when the child's age is lower than the age range for the MLU stage, the appropriate conclusion is that the child's production is advanced for his or her age. According to Miller and Chapman, these age ranges also can be translated into developmental-age expectations. For example, a 5-year-old child who is developmentally at a 2-year-old level would be expected to produce utterances typical in length and complexity of Late Stage I/Early Stage II. Thus, the MLU stage assignment is pivotal in the interpretation of the child's age level and structural complexity.

The age of the child in the sample transcript is 28 months. On the basis of the predicted ages for Brown's stages (Miller & Chapman, 1981), this child falls within Stage II. And the MLU stage is Stage II. Thus, Bridget is producing utterances that are of an appropriate length for her age. And from the previous comparisons, it can be concluded that she is producing utterances that reflect an appropriate amount of variability in developmental complexity. The sample transcript reflects typical development of this child's syntax.

Implications for Intervention

In contemplating the previous comparisons, one might have some cause for concern. First, if the Most Typical Stage for some or all of the syntactic structures analyzed is lower than the MLU stage, it can be concluded that a delay in some aspect of syntax production exists. Second, if no gap is present between the Most Typical Stage and the Most Advanced Stage for most or all of the syntactic structures analyzed, it can be concluded that a delay in some aspect of syntax production exists. Third, if chronological age (or cognitive level) is higher than the age range for the MLU stage, it can be concluded that a delay in language production exists.

As suggested by Fey (1986), factors in addition to MLU stage, Most Typical Stage, and Most Advanced Stage must be considered before concluding that the delay warrants intervention. These include no change versus dramatic change in language production during the past few months; negative versus positive reactions by parents and other caregivers to the child's communication attempts; history of middle-ear problems in the child versus no such history; and nonstimulating versus stimulating linguistic environments. A child with a depressed MLU in combination with recent dramatic gains in language production and a stimulating linguistic environment may not be a candidate for intervention. On the other hand, a child with a low MLU, recurrent ear infections, and parents who are reacting negatively to the delay may need intervention.

How is the information from syntactic analysis procedures used in planning intervention of the observed delays? While this could be the topic of another extensive volume, the implication is obvious. Based on the sequence of accomplishments in normal language acquisition, forms that would appear next in the sequence to increase the length and complexity of the child's utterances can be taught. This may appear to oversimplify the process, but clinical experience has shown that from the detailed analysis of syntactic aspects of language production, the forms likely to emerge next are quite predictable. Advances are likely to be seen first in structures where a gap exists between the Most Typical Stage and the Most Advanced Stage. It also has been shown that the forms occurring next in the developmental sequence can be taught even when no gap exists between the Most Typical Stage and the Most Advanced Stage.

Consideration of as many structures as have been examined in this analysis has three purposes. First, variability in performance of each structure is assumed; therefore, data on as many structures as it is possible to obtain are necessary to capture both variability and consistency. Second, stage assignments for individual structures are considered estimates of overall production abilities; therefore, data on as many structures as it is possible to obtain are necessary to be confident of the estimates. Third, each structure provides the basis for a set of intervention goals and objectives; therefore, data on as many structures as it is possible to obtain are necessary for appropriate intervention. Only with such extensive analysis is documentation of the nature of the delay possible. The goals and objectives for intervention of the identified delay are the logical outgrowth of this extensive syntactic analysis.

CHAPTER 4
Pragmatic ANALYSIS

Introduction

Language as Communication

Language acquisition is not simply learning semantic rules and syntactic rules: It is the process of learning to communicate with others. As Tomasello (1992) wrote, "Language is social behavior. Its structures are social conventions. Its functions all derive in one way or another from communication. It can be acquired only through social interaction with human beings" (p. 67).

This view of language as social behavior illustrates its complexity, for language is more than the use of the phonological, morphological, semantic, and syntactic aspects of language— "Language is communication within a social context" (Duchan, 1984). The "meeting of meaning" between two or more persons in a social context results in communication. It is this meeting of meaning between young children and adults for purposes of communication that is the focus of this chapter.

Since the rules of language encompass social rules, an analysis of language abilities that does not document pragmatic structures and functions is incomplete. Documentation of the child's ability to appropriately use semantic and syntactic aspects of the language system within a communicative context is essential for full understanding of language production abilities. Because of this, *Guide to Analysis of Language Transcripts* examines the child's pragmatic abilities within this communicative context, describing the child's abilities in relation to a conversational co-participant. Only within this exchange can we examine the conversational contingencies that affect the child's contributions.

The use of language for communication must be examined within the context of conversation. According to Hoskins and Noel (2011), "if pragmatics is the study of language in context, then that context is conversation" (p. 7). The ability to communicate within conversation is thought to develop from mutual focus and joint activity in which both participants engage in interaction (Bates, 1976; Bruner, 1975; Wells, 1981). These authors contend that the components and structures of language are not learned in isolation. The phonological, semantic, and syntactic/morphological components of language are acquired in social, communicative interactions. This is true for the pragmatic components of language as well: The child learns the pragmatic rules of language while engaged in conversation.

According to Hoskins and Noel, to participate in conversation,

> a person must engage in joint attention, take the perspective of another and, thereby, choose an appropriate topic. One must have an organized set of concepts from which to draw topics and the vocabulary to express those concepts. Moreover, one must be able to retrieve those words and formulate sentences and connected language to initiate and ultimately maintain conversation. (2011, p. 6)

This description of conversation highlights how the components of language function together, and it explains why the examination of the pragmatic aspects of communication is critical. For children between the ages of 1 and 5 years, this examination must focus on conversation between children and familiar adults.

This is the reason both participants within the conversations (i.e., the child and a familiar adult) are examined in the analyses described in this chapter.

Larson and McKinley (1998) contended that conversations can be analyzed on at least three levels: (1) a macrolevel, which provides the conversational framework; (2) a midlevel, which specifies the pragmatic behaviors used; and (3) a microlevel, which examines the linguistic and paralinguistic behaviors employed. The procedures demonstrated in this chapter parallel the macro- and midlevels of analysis described by Larson and McKinley and the role of the conversational co-participants as described by Anderson-Wood Smith (1997) and Hoskins and Noel (2011). As the child engages in conversation, the components of language come together at the various levels of the conversation to result in mutual exchanges of meaning.

Pragmatic Language Disorders

While it appears that delays in pragmatic (i.e., conversational) development may co-occur with delays in semantic or syntactic development, it appears that delays may also occur in isolation (Craig, 1991; Paul & Norbury, 2012). In the *Diagnostic and Statistical Manual of Mental Disorders* (5th edition; DSM-5), the American Psychiatric Association (2013) listed new criteria for identifying a social (pragmatic) communication disorder. For the child whose semantic and/or syntactic delays have previously been identified, failure to examine pragmatic aspects of production results in an incomplete description of the language production disorder. This failure may result in overlooking factors contributing to the semantic and/or syntactic delays and stylistic variations of the conversational co-participant that may be hindering development. In addition, failure to examine the pragmatic aspects of the child's linguistic production system may result in overlooking the child with normal semantic and syntactic skills who has problems with some aspect of pragmatic production. This oversight may result in the child's language disorder persisting until the impact on academic performance becomes apparent. Either scenario can be avoided by conducting a thorough examination of the pragmatic aspects of language production.

Procedures similar to those presented in this chapter have been described in the literature as revealing developmental changes in pragmatic aspects of oral language and/or deviation from what is considered to be typical conversation (Damico, 1991; Larson & McKinley, 1998; Penn, 1988; Prutting & Kirchner, 1987; Roth & Spekman, 1984; Strong, 1998; Wetherby & Prizant, 1992; Wetherby & Prutting, 1984). Numerous studies have described differences in pragmatic aspects of oral language for individuals with a language disorder. Table 4.1 summarizes some of the potential difficulties of children with specific language impairment (SLI) as compared to children with typical language development. The formats for identifying each of the characteristics described differ for each author. Additional pragmatic characteristics of children with language disorders may include restricted use of linguistic forms, difficulty entering ongoing social interactions, difficulty with topic maintenance and responsiveness to conversational partners, and difficulty participating in cooperative groups (Brinton, Fujiki, Spencer, & Robinson, 1997; Gerber, Brice, Capone, Fujiki & Timler, 2012; Liiva & Cleave, 2005; Toe, Rinaldi, Caselli, Paatsch, & Church, 2016; van Balkom, Verhoeven, & van Weerdenburg, 2010). Some of the characteristics can be identified using the procedures described in this chapter.

Further, a number of studies have investigated the pragmatic functions and discourse characteristics typical of young communicators who are at risk for or diagnosed with autism spectrum disorder (ASD). Research has consistently documented the differences in the pragmatic functions of early communicative acts used by children with a diagnosis of ASD, as compared to the communicative acts used by both typically developing children and children with language delays and disorders (Mundy, Sigman, & Kasari, 1990; Wetherby, Watt, Morgan, & Shumway, 2007). Descriptions of discourse-level deficits commonly associated with ASD are also available in the literature. For example, children with autism have been found to have significantly fewer contingent responses during conversation (Hale & Tager-Flusberg, 2005). As discussed in detail later in this chapter, use of the procedures described in this chapter may be helpful in assisting speech–language pathologists to identify young children who may be at risk of a diagnosis of ASD.

Despite the attention given in recent years to the analysis of pragmatic aspects of conversation, no real normative data have emerged. According to Brinton (1990), the flurry of activity described as the "pragmatic revolution" has not yielded its primary goal: making clinical research and intervention easier. Specific typologies of conversational moves and variations in specificity, conciseness, and style have been identified as occurring in individuals with a language disorder (Brinton & Fujuki, 1984, 1989; Brinton, Fujuki, Loeb, & Winkler, 1986; Brinton, Fujuki, & Powell, 1997; Brinton, Fujuki, & Sonnenberg, 1988; Craig, 1991; Fey & Leonard, 1983; Liiva & Cleave, 2005; McTear, 1985; McTear & Conti-Ramsden, 1991; Prutting & Kirchner, 1987; Rice, Sell, & Hadley, 1990; van Balkom et al., 2010). However, the emergence of data implicating differences in typologies of conversational moves and/or variations in specificity, conciseness, or style still leaves us with many unanswered questions. The speech–language pathologist is still "in the position of being able to identify problems, without being able to evaluate their significance" (Anderson-Wood & Smith, 1997, p. 28). Many of the pragmatic problems cited in Table 4.1 can be recognized by using the procedures presented in this chapter, including speech acts analysis (Dore, 1974), conversational acts analysis (Dore, 1978), conversational moves analysis (Martlew, 1980), and appropriateness judgments (Retherford, 1980).

Narrative Analysis Procedures

Analysis of children's abilities to relate past events in storytelling frameworks has received considerable attention in recent years. Procedures for examining the structure of narratives have been based on loose guidelines of having children tell about their favorite book or summer vacation and/or tell versus retell versions of wordless picture books (e.g., Bishop & Edmundson's, 1987, use of Renfrew's, 1969, *Bus Story*; Stein & Glenn's, 1979, use of Mayer's, 1973, *Froggie on His Own*). Work in this area is promising in that various subgroups of children with language disorders may be distinguished on the basis of narrative analysis (Anderson-Wood

TABLE 4.1

Pragmatic Characteristics of the Child With Specific Language Impairment

Conversational function	Linguistic form
Requesting	Requests for clarification may be inadequate and grammatically incomplete.
Commenting	Comments may be stereotypic and prone to false starts, mazes, and other forms of dysfluency.
Referencing presuppositions	Presuppositions depend less on pronominals.
Turn taking	Comments relate to preceding discourse and more substitution devices and more inadequate forms are used.
	Turns involve less other-directed speech and are shorter in length.
	Fewer turns are taken and utterances are less "adjacent," so the turn-taking response to the previous speaker takes longer.
	Interruptions are infrequently used to gain the turn at speaking.
	Topic is poorly maintained.
Responding	Responses to requests for clarification are structurally diffuse and less focused.
	Responses to other types of speech acts can be unrelated, inappropriate, and variable.
Narratives	Narratives are less complete, less elaborate, and include different distributions of cohesive ties.
Speech adjustments	Speech style modifications reflect fewer internal state questions and less adjustment of utterance length and complexity.

Note. Modified from Craig, H. (1991). Pragmatic Characteristics of the Child with Specific Language Impairment: An Interactionist Perspective. In T. Gallagher (Ed.), *Pragmatics of Language: Clinical Practice Issues* (pp. 163–198). San Diego, CA: Singular.

& Smith, 1997; Carpenter, 1991; Griffith, Ripich, & Dastoli, 1986; Colozzo, Gillam, Wood, Schnell, & Johnston, 2011; Hughes, McGillivray, & Schmidek, 1997; Liles, 1985a, 1985b, 1987; Merritt & Liles, 1987; Roth, 1986; Smith & Leinonen, 1992; Schneider & Hayward, 2010; Strong, 1998; Thorne, Coggins, Carmichael Olson, & Astley, 2007; Thorne & Coggins, 2016). Collection and analysis of narrative samples are recommended for children who demonstrate difficulties with any aspect of pragmatic analysis described and/or analyzed in Chapter 4. However, it is not within the scope of *Guide* to present procedures for analyzing narratives and the normative data that exist; Hughes et al. (1997) and Strong (1998) have delineated a variety of descriptive analyses for narration.

Pragmatic Analysis Procedures

The pragmatic analysis procedures in Chapter 4 are compatible with the semantic and syntactic analysis procedures described in the preceding two chapters. It would be appropriate to analyze first semantic, then syntactic, and then pragmatic aspects of an obtained language transcript. While it is not necessary to complete the analyses in this order, following this order may be the most productive because it would provide a systematic organizational framework. Analysis information from Chapters 2, 3, and 4 should be combined to identify and diagnose language production problems and delays. The composite analysis information should also be combined with information obtained from narrative samples and standardized tests to build a detailed picture of the child's communicative strengths and weaknesses, which should then be used to develop an intervention plan that includes specific goals and objectives to address any language production difficulties.

The analysis procedures described in this chapter are based on information provided by Dore (1974, 1978), Martlew (1980), and Retherford (1980) and on variables identified by Grice (1975), Keenan and Schieffelin (1976), and Shatz and Gelman (1973). The procedures are designed to be used with transcripts obtained from children at the one-word stage and beyond, including transcripts obtained from children functioning within Brown's stages of syntactic development. Not all analysis procedures described should be used for analysis of every transcript. Some procedures are appropriate for use with transcripts obtained from children at the one-word stage (Dore's primitive speech acts, 1974), and other procedures are appropriate for use with transcripts obtained from children producing utterances longer than one word in length (Dore's conversational acts, 1978; Martlew's conversational moves, 1980; and Retherford's appropriateness judgments, 1980). Decisions about which procedure to use with a child can be made only after gaining familiarity with each procedure.

Our examination of the pragmatic aspects of language production parallels two of the three major levels of distinction described by Larson and McKinley (1998). The first distinction is between the particular function of each utterance (i.e., its purpose or intent) and the role of each utterance in the development of the overall conversation—at the macrolevel. This distinction has been recognized in the procedures developed for this chapter. The first two procedures—Dore's primitive speech acts and Dore's conversational acts—examine the communicative functions of utterances within children's conversation. The last two procedures—Martlew's conversational acts and Retherford's appropriateness judgments—investigate the discourse relations within children's conversation.

The second distinction is between quantitative and qualitative analyses—termed "midlevel analysis" by Larson and McKinley (1998). For many of the analysis procedures described in the previous two chapters, instances of each utterance type were tallied, analyzed on the basis of the frequency of occurrence of each type, and then compared to frequency-of-occurrence normative data. This type of quantitative analysis ensures reasonably reliable conclusions about semantic and syntactic abilities. However, for some analysis procedures, particularly in the area of pragmatics, quantitative measurements are still not possible. Thus, qualitative analyses are employed. Although conclusions drawn from qualitative analyses may not be as reliable as those drawn from quantitative procedures, the importance of qualitative measures cannot be denied. In the case of the role that individual utterances play in ongoing discourse, it is not possible to say that a particular number of topic initiations is "typical." Judgments are made regarding the appropriateness of conversational moves, and the overall conclusion is based on individual judgments of appropriateness. These types of judgments may be more difficult for the beginning speech–language pathologist to make, but with practice, speech–language pathologists become better at drawing conclusions from qualitative analyses.

The third and final distinction is between the role of the child and that of the conversational co-participant. Analyzing children's conversational contributions without examining and describing what occurred linguistically before and after each utterance would be incomplete (Anderson-Wood & Smith, 1997; Hoskins & Noel, 2011). However, we are in no better position to judge the developmental adequacy or significance of the adult's contributions when conversing with a child than we are to judge the child's contributions. Therefore, the analysis procedures described for child utterances are also used for adult contributions. However, adult utterance types and frequencies will be compared not to normative data, but rather to child utterance types and frequencies, to permit an examination of the conversation at large. According to Smith and Leinonen (as cited in Anderson-Wood & Smith, 1997), it is clear that each conversational co-participant "can do things that either help or hinder the process of communication" (p. 50). Thus, while it may not be possible to draw definitive conclusions from a description of the adult's utterance types and frequencies, such a description helps in analyzing the child's utterance types and frequencies more completely. It may also be possible to describe specific exchanges that are problematic for one or both of the participants. As a result, SLPs will have a more thorough description of the child's participation in conversation than would be possible without examining the conversational co-participant.

Documentation of pragmatic analysis as a diagnostic tool remains difficult. The research data are sketchy quantitatively and demonstrate extreme variability, thus preventing comparison of language samples to existing norms or making the comparison questionable. Perhaps, at best,

> all a speech–language pathologist can do is look at the range of normal behavior and make some educated guesses as to what normal behavior might be. Another possibility . . . is to look at the child's use of language content and form. Bottom of the range performance should be interpreted as normal if the child's language in other areas is [appropriate]. (Fey, personal communication, September 1987)

Although pragmatic analysis is still in its infancy, this chapter presents several pragmatic analysis procedures that can provide descriptive data and limited quantitative, albeit extremely variable, data.

Some procedures described in this chapter are demonstrated on the sample transcript used in the preceding chapters (Bridget's transcript) and some are demonstrated using a transcript of a girl named Sara (found in Appendix E). The reasons for this transcript variance will become clear as each analysis procedure is considered. Blank forms for the analysis procedures described in this chapter are provided in Appendix D (online) and can also be printed from the *Guide Practice* web-based program.

Dore's Primitive Speech Acts

The first procedure that we use to analyze the pragmatic content of language transcripts is based on a set of categories developed by Dore (1974). These categories were used to code young children's utterances as they began to acquire language and are based on Dore's interpretation of Searle's (1969) speech acts, which Searle contended are those that adults perform when communicating. A *speech act*, according to Dore, is a linguistic unit of communication consisting of conceptual information (i.e., a *proposition*) and an intention (i.e., the *illocutionary force*). The proposition and illocutionary force are expressed according to conventional grammatical and pragmatic rules. Searle's speech acts require the speaker to have fairly complex language, but Dore (1974) claimed that the foundations for speech acts are laid in the young child's early communicative attempts. In fact, Dore asserted that children can perform "primitive speech acts" before they have acquired sentence structures. According to Dore, *a primitive speech act* is "an utterance, consisting formally of a single word or a single prosodic pattern which functions to convey the child's intentions before he acquires sentences" (p. 345). Table 4.2 lists and summarizes Dore's primitive speech acts.

A few utterances are provided for practice in assigning Dore's (1974) primitive speech acts before attempting to categorize the utterances in the sample transcript. Some of the example utterances used for practice with Bloom's and Nelson's procedures in Chapter 2 are provided, along with a few others. In Example 4.1, cover the right side of the page and categorize each example utterance using one of Dore's nine primitive speech acts. Linguistic and nonlinguistic contexts are provided for each practice utterance, since this information is crucial for coding. When you are finished, check your results with those provided in the shaded section.

TABLE 4.2

Primitive Speech Acts

Labeling	One or more words that function as a label produced while attending to an object. The child's word or words may label a part of the event or a situation. The child does not address the adult or wait for a response.
Repeating	One or more words or a prosodic pattern that repeats part of the adult utterance and is produced while attending to the adult utterance. The child does not address the adult or wait for a response.
Answering	One or more words that respond to an adult question or statement and are produced while attending to the adult utterance. The child addresses the adult but does not necessarily wait for a response.
Requesting Action	One or more words or a prosodic pattern that functions as a request for an action and is produced while attending to an object or an event. The child addresses the adult and waits for a response. Often, the production is accompanied by a gesturing signal.
Requesting Answer	One or more words that function as a request for an answer. The child addresses the adult and waits for a response. The child may gesture toward an object.
Calling	One or more words that are used to obtain another's attention. The child addresses the adult (or other participant) and waits for a response.
Greeting	One or more words that are used to mark arrival or leave-taking and are produced while attending to the adult or an object. The child addresses the adult or object and does not necessarily wait for a response.
Protesting	One or more words or a prosodic pattern that expresses disapproval of or dislike for an object or an action and is produced while attending to the adult. The child addresses the adult but does not necessarily wait for a response.
Practicing	One or more words or a prosodic pattern that is not contingent on preceding utterances and is produced while attending to an object or an event. The child does not address the adult and does not wait for a response. Dore suggests that this is a "catch-all" category that should be used whenever an utterance cannot be assigned clearly to another category.

Note. Adapted from "A Pragmatic Description of Early Language Development," by J. Dore, 1974, *Journal of Psycholinguistic Research, 4*, 343–350; and *Speech Acts*, by J. Searle, 1969, Cambridge, MA: Cambridge University Press.

Explanations are provided to help clarify discrepancies. You may also wish to turn to the *Guide Practice* web-based exercises for additional practice.

Example 4.1 and the web-based examples should be helpful as you code the utterances in Bridget's transcript. Using Dore's Primitive Speech Acts Analysis form (found in Appendix D, online), progress through Bridget's transcript and examine each child utterance to determine the type of primitive speech act it represents. Categorize each utterance, remembering that Dore supports the notion of using the **practicing** category as a "catchall" category. Record the utterance number next to the appropriate speech act on Dore's Primitive Speech Acts Analysis form. (In the next section, you will learn about Dore's conversational acts, which will be used to code both the child's and the adult's utterances.) When all child utterances have been coded, count the number of each speech act and enter them in each Total space. Calculate the percent of total utterances (in this case 100 utterances) that accounts for each speech act and enter those percentages in each percentage space. Then compare your analysis with Form 4.1.

The completed analysis form for the sample transcript shows that 19 of Bridget's utterances were examples of **labeling**, one utterance was an example of **repeating**, 41 utterances were examples of **answering**, 20 utterances were examples of **requesting action**, 14 utterances were examples of **requesting answer**, one utterance was an example of **calling**, two utterances were examples of **greeting**, one utterance was an example of **protesting**, and one utterance was an example of **practicing**.

EXAMPLE 4.1

PRIMITIVE SPEECH ACTS

(C picks up toy horse) horsie/	**LABELING** The child produced this utterance while attending to the horse, and it is assumed that he is labeling the horse.
(C hears door opening) Dada/	**LABELING, CALLING, OR GREETING** Without additional context information, it is impossible to differentiate these three categories; this underlines the necessity of noting complete contextual information.
(C picks up big toy horse) big/	**LABELING** The child says this while attending to the horse and is labeling a feature.
(C reaches for cup on table) cup↑/	**REQUESTING ACTION** The child appears to desire the cup, which is out of reach. He then labels the desired cup and, by reaching, indicates the desire for the action of bringing it within reach.
(C reaches up to M, who has entered bedroom) up/	**REQUESTING ACTION** This utterance is also an example of a request for an action, but the child labels the action instead of the object of the action.
(dog barking in background) Dee Dee/	**LABELING OR CALLING** The child appears to be either labeling the dog or calling the dog; additional context would need to be considered before coding the utterance.
(C takes a drink from cup) juice/	**LABELING** The child is labeling the substance.
(M says, "Where is that shoe?"; C points to chest of drawers and says) there/	**ANSWERING** The child is responding directly to the adult's question.
(C points to self in mirror) Baby/	**LABELING** The child is labeling himself. Recall from the practice examples for Bloom's and Nelson's analyses that this child refers to himself as "Baby."
(C hands empty cup to M) drink/	**REQUESTING ACTION** The child is asking his mother to get him a drink.
(M attempts to wipe C's face) no/	**PROTESTING** The child is protesting his mother's attempt to wipe his face.
(C is holding box; M says, "What's in there?") kiki/ [cookie]	**ANSWERING** The child is responding to his mother's question.
(C pulls block from bag) bɑ/ [block]	**LABELING** The child is attending to the object retrieved from the bag and is labeling it.
(C holds up toy sheep and looks at M) moo↑/	**REQUESTING ANSWER** The child is asking his mother to confirm the label for the toy animal.
(C reaches arms up to M, who is standing by door) /ʌ/ [up]	**REQUESTING ACTION** The child is requesting that his mother pick him up.

(continues)

EXAMPLE 4.1 (continued)

(M places C in bed and turns to leave, saying, "Sleep tight, Megan") naɪ naɪ/ [night-night]	**GREETING** Remember, this category is used both for arrivals and departures.
(C is playing in crib after nap and bats at mobile hanging above bed) bwɪ/ [XXX]	**PRACTICING** The child is not addressing anyone, and therefore appears to be practicing some aspect of language.
(C is playing in crib after nap; M walks by the bedroom door) mɑ/ [mom]	**CALLING** The child is calling for his mother. This utterance appears to be more clearly an example of calling instead of labeling because the child uses more emphasis in saying /mɑ/.
(M stands up and says, "Let's have some cookies") kiki/ [cookie]	**REPEATING** The child is repeating part of the mother's utterance without addressing her.
(M asks C, "Do you want some cookies?") ya/	**ANSWERING** The child is responding directly to the mother's question.

TABLE 4.3

Percentage of Total Utterances Accounted for by Primitive Speech Act Types for Bridget (Age 2 Years 4 Months)

Act type	% total (based on 100 utterances)	
Labeling	19	
Repeating	1	
Answering	41	
Requesting Action	20	
Requesting Answer	14	34
Calling	1	
Greeting	2	
Protesting	1	
Practicing	1	

As can be seen in Table 4.3, Bridget used the primitive speech acts of **labeling** and **answering** for 60% of her utterances. When the two requesting categories—**requesting action** and **requesting answer**—are added to this percentage, these four acts account for 94% of the child's utterances.

When these results are compared to results obtained by Dore (1974), substantial differences can be found. Table 4.4 summarizes the distribution of primitive speech acts for two children, each 15 months of age, used in Dore's study. The analysis was based on 81 utterances for one child and 80 utterances for the other. While there are differences between the two children on whom Dore reported, there are more substantial differences between Dore's subjects and Bridget, the 28-month-old child in the sample transcript. For example, the primitive speech act **repeating** accounted for 39.5% and 28.7% of utterances for Dore's subjects, but only 1% of utterances in Bridget's transcript. In addition, **answering** accounted for 14.8% and 10% of utterances for Dore's subjects, but 41% of utterances in Bridget's transcript. The observed differences could be the result of

FORM 4.1   Name of Child **Bridget**

DORE'S PRIMITIVE SPEECH ACTS ANALYSIS

Act	Child Utterance Number	Total	%
Labeling	1, 8, 13, 17, 18, 20, 27, 32, 40, 41, 46, 61, 62, 65, 83, 84, 86, 94, 99	19	19
Repeating	50 — *Not labeling, because in the preceding turn, M asks about the stroller*	1	1
Answering	2, 3, 4, 5, 9, 12, 21, 25, 30, 33, 34, 36, 37, 42, 43, 44, 45, 47, 48, 49, 51, 55, 56, 57, 58, 63, 64, 69, 75, 76, 77, 78, 79, 80, 81, 82, 85, 92, 93, 95, 97	41	41
Requesting Action	6, 10, 11, 14, 15, 22, 26, 28, 31, 38, 52, 53, 70, 72, 73, 87, 88, 89, 90, 100 — *Directs adult to look at tail, not simply to answer*	20	20
Requesting Answer	7, 16, 19, 23, 24, 29, 35, 59, 60, 66, 68, 74, 91, 96	14	14
Calling	71	1	1
Greeting	54, 98	2	2
Protesting	39	1	1
Practicing	67	1	1

either the question-asking performance of the child's conversational partner or the developmental levels of the children (i.e., MLU, semantic, or syntactic aspects reflecting a higher developmental level). Bridget appears to be using a more conversational interaction style while communicating, as evidenced by the high percentage of **requesting** and **answering** speech acts. Dore's children used primarily **labeling** and **repeating**, both decidedly less conversational in style, although Bridget's **labeling** slightly exceeded Dore's Child J.

Other differences between Dore's (1974) subjects and Bridget were noted but do not appear to be as substantial as these differences, primarily because of the variability between Dore's two subjects. In fact, Dore noted that his two subjects had different styles of language use. The child identified as "M" in Table 4.4 apparently used language at this stage of development to declare things about her environment. The child identified as "J" apparently used language to manipulate other people. This variation may be similar to variation in semantic use at the one-word stage, as described in Chapter 2. For purposes of the present analysis, however, we are more concerned with the differences between Bridget's transcript and the results of Dore's analysis. There is a notable age difference between Bridget and the children studied by Dore. Dore's subjects were just into the one-word stage at 15 months. Bridget is beyond the one-word stage at age 28 months. The differences in frequency of use of various speech acts are obvious for these children. As a result, analysis of Dore's primitive speech acts may not be the most revealing for children beyond the one-word stage. Such analysis, then, should be reserved for children at the one-word stage, where it can be used to identify differences in styles of language, differences that may be the result of a language delay and/or disorder, and differences in how the adult interacts with child.

Coggins and Carpenter (1981) proposed a variation of Dore's (1974) system. Their Communicative Intention Inventory is based on the writings of Bates (1976), Greenfield and Smith (1976), and Halliday (1977). The instrument uses a criterion-referenced approach (i.e., determining how well a child has established a particular behavior) rather than a norm-referenced approach (i.e., comparing the behavior of one child with that of other children). Although Coggins and Carpenter published selected percentile ranks and a standard error of measurement for the frequency of each of eight categories of communicative intentions, the data were intended not as reference norms but as a means "to provide the user with a perspective regarding the frequency of a set of intentional behaviors in a group of normal 16-month-old children who communicate primarily vocally and gesturally and are beginning to convey their intentions verbally" (p. 249). The inventory includes these eight intentional categories: comment on action, comment on object, request for action, request for object, request for information, answering, acknowledging, and protesting. These eight categories were selected because they are likely communicative acts to occur in a clinical setting. Direct comparison

TABLE 4.4

Percentage of Total Utterances Accounted for by Primitive Speech Act Types for Two Children, Age 1 Year 3 Months

	Child M (% based on 81 utterances)	Child J (% based on 80 utterances)
Labeling	34.6	17.5
Repeating	39.5	28.7
Answering	14.8	10.0
Requesting (action and answer)	7.4	26.2
Calling	0	11.2
Greeting	1.2	6.2
Protesting	2.5	0
Practicing	0	0

Note. Recomputed from totals provided by Dore (1974).

with Coggins and Carpenter's frequency data is possible only if a 45-minute sample of the child and a familiar adult's interaction is videotaped in a clinical setting. Coggins and Carpenter noted that "deviations from these guidelines (i.e., conditions under which the sample is obtained) may lead to erroneous estimates of what intentions a child is capable of communicating" (p. 239).

While Coggins and Carpenter's (1981) Communicative Intention Inventory has special merit for analyzing timed language samples obtained in a clinical setting, it is not appropriate to use with the 100-utterance samples in *Guide*. Coggins and Carpenter's system does not analyze the communicative intent of each utterance, but rather the intentional behaviors displayed (e.g., if the child repeats the word *drink* three times while drinking a glass of juice and looking toward the mother, those three utterances are tallied as one verbal comment on action, not three). Readers are urged to study Coggins and Carpenter's Communicative Intention Inventory and to apply it when appropriate, but its use will not be demonstrated with the language transcripts in *Guide*.

Perhaps more revealing than a comparison of the frequency of occurrence of specific speech acts used by Bridget to Dore's (1974) two subjects is a comparison of Bridget's use of specific speech acts to her mother's use of specific conversational acts. **Answering** characterized 41% of Bridget's turns; this was her most frequently occurring conversational act. A quick look ahead reveals that the act of **request** characterized 61% of Bridget's mother's turns; this was her most frequently occurring conversational act. It appears that Bridget responded to more than half of her mother's requests and that these exchanges accounted for almost half of the interaction. Is this good? At the very least, it suggests that Bridget is participating in this conversation with her mother and is often responding when asked to respond.

Is Bridget's mother's use of **request** hindering Bridget's language development? We can't say for sure since Dore's (1978) **request** includes both yes/no and *wh-* questions. It would be important to follow this level of description of conversational act use with a detailed examination of the nature of **request** by Bridget's mother.

In her summary of the literature on parent–child interaction comparing parents of children developing typically to parents of children with a language disorder, Cross (1984) found substantial differences in the sentence types used. Parents of children with a language disorder were more likely to use *wh-* questions than were parents of typically developing children. Parents of children with a language disorder were less likely to use yes/no questions that typically recast (i.e., rephrase) their own children's utterances. These recasts have a positive correlation with children's elaboration of the auxiliary verb system.

We must again consider the age difference between Dore's (1974) subjects and Bridget. Whereas an analysis of the use of primitive speech acts by children at the one- and early two-word stage may be useful, Bridget is more than 1 year older than Dore's subjects. We may be able to clarify the interaction between Bridget and her mother more thoroughly by using Retherford's (1980) appropriateness judgments, discussed later in this chapter.

Analysis of Dore's primitive speech acts may reveal a pattern that points to the possibility of an ASD diagnosis. Young children who have a diagnosis of ASD have been found to communicate less frequently for the purpose of joint attention and more frequently for the purpose of behavioral regulation (Maljaars, Noens, Jansen, Scholte, & van Berkelaer-Onnes, 2011; Mundy, Sigman, & Kasari, 1990; Shumway & Wetherby, 2009; Stone, Ousley, Yoder, Hogan, & Hepburn, 1997; Wetherby, Cain, & Yonclas, 1988). A limited use of communication for the purpose of joint attention has been found to be one of the most sensitive discriminators of ASD in young children and can be used to distinguish young children with ASD from children with language delays or other developmental delays (Dawson, et al., 2004; Mundy et al., 1990; Wetherby et al., 2007).

Research studies that have documented this difference have used Bruner's communicative intentions (Bruner, 1981; Shumway & Wetherby, 2009). Although this taxonomy differs slightly from Dore's primitive speech acts, the reader of *Guide to Analysis of Language Transcripts* can use information gained from Dore's primitive speech acts to make judgments about the child's use of joint attention, social interaction, and behavioral regulation. Doing so requires familiarity with Bruner's major communicative functions: behavioral regulation, social interaction, and joint attention. According to Bruner (1981) and Wetherby and Prizant (2002):

> *Behavioral regulation* acts are used to regulate the behavior of another person. Behavioral regulation acts include gestures, communicative vocalizations, and words used to get another person to do something (request) or to stop doing something (protest).

Social interaction acts are used to call attention or maintain another person's attention to oneself. When children communicate for the purpose of social interaction, they are attempting to get another person to look at or notice him or her. These acts include requesting social routines, calling, greeting, showing off, and requesting permission.

Joint attention acts are used to direct another person's attention to an object, event, or topic. Joint attention acts are used to get another person to look at or notice something outside of oneself. Joint attention acts include commenting on an action, object, or topic, and requesting information.

By age 12 months, a range of functions should be exhibited in typically developing children; by 15 months, behavioral regulation, social interaction, and joint attention should be used consistently with a variety of means (Crais, Watson, Baranek, & Reznick., 2006; Wetherby et al., 1988). Of these three major categories, behavioral regulation and joint attention are used most frequently in typically developing children who are in the prelinguistic, one-word, and multiword phase of language development; requesting and commenting are the most frequent specific communication acts used within those broad categories (Wetherby et al., 1988). Research on young children who have received, or will receive, a diagnosis of ASD indicates that these children are much less likely to use communication for the purpose of joint attention and more likely to use communication for behavioral regulation. A young child whose communication profile reveals high levels of requesting combined with low levels of commenting may be at risk for a diagnosis of ASD (Bruinsma, Koegel, & Koegel, 2004; Maljaars, et al. 2011; Wetherby et al., 2007).

The results from an analysis of Dore's primitive speech acts can be used to provide insight into a child's use of communication for the purpose of joint attention as compared to his or her use of communication for the purpose of behavioral regulation. Specifically, Dore's categories of **labeling** and **requesting answer** are likely to fall mainly within the communicative function of joint attention, especially if the child is specifically addressing an adult while engaged in these acts. Dore's categories of **requesting action** and **protesting** are likely to be categorized into the communicative function of behavioral regulation. Dore's categories of **calling** and **greeting** would likely be categorized into the communicative function of **social interaction**. Dore's category of **answering** is not as easily categorized; depending on the question being answered, the communicative function may be different. A child who answers the question, "What do you want?" may be demonstrating behavioral regulation, while a child who answers the question, "What is that?" or who answers a specific question to continue a topic of conversation may be demonstrating joint attention. The utterances that fall into the category of **answering**, then, would need to be reanalyzed to determine which communicative function they served within the specific language sample being analyzed.

Bridget's communicative profile in Table 4.3 provides an example. Note that 19% of her utterances were coded as **labeling**, while 14% of her utterances were coded as **requesting answer**, both of which could be recategorized into joint attention. Combined, these two communicative acts compose 33% of her overall utterances. However, it is also important to look at her use of **answering**, which makes up a full 41% of her communicative profile. Whenever Bridget is answering a question to comment on an object, action, or topic, her **answering** utterances could be considered joint attention. For example, in utterance #36, Bridget answers the adult question "What happened?" by saying "I kick 'em." In this instance, Bridget's utterance serves to direct an adult's attention to the topic of conversation (the circus man) and could be considered joint attention. Returning to her transcript and further analyzing the utterances that had been coded as **answering**, 37 of these 41 utterances appear to fall within the communicative function of joint attention; this represents 37% of utterances in the language sample. When combined with the 33% of communicative acts that are coded **labeling** and **requesting answer**, this increases the percentage of her use of the communicative function of joint attention to 70%.

Bridget also uses **requesting action** 20% of the time and **protesting** 1% of the time. When these percentages are combined with the 4% of **answering** utterances that likely fall into the category of behavioral regulation, Bridget appears to use the communicative function of behavioral regulation 25% of the time in her language sample. Finally, her **calling** (1%) and **greeting** (2%) utterances could be combined to suggest that she uses the communicative function of social interaction a total of 3% of the time.

This analysis of Bridget's sample indicates that she is, indeed, using all three major communicative functions: joint attention, social interaction, and behavioral regulation. Further, she is using joint attention at a much higher rate (70% of her utterances) than she uses behavioral regulation (25%); this profile fits with the typical development of pragmatics at a young age.

If a child's communication profile revealed a lack of diversity in use of the major communicative functions or a significantly low percentage use of communicative acts for joint attention (e.g., labeling, answering, requesting answer), this might indicate ASD. It should be noted, however, that the guidelines for the communication samples in the research that examined communicative acts in young children with ASD differed from language sampling guidelines in *Guide to Analysis of Language Transcripts* in three important ways. First, communication samples gathered during research on the communicative acts of children with ASD generally contained nonverbal gestures, intentional vocalizations, and verbalizations; language samples gathered using *Guide* typically only include verbalizations. Second, many of the research studies that examined the communicative acts of children with ASD included both unstructured language samples and structured communication temptation situations, while language samples gathered using *Guide* are typically unstructured. Third, as part of the definition of **labeling**, Dore (1974) includes that the child does not address the adult or wait for a response. This wording makes it unclear whether a child's use of a label, according to Dore, would be truly considered an attempt to initiate joint attention.

Due to those differences, caution should be exercised when interpreting utterances based on Dore's primitive acts, particularly when used to identify potential ASD. Should a speech–language pathologist determine that a concern regarding ASD exists, he or she may want to gather and analyze a language sample in a way that is more consistent with the methodology used in research studies investigating the nonverbal and verbal communicative acts of young children. It may be helpful to review Shumway and Wetherby's (2009) research on communicative acts of children with ASD in the second year of life and Wetherby and Prizant's (1998) article on the profiles of children's communicative competence. Assessment tools that are specifically designed to assess both nonverbal and verbal communicative acts of young children might also be used. One such example is the *Communication and Symbolic Behavior Scales* (Wetherby & Prizant, 2002).

Dore's Conversational Acts

Another of Dore's analysis procedures (1978) may be more appropriate for the developmental level of the child (Bridget) in the sample transcript. This analysis procedure, like the preceding, examines the communicative functions of utterances based on the form of those utterances and their use in conversation. The procedure is based on what Dore defines as a conversational act. A *conversational* act consists of a proposition, a grammatical structure, and the illocutionary force. The *proposition* refers to the conceptual information in the utterances; that is, what the utterance means. The *illocutionary force* refers to how the speaker intends his utterance to be taken. Dore (1978) contended that the *grammatical structure* of the utterance alters the illocutionary force of the proposition. Therefore, all three components must be assumed to work together in communication.

Table 4.5 is a combination of definitions of conversational acts and conversational moves. The first section of the table lists and defines Dore's (1978) conversational acts. Within each act's definition are subcategories to help identify utterances that are examples of the act. Because the breakdown of subcategories within each conversational act is primarily the result of variations in form, semantic content, and/or minor shades of intention, only the major category distinctions are used in this analysis.

Categorizing a few utterances for practice should be helpful before turning back to the sample transcript. Some of the same utterances used for practicing Dore's (1974) primitive speech acts are provided in Example 4.2, and then a few more examples are considered. Dore's (1978) conversational acts should be used for both adult and child utterances in transcripts with child utterances that are longer than one word. Adult examples have been interspersed for practice. As previously, cover the right side of the page, categorize each utterance, and then check your results with those in the shaded section. You will find additional practice opportunities in the *Guide Practice* web-based exercises. Exercises 1–4 use Dore's primitive speech acts for the child. Exercises 5–8 use Dore's conversational acts for both the child and the adult.

TABLE 4.5

CONVERSATIONAL ACTS & CONVERSATIONAL MOVES

Conversational Acts[a]

REQUEST:	Utterance used to request information, action, or acknowledgment—including yes/no questions that seek true/false judgments; *wh-* questions that seek factual information; clarification questions about the content of a prior utterance; action requests in the form of questions or directives that seek action from the listener; permission requests; and rhetorical questions that seek acknowledgment from the listener permitting the speaker to continue.
RESPONSE TO REQUEST:	Utterance following a request that responds directly to the request—including yes/no answers that supply true/false judgments; *wh-* answers that supply solicited factual information; clarifications that supply relevant repetition; compliances that verbally express acceptance, denial, or acknowledgment of a prior action or permission request; qualifications that supply unexpected information in response to the soliciting question; and repetitions of part of prior utterances.
DESCRIPTION:	Utterance used to describe verifiable past and present facts—including identifications that label objects, events, etc.; descriptions of events, actions, propositions, etc.; descriptions of properties, traits, or conditions; expression of locations or directions; and reports of times.
STATEMENT:	Utterance used to state facts, rules, attitudes, feelings, or beliefs—including expressions of rules, procedures, definitions, etc.; evaluations that express attitudes, judgments, etc.; internal reports of emotions, sensations, and mental events, such as intents to perform future actions; attributions that report beliefs about others' internal states; and explanations that express reasons, causes, and predictions.
ACKNOWLEDGMENT:	Utterance used to indicate recognition of a response or nonrequest utterance—including acceptances that neutrally recognize answers and nonrequests; approvals/agreements that positively recognize answers or nonrequests; disapprovals/disagreements that negatively evaluate answers or nonrequests; and returns that acknowledge rhetorical questions and some nonrequests.
ORGANIZATIONAL DEVICE:	Utterance used to regulate interaction and conversation—including boundary markers that indicate openings, closings, and other significant points in the conversation; calls that solicit attention; speaker selections that explicitly indicate the speaker of the next turn; politeness markers that indicate politeness; and accompaniments that maintain verbal contact.
PERFORMATIVE:	Utterance that is accomplished by being said—including protests that register complaints about the listener's behavior; jokes that display nonbelief toward a proposition for humorous effect; claims that establish rights; warnings that alert the listener of impending harm; and teases that taunt or playfully provoke the listener.
MISCELLANEOUS:	Utterance that is uninterpretable because it is unintelligible, incomplete, or anomalous or because it contains no propositional content, such as an exclamation.

Conversational Moves[b]
(With Letter Identification for Coding)

INITIATING MOVES

New Topic Introduction (N):	A new topic is introduced into the conversation.
Restarting Old Topic (R):	A previous topic is reintroduced into the conversation.
Eliciting Verbal Response (E):	The speaker invites the other participant to respond verbally, including questions.
Intruding (I):	The speaker intrudes into the conversation in an inappropriate manner or at an inappropriate time; topic may be irrelevant or a turn out of place.

RESPONDING MOVES

Acknowledging (A):	The previous speaker's utterance is acknowledged through brief remarks.
Yes/No Responses (Y):	Simple affirmation or negation of previous speaker's turn.
One-Word Answers (O):	Brief responses contingent on previous speaker's utterance; "sit" and "sit down" would both be coded O in response to "What do you want him to do?"
Repeating (R):	The previous utterance is repeated partially or wholly, with or without additional information.
Sustaining Topic (S):	The topic is maintained by reformulating content without adding new information.
Extending Topic (E):	The topic is maintained but new information is added.
False Starts	An utterance is begun but is not completed; thus there is neither an **initiating move** nor a **responding move**. If utterances have been numbered according to the rules described in Chapter 1, no FALSE STARTS would appear numbered in a transcript.

[a]Adapted from Dore, J. (1978). Variation in Preschool Children's Conversational Performances. In K. Nelson (Ed.), *Children's Language: Vol. 1* (pp. 397–444). New York, NY: Gardner Press. [b]Adapted from Martlew, M. (1980). Mothers' Control Strategies in Dyadic Mother/Child Conversations. *Journal of Psycholinguistic Research, 9*(4), 327–346.

In many cases, conversational acts coding is easier for utterances longer than two or three words in length because there is more language on which to base the category judgments. It also should be apparent that the major developmental change in use of conversational acts occurs when the child is able to produce **statements**, which reflect the child's greater awareness of rules, internal states, attitudes, and feelings.

Now, code the sample transcript of Bridget using Dore's Conversational Acts Analysis form (found in Appendix D, online). Progress through the transcript and determine the appropriate conversational act that characterizes each utterance. Record the utterance number next to the conversational act on the analysis sheet and calculate as you did for Dore's Primitive Speech Acts analysis. Do this for both conversational co-participants. When finished, check your results with Form 4.2.

Because we used 100 of Bridget's utterances in our analysis, the following frequency counts can be considered percentages as well. Analysis of the conversational acts used by Bridget reveals use of 31 **requests**,

EXAMPLE 4.2

CONVERSATIONAL ACTS	
(C picks up toy horse) horsie/	**DESCRIPTION** The child labels an object, the horse. Most utterances previously identified as **labeling** will now be **description**.
(C hears door opening) Dada/	**DESCRIPTION OR ORGANIZATIONAL DEVICE** The problem previously encountered when differentiating primitive speech acts exists here as well. Without additional contextual information, it is impossible to differentiate these two categories.
(C reaches for cup on table) cup/	**REQUEST** The child is requesting his cup. Dore (1978) does not differentiate types of requests for conversational acts analysis.
(M hands cup to child) Here's your cup/	**DESCRIPTION** The adult extends the child's topic by interpreting his request.
(C reaches up to M, who has entered bedroom) up/	**REQUEST** The child appears to be requesting to be picked up. Again, it is not necessary to differentiate types of requesting.
(dog barking in background) Dee Dee/	**DESCRIPTION OR ORGANIZATIONAL DEVICE** If the child is labeling the dog, then it is coded **description**. If the child is calling the dog, then it is coded **organizational device**. Analysis of additional context would determine which way to code it.
(C takes a drink from cup) juice/	**DESCRIPTION** This utterance identifies the substance as juice.
(M says, "Where is that shoe?"; C points to chest of drawers and says) there/	**RESPONSE TO REQUEST** Because the mother has asked a question, the child's utterance is considered to be a response to that question, rather than a **description** of the object's location.
(C points to self in mirror) Baby/	**DESCRIPTION** Again, the child is labeling himself; therefore this utterance is considered to be a **description**.
(C hands empty cup to M) drink/	**REQUEST** The child is requesting that his mother fill his empty cup.
(M attempts to wipe C's face) no/	**PERFORMATIVE** This type of conversational act refers to those utterances that are accomplished simply by being said. Perhaps one of the simplest forms of **performative** is the protest, which this utterance is an example of.
(C is holding box; M says, "What's in there?") /kiki/ [cookie]	**RESPONSE TO REQUEST** The child is responding directly to the mother's request.
(C pulls block from bag) /bɑ/ [block]	**DESCRIPTION** The child is labeling the block he has pulled from the bag.
(C holds up toy sheep and looks at M) /moot/	**REQUEST** The child is asking his mother to confirm his label for the toy animal.

EXAMPLE 4.2 (*continued*)

(C reaches arms up to M, who is standing by door) /ʌ/ [up]	**REQUEST** The child is asking his mother to pick him up. All types of requests, including requests for labels and for action, are labeled **request**.
(M places C in bed and turns to leave, saying, "Sleep tight, Megan") /naɪ naɪ/ [night-night]	**ORGANIZATIONAL DEVICE** Types of greetings—including closings—are labeled in this manner, primarily because of the way in which they regulate conversation.
(C is playing in crib after nap and bats at mobile hanging above bed) /bwɪ/ [XXX]	**MISCELLANEOUS** This category is used for a variety of types of utterances. In this case, it is used to indicate that the propositional content of the utterance is unclear.
(C is playing in crib after nap; M walks by the bedroom door) /mɑ/ [mom]	**ORGANIZATIONAL DEVICE** The child is soliciting his mother's attention.
(M stands up and says, "Let's have some cookies") /kiki/ [cookie]	**RESPONSE TO REQUEST** The child's utterance indicates acceptance of the request and readiness for cookies.
(M asks C, "Do you want some cookies?") ya/	**RESPONSE TO REQUEST** Again, the child is responding directly to the request regarding his desire for cookies.
(C picks up toy sheep that's in corral with cows) that's not a cow/	**DESCRIPTION** This utterance describes a verifiable fact regarding the sheep.
(M looks at toy sheep) cows don't have wool/	**STATEMENT** This utterance states a fact about cows.
(C picks up two cylinder-shaped blocks) these are the ones what we need/	**STATEMENT** This utterance expresses a need statement that reports on an internal state. Because it is not verifiable, it is not a **description**.
(C and M are playing with playground set; M puts boy doll on top of pavilion; C says) you're a silly mommy/	**PERFORMATIVE** The child is teasing his mother for her silly behavior. The utterance accomplishes the tease simply by being said.
(M responds) I am?	**REQUEST** This utterance rhetorically requests clarification of the child's utterance.
(C and M are playing with playground set; C takes doll off swing and says) he's not feeling very good/	**STATEMENT** This utterance reports the child's belief about the internal state of the doll. Thus, it is an example of a **statement** and not a **description**.
(C pulls toy sandbox out of box and holds it up) wow!/	**MISCELLANEOUS** This utterance is an exclamation, which Dore considers to have no propositional content.
(M picks up table) I'm going to put the table in the shelter/	**STATEMENT** The mother states her intention to put a table in the shelter.
(C looks at table) okay/	**ACKNOWLEDGMENT** The child's utterance is indicating acceptance of the mother's utterance.
(M and C are playing with playground set; one of the dolls falls off swing; C picks it up and says) this one fell off 'cuz he weren't hanging on/	**STATEMENT** This utterance states the facts of the situation (the doll fell off the swing) but goes on to explain the reason for it ('cuz he weren't hanging on). Because of the inclusion of an explanation, this utterance is an example of a **statement** instead of a **description**.

Guide to Analysis of Language Transcripts

FORM 4.2   Name of Child __Bridget__

DORE'S CONVERSATIONAL ACTS ANALYSIS

Total	%	Adult Utterance Number	Act	Child Utterance Number	Total	%
122	61	1, 2, 3, 4, 6, 8, 10, 11, 14, 15, 16, 17, 19, 20, 24, 26, 27, 28, 29, 30, 32, 33, 34, 36, 37, 38, 39, 41, 42, 44, 47, 50, 52, 53, 54, 55, 56, 58, 59, 60, 62, 63, 65, 68, 70, 71, 72, 73, 75, 76, 77, 78, 79, 80, 81, 82, 84, 85, 87, 89, 90, 91, 92, 93, 94, 96, 98, 99, 100, 105, 106, 107, 108, 110, 112, 115, 117, 119, 120, 121, 123, 126, 127, 128, 129, 130, 132, 135, 140, 141, 142, 143, 144, 145, 146, 147, 148, 149, 150, 152, 153, 158, 161, 162, 164, 167, 176, 177, 178, 179, 180, 181, 182, 183, 184, 186, 188, 189, 192, 196, 197, 198	Request	6, 7, 11, 15, 16, 19, 22, 23, 24, 26, 28, 29, 31, 35, 38, 52, 53, 59, 66, 68, 70, 72, 73, 74, 87, 88, 89, 90, 91, 96, 100	31	31
5	2.5	5, 23, 31, 133, 172 *(The information before s/c is ignored.)*	Response to Request	2, 3, 4, 5, 9, 12, 21, 25, 30, 33, 34, 36, 37, 42, 43, 44, 45, 47, 48, 49, 51, 55, 56, 57, 58, 64, 69, 75, 76, 77, 78, 79, 80, 81, 92, 93, 95, 97	38	38
22	11	13, 21, 22, 25, 43, 46, 48, 51, 86, 88, 102, 109, 111, 113, 124, 151, 155, 157, 165, 166, 193, 194	Description	8, 13, 14, 17, 20, 27, 32, 40, 41, 46, 50, 60, 61, 65, 83, 84, 86, 94	18	18
18	9	35, 57, 66, 95, 97, 103, 118, 131, 136, 137, 138, 139, 160, 169, 187, 190, 199, 200	Statement	18, 39, 62, 99	4	4
11	5.5	7, 9, 12, 40, 49, 61, 67, 69, 83, 104, 154 *(M appears to be acknowledging B's choice of object.)*	Acknowledgment	82, 85	2	2
8	4	114, 116, 122, 134, 159, 163, 185, 195	Organizational Device	10, 54, 63, 71, 98	5	5
3	1.5	74, 125, 191	Performative	1	1	1
11	5.5	18, 45, 64, 101, 156, 168, 170, 171, 173, 174, 175	Miscellaneous	67	1	1

38 **responses to requests**, 18 **descriptions**, four **statements**, two **acknowledgments**, five **organizational devices**, one **performative**, and one **miscellaneous**.

Bridget's mother used 122 **requests**, or 61% of her utterances; five **responses to requests**, or 2.5% of her utterances; 22 **descriptions**, or 11% of her utterances; 18 **statements**, or 9% of her utterances; 11 **acknowledgments**, or 5.5% of her utterances; eight **organizational devices**, or 4% of her utterances; three **performatives**, or 1.5% of her utterances, and 11 **miscellaneous**, or 5.5% of her utterances.

Although Dore does not provide frequency-of-occurrence data for use of conversational acts, he does provide guidelines to aid in interpretation. However, before interpreting the analysis of Bridget's transcript, take a look at another transcript obtained from an older child (Sara), which is provided for comparison. Using Sara's transcript from Appendix E and another blank Dore's Conversational Acts Analysis form, categorize each mother and child utterance. This child's utterances are longer and may be easier to code than the utterances in Bridget's transcript, and the results obtained should be very different. Compare your results with Form 4.3.

Results of this analysis reveal several differences: Seven of Sara's utterances were **requests**, 67 were **responses to requests**, 12 were **descriptions**, 11 were **statements**, none were **acknowledgments** or **organizational devices**; two were **performatives**, and one was **miscellaneous**. The most obvious difference between the girls in these two transcripts is in their use of **responses to requests** and **requests**: 67% of Sara's utterances were **responses to requests**, whereas only 38% of Bridget's utterances were **responses to requests**. **Requests** characterized only 7% of Sara's utterances but 31% of Bridget's.

There are differences between the girls' mothers as well. Sara's mother produced 91 **requests**, or 79.8% of her 114 utterances; four **responses to requests** (3.5%), no **descriptions** (0%), eight **statements** (7%), 9 **acknowledgments** (7.9%); one **organizational device** (.9%), no **performatives** (0%), and one **miscellaneous** (.9%). Thus, **requests** accounted for 61% of the utterances used by Bridget's mother and 79.8% of the utterances used by Sara's mother.

Dore (1978) and others (Bloom, Rocissano, & Hood, 1976; Brinton & Fujiki, 1984; Ervin-Tripp & Mitchell-Kernan, 1977; Garvey, 1975) have reported that the ability to appropriately initiate conversation increases as the child's developmental level increases. Using requests is one way of initiating conversation. Sara is older than Bridget, yet Bridget uses more than 4 times as many **requests**. So does this mean that Sara is pragmatically delayed? Not necessarily. There are other ways of initiating conversation besides asking questions. Dore contends that **descriptions**, **statements**, and **performatives** also may function to initiate conversation and some researchers identify other conversation initiators. But if the totals for each of these categories are added to each child's total number of **requests**, the difference between the two children is even greater. A total of 54 of Bridget's utterances were conversational acts that could function to initiate conversation, but only 32 of Sara's utterances could function in that capacity. Still, this does not prove that Sara is pragmatically delayed. In fact, it may indicate a greater attention to the cohesiveness of ongoing conversation. Bloom et al. (1976) reported a decrease in spontaneous, noncontingent speech in children 21–36 months of age and an increase in topically cohesive speech. With this in mind, should both Bridget and Sara be considered developmentally typical in their patterns of initiating and responding? Before any conclusion can be drawn, two other points must be considered.

First, Sara's tendency to respond is the result of a mother who asks a considerable number of questions. Of the 114 utterances that Sara's mother produced, 79.8% were **requests**, compared to only 61% of the 200 utterances of Bridget's mother. In fact, if Sara had responded to all of her mother's questions, her total number of responses would be even greater. To conclude that Sara is pragmatically delayed because the majority of her utterances were **responses to requests** would be inappropriate, since her mother appears to be responsible for this high number of responses. It would be important to obtain another language sample, as suggested in Chapter 1, with Sara interacting with another familiar individual. Only then could it be determined if she is able to maintain a topic without questions to direct her.

The second point to consider before drawing a conclusion regarding the pragmatic abilities of these children is the setting in which the samples were obtained. While both were free-play situations, Sara's mother apparently felt a greater need to direct the interaction. As mentioned earlier in this chapter, Cross (1984) identi-

FORM 4.3 Name of Child: Sara

DORE'S CONVERSATIONAL ACTS ANALYSIS

Total	%	Adult Utterance Number	Act	Child Utterance Number	Total	%
91	79.8	1, 2, 3, 4, 5, 6, 7, 8, 9, 10, 11, 12, 13, 14, 15, 16, 17, 18, 19, 21, 22, 24, 25, 26, 29, 30, 31, 33, 36, 37, 38, 39, 42, 43, 44, 45, 47, 50, 51, 52, 53, 55, 56, 58, 59, 60, 61, 62, 63, 65, 66, 67, 68, 69, 70, 71, 73, 74, 75, 76, 77, 78, 79, 80, 81, 82, 83, 86, 87, 88, 89, 90, 91, 92, 93, 94, 96, 98, 99, 100, 102, 104, 105, 107, 108, 109, 110, 111, 112, 113, 114	Request	30, 37, 39, 47, 58, 62, 98	7	7
4	3.5	48, 49, 57, 72	Response to Request	1, 2, 3, 4, 5, 7, 8, 9, 11, 12, 13, 16, 18, 19, 20, 21, 24, 25, 28, 29, 31, 33, 34, 35, 38, 40, 41, 42, 43, 45, 46, 48, 49, 51, 52, 54, 55, 56, 57, 59, 60, 61, 63, 64, 65, 66, 69, 70, 71, 72, 75, 77, 78, 79, 81, 82, 84, 85, 87, 88, 89, 93, 94, 95, 96, 99, 100	67	67
0	0		Description	6, 15, 17, 23, 44, 53, 73, 74, 76, 80, 91, 97	12	12
8	7	20, 23, 35, 41, 64, 85, 101, 106	Statement	10, 22, 26, 32, 36, 50, 67, 83, 86, 90, 92	11	11
9	7.9	27, 28, 34, 40, 54, 84, 95, 97, 103	Acknowledgment		0	0
1	.9	46	Organizational Device		0	0
0	0		Performative	14, 68	2	2
1	.9	32	Miscellaneous	27	1	1

fied differences in the interaction patterns of parents and their children with language disorders compared to parents of children without language disorders. Of the differences noted, most relevant here are the increased use of *wh-* questions and the decreased use of declarative forms for the functions of commenting and stating. Sara's mother produced **requests** 79.8% of the time, produced **statements** 7% of the time, and produced no **descriptions**. Compare these percentages to those of Bridget's mother, who produced **requests** 61% of the time, **descriptions** 11% of the time, and **statements** 9% of the time. Whether the differences noted by Cross as well as those noted here implicate parents causally in a child's language disorder has not been documented. But the interaction style of Bridget conversing with her mother is very different from the interaction style of Sara conversing with her mother. Again, to determine whether Sara does not initiate conversation more frequently than the present sample indicates, it would be important to obtain another sample in a different setting (in addition to the sample obtained with another familiar individual, mentioned earlier).

Overall, Dore's (1974) primitive speech acts analysis and Dore's (1978) conversational acts analysis provide information that, when taken together with data obtained from semantic and syntactic analyses, can be used to describe a child's language production. Identification of a pragmatic delay or potential disorder cannot be made using conversational acts analysis and one language sample. With primitive speech acts analysis, only one sample was necessary to draw conclusions. With Dore's conversational acts analysis, however, it is necessary to obtain at least two additional samples of a particular child's language production abilities: one in a different setting and another with at least one other participant.

Martlew's Conversational Moves

The next analysis procedure that we demonstrate is based on a set of discourse categories described by Martlew (1980). Her conversational moves categories were used to code the utterances of children developing typically and those of their mothers at two points in time: when the children were approximately 3 years of age, and 1 year later when the children were approximately 4 years of age. Because Sara's age more closely matches the ages of Martlew's subjects, Sara's transcript is analyzed.

Martlew's categories differentiate types of **initiating moves** and types of **responding moves**. While the subcategories of Martlew's conversational moves are not dissimilar to Dore's (1978) conversational acts, the focus in examining **initiating moves** versus **responding moves** is to document discourse abilities. The unit of analysis continues to be the utterance, but because the role utterances play in initiating and responding to topics is examined, the results are closer to an account of the discourse relations of the conversation. This is particularly true when we examine both speakers participating in the conversation. Table 4.5 lists and describes the categories of conversational moves that Martlew posits. The names for many of the categories have been changed in *Guide* to aid in recall for coding.

Because the coding of an utterance is based primarily on the immediately preceding utterance of the conversational co-participant, but also at times on utterances several speaking turns prior to the utterance under consideration, it is impossible to present single-utterance examples for practice. The descriptions of Martlew's (1980) conversational moves in Table 4.5 should be sufficiently clear for successful coding of utterances from the sample transcript, without the benefit of practice examples. In addition, final analysis of results is based on the broad categories of **initiating moves** and **responding moves**; consequently, minimal variation in use of subcategories can be allowed. The online exercises do provide practice in analysis of conversational moves and appropriateness judgments analysis.

Use Sara's transcript (from Appendix E) and a blank Conversational Moves and Appropriateness Judgments Analysis form in (found in Appendix D, online) to code the conversational moves of Sara and her mother according to the modified Martlew (1980) categories. The first two columns on each half of the form are to be used to record the letter code given in the second half of Table 4.5 for the types of **initiating moves** and **responding moves**. For example, if Sara produced an utterance considered a new topic introduction, record an "N" under the Initiating Moves column on the Child portion of the form, next to the appropriate utterance number. Progress through the transcript and code each utterance, considering its role in relation to preceding utterances. When finished, check your results with Form 4.4. Then, count and record the resulting information

FORM 4.4

Name of Child: Sara

CONVERSATIONAL MOVES AND APPROPRIATENESS JUDGMENTS ANALYSIS

	ADULT						CHILD				
	Conversational Moves		Appropriateness Judgments				Conversational Moves		Appropriateness Judgments		
UTT#	Initiating Moves	Responding Moves	Referent Specificity	Contributional Conciseness	Communication Style	UTT#	Initiating Moves	Responding Moves	Referent Specificity	Contributional Conciseness	Communication Style
1	N					1		O			
2	E					2		E			
3	E					3		R			
4	E					4		E			
5	E					5		E			
6	E					6		E			
7	E					7		E			
8	E					8		O			
9	E					9		E			
10	E					10		R			
11	E					11		E			
12	E					12		O			
13	E					13		O			
14	E					14		E			
15		E				15	N				
16	E					16		E			
17	E					17		E			
18	E					18		O			
19	E					19		E			
20		E				20		E			
21	E					21		E			
22	E					22		E			
23		E				23		E			
24	E					24		E			
25	E					25		R			

FORM 4.4

CONVERSATIONAL MOVES AND APPROPRIATENESS JUDGMENTS ANALYSIS (continued)

	ADULT						CHILD				
	Conversational Moves		Appropriateness Judgments				Conversational Moves		Appropriateness Judgments		
UTT#	Initiating Moves	Responding Moves	Referent Specificity	Contributional Conciseness	Communication Style	UTT#	Initiating Moves	Responding Moves	Referent Specificity	Contributional Conciseness	Communication Style
26	E					26		E			
27		R				27		R			
28		A				28		O			
29	E					29		E			
30	E					30	E				
31	E					31		O			
32		E				32		E			
33	E					33		O			
34		A				34		E			
35		E				35		O			
36	E					36	N				
37	E					37	N				
38	E					38		Y			
39	E					39	E				
40		A				40		O			
41		A				41		O			
42	E					42		Y			
43	E					43		O			
44	E					44		E			
45	E					45		O			
46	E					46		E			
47	E					47	E				
48		E				48		O			
49		Y				49		O			
50	E					50		E			

FORM 4.4

CONVERSATIONAL MOVES AND APPROPRIATENESS JUDGMENTS ANALYSIS (*continued*)

	ADULT						CHILD				
	Conversational Moves		Appropriateness Judgments				Conversational Moves		Appropriateness Judgments		
UTT#	Initiating Moves	Responding Moves	Referent Specificity	Contributional Conciseness	Communication Style	UTT#	Initiating Moves	Responding Moves	Referent Specificity	Contributional Conciseness	Communication Style
51	E					51		O			
52	E					52		E			
53	E					53	N				
54		A				54		E			
55	E					55		E			
56	E					56		S			
57		E				57		E			
58	E					58		E			
59	E					59		O			
60	E					60		E			
61	E					61		Y			
62	E					62	E				
63	E					63		E			
64		E				64		S			
65	E					65		Y			
66	E					66		E			
67		S				67		E			
68	E					68		E			
69	E					69		E			
70	E					70		E			
71	E					71		O			
72		E				72		E			
73	E					73		E			
74	E					74		R			
75	E					75		E			

FORM 4.4

CONVERSATIONAL MOVES AND APPROPRIATENESS JUDGMENTS ANALYSIS (*continued*)

	ADULT						CHILD				
	Conversational Moves		Appropriateness Judgments				Conversational Moves		Appropriateness Judgments		
UTT#	Initiating Moves	Responding Moves	Referent Specificity	Contributional Conciseness	Communication Style	UTT#	Initiating Moves	Responding Moves	Referent Specificity	Contributional Conciseness	Communication Style
76	E					76		E			
77	E					77		E			
78	E					78		O			
79	E					79		E			
80	E					80	R				
81	E					81		E			
82	E					82		S			
83	E					83	N				
84		R				84		Y			
85		E				85		O			
86	E					86		E			
87	E					87		O			
88	E					88		Y			
89	E					89		E			
90	E					90		E			
91	E					91		E			
92	E					92		E			
93	E					93		E			
94	E					94		O			
95		A				95		O			
96	E					96		O			
97		A				97		E			
98	E					98	E				
99	E					99		E			
100		E				100		O			

(*continues*)

FORM 4.4

CONVERSATIONAL MOVES AND APPROPRIATENESS JUDGMENTS ANALYSIS (continued)

	ADULT						CHILD				
	Conversational Moves		Appropriateness Judgments				Conversational Moves		Appropriateness Judgments		
UTT#	Initiating Moves	Responding Moves	Referent Specificity	Contributional Conciseness	Communication Style	UTT#	Initiating Moves	Responding Moves	Referent Specificity	Contributional Conciseness	Communication Style
101		S									
102	E										
103		A									
104	E										
105	E										
106	N										
107	E										
108	E										
109	E										
110	E										
111	E										
112	E										
113	E										
114	E										

on the Conversational Moves and Appropriateness Judgments Summary form. (Check results with Form 4.4. You will find a blank form in Appendix D.)

Review of the summary form for Sara's transcript shows that 11 (11%) utterances were types of **initiating moves,** and 89 (89%) utterances were types of **responding moves.** Sara's mother produced utterances that were types of **initiating moves** 78.9% of the time and utterances that were types of **responding moves** 21.1% of the time. When these results are compared to those obtained by Martlew (1980), there are differences. Table 4.6 summarizes the frequency of use of individual conversational moves as percentages of total utterances for eight mothers and their children at approximately 3 years of age, and then again at approximately 4 years of age, while engaged in free-play conversation.

As can be seen in Table 4.6, 28.2% of the children's utterances at approximately 3 years of age were types of **initiating moves.** One year later, 25.5% of their utterances were types of **initiating moves.** At approximately 3 years of age, 66.7% of their utterances were types of **responding moves**; at approximately 4 years, 68.2% were types of **responding moves.** In fact, Martlew (1980) reported that for this group of mothers and children, **initiating moves** accounted for approximately 30% of utterances, and **responding moves** accounted for approximately 70% of utterances of the children and their mothers at both points in time. Changes that occurred were primarily in the use of individual categories. Overall distribution of utterances between **initiating** and **responding moves** remained relatively constant over time.

Sara used substantially fewer **initiating moves** and more **responding moves** than did Martlew's (1980) subjects. Should it be concluded that Sara is pragmatically delayed or disordered on the basis of this comparison? These concerns are similar to those that were raised as a result of Dore's (1978) conversational acts analysis. In that case, as now, it is important to consider the mother's role in these results. The distribution of **initiating moves** and **responding moves** for Sara's mother is even more dissimilar to Martlew's subjects than Sara's distribution was. In fact, Sara's mother produced utterances that reflected a reversal of the 30%/70% distribution that Martlew found: 78.9% of Sara's mother's utterances were **initiating moves** and 21.1% were

TABLE 4.6

Percentage of Total Utterances Accounted for by Conversational Moves for Eight Children at Two Points in Time

	Time 1		Time 2	
Initiating Moves	Mothers	Children (% at 3 years 3 months)	Mothers	Children (% at 4 years 3 months)
New Topic Introduction	4.0	5.1	2.1	2.5
Restarting Old Topic	4.0	7.8	5.3	8.7
Eliciting Verbal Response	25.1	14.4	25.0	13.6
Intruding	0.7	0.9	0.8	0.7
TOTAL	33.8	28.2	33.2	25.5
Responding Moves*				
Acknowledging	8.6	2.8	9.0	3.9
Yes/No Responses	4.0	10.3	5.8	15.1
One-Word Answers	1.8	10.3	1.4	8.9
Repeating	6.5	3.8	5.7	4.0
Sustaining Topic	15.4	9.4	15.7	9.2
Extending Topic	10.7	5.0	13.4	6.1
TOTAL*	64.4[a]	66.7[b]	64.9[c]	68.2[d]
False Starts		4.8		6.4

Note. Adapted from Martlew, M. (1980). "Mothers' Control Strategies in Dyadic Mother/Child Conversations," *Journal of Psycholinguistic Research, 9*(4), pp. 327–346.

[a]This total includes 17.4% comments. [b]This total includes 25.1% comments. [c]This total includes 13.7% comments. [d]This total includes 21.0% comments.

*The totals for responding moves include a subcategory called "Comments," which Martlew does not define in her responding moves.

responding moves. Martlew reported that the mothers in her study tended to ensure the maintenance of the conversation and the interchange between speakers. Clearly, Sara's mother appeared to be attempting to maintain the ongoing conversation and to promote an exchange of speaker–listener roles. However, her strategy for doing this included greater use of **initiating moves** than did the mothers in Martlew's study.

So is this mother-and-child pair pragmatically delayed or potentially disordered? The same conclusion that was drawn following Dore's (1978) conversational acts analysis holds here as well. Before a conclusion can be reached a minimum of two additional samples are needed: one obtained from Sara and her mother while interacting under conditions other than free play, and one obtained from Sara while interacting with another familiar adult. If the distribution of **initiating moves** and **responding moves** in the additional samples is similar to the distribution obtained in the sample transcript, it would be appropriate to conclude that Sara has a limited repertoire of means available to her for initiating speaking turns. In other words, if changes in condition and/or conversational co-participant do not result in significant changes in the distribution of **initiating moves** and **responding moves**, the prudent conclusion would be that Sara's participation in conversation is restricted. This apparent pragmatic delay/disorder would warrant attention in intervention.

Perhaps a comparison of each conversational co-participant's use of the individual conversational moves making up the **initiating moves** and **responding moves** categories would be helpful. The percentages for use of individual **initiating moves** obtained for Sara were as follows: 5% (5 ÷ 100 total utterances) new topic introduction, 1% restarting old topic, 5% eliciting verbal response, and 0% intruding. The percentages for use of individual **responding moves** were 0% acknowledging, 6% yes/no responses, 25% one-word answers, 5% repeating, 3% sustaining topic, and 50% extending topic. There were no instances of false starts. The most striking differences between Sara's totals and totals for Martlew's (1980) subjects at either point in time are in the use of one-word answers and extending topic. Sara used 25% one-word answers, and Martlew's subjects used 10.3% at approximately 3 years and 8.9% at approximately 4 years. In addition, Sara used 50% extending topic utterances, while Martlew's subjects used 5.0% at approximately 3 years and 6.1% at approximately 4 years.

The percentages for use of **initiating moves** for Sara's mother were as follows: 1.8% new topic introduction and 77.2% eliciting verbal response. There were no instances of restarting old topic or intruding. The percentages for use of individual **responding moves** were 7.0% acknowledging, .9% yes/no responses, 1.8% repeating, 1.8% sustaining, and 9.6% extending topic. There were no instances of one-word answers. The most striking difference between Sara's mother and the mothers in Martlew's (1980) study is in the use of the **initiating moves** category of eliciting verbal response. While this was the most frequently occurring category of **initiating moves** for Martlew's mothers, their total use of 25.1% falls far short of the 77.2% that Sara's mother used.

So how is the disparity between our dyad and Martlew's (1980) dyads to be reconciled? Sara's mother, like the mothers in Martlew's study, facilitated the child's participation in the conversation. Her strategy for accomplishing this clearly differed from that of the mothers in Martlew's study. Nevertheless, can we conclude that her strategy for facilitating Sara's participation in conversation was, in fact, hindering Sara's pragmatic development or her overall language development? Clearly not. But these data support the contention that more transcripts must be obtained. Verification of the ability to control the conversation less, by using fewer **initiating moves**, and to respond to Sara more by using more **responding moves**, would be essential. It is crucial that definitive conclusions about child conversational abilities as well as adult conversational tendencies not be made on the basis of a single transcript.

Another point to consider is the ambiguity in Martlew's (1980) data. As noted in a footnote to Table 4.6, Martlew reports frequency-of-occurrence data for a conversational move that she does not define. This move, which she labels as "comments," occurred with the greatest frequency of either group of children for her **responding moves**. If the percentages obtained for comments and extending topic utterances are added together, the resulting total approaches the total extending topic utterances obtained for Sara. Clearly, the percentages of 30.1% and 27.1% are a long way from Sara's 50%, but these figures make more sense than the extending topic percentages of 5.0% and 6.1% shown in the table. The inclusion of another category that reflects responding to the conversational co-participant may explain the differences between Sara and the children in Martlew's study. However, it does not explain the differences between Sara's mother and the mothers in Martlew's study.

It is obvious that additional samples must be obtained, including one with Sara participating in a conversation with another adult and one in another setting. In addition, the use of frequency-of-occurrence data on individual conversational moves may not be a valid tool to identify differences in pragmatic abilities. Judgments are best made on overall use of the broader categories of **initiating moves** versus **responding moves**. The use of individual moves may support overall conclusions but should not be considered diagnostic in and of itself.

Another consideration for using Martlew's conversational moves includes the value of this assessment in relation to the assessment of and intervention with children with ASD. Children with a diagnosis of ASD have been found to have distinct and pervasive patterns when engaged in discourse. Further, a thorough assessment of discourse is a recommended part of the diagnostic process for children with a suspected ASD diagnosis (Hale & Tager-Flusberg, 2005). Analysis of discourse using Martlew's conversational moves may provide insight into the diagnostic process for children who are suspected of being on the autism spectrum.

The most obvious way in which children with ASD may different in their use of Martlew's conversational moves is in the category of **repeating**. Children with a diagnosis of autism frequently engage in atypical use of echolalia (Stiegler, 2015; Woods & Wetherby, 2003). Echolalia may be immediate or delayed; immediate echolalia is generally considered to be a repetition of the preceding utterance. A child who frequently uses immediate echolalia will have a higher percentage of **repeating**, which may also lead to a higher percentage of **responding moves**.

Even if children with a diagnosis of ASD do not use immediate echolalia on a frequent basis, they may still present with differences in their use of conversational moves. Specifically, children with a diagnosis of ASD use many fewer contingent utterances in conversation. This has been found to be true across settings and conversational partners (Hale & Tager-Flusberg 2005). Looking at Martlew's conversational moves, one might expect to see this very particular pattern appear in a number of different ways. First, a child with a diagnosis of ASD may have a higher frequency of **intrusions**, which are defined as utterances that contain a topic that is irrelevant or a turn that it out of place. Second, children with ASD may be more likely to frequently introduce new topics into the conversation, which may show up in higher percentage of **new topic introductions**. Taken together, an increase in these categories may lead to a greater percentage of **initiating moves**. Careful consideration of these categories may prove helpful for diagnostic assessment, establishment of baseline data, and progress monitoring for children with ASD.

Retherford's Appropriateness Judgments

This next set of analysis procedures was developed by Retherford in 1980 for use in the first edition of *Guide to Analysis of Language Transcripts* (1987) and encompasses appropriateness judgments relative to three conversational variables: (1) referent specificity, (2) contributional conciseness, and (3) communication style. Although little support for the reliability of appropriateness judgments exists in the literature, the three analysis procedures described in the following sections are useful for descriptive purposes. The selection of these three variables from a variety of options discussed in the literature is an attempt to capture those aspects of conversation that may be problematic for children with a language delay and/or disorder. A lack of appropriateness in regard to these variables is fairly easy to identify. In addition, it appears that problems in each of these areas can be treated. Clinical experience has shown that behaviors to increase the level of appropriateness in each of these areas can be taught. Each of Retherford's (1980) appropriateness judgments is considered individually as the sample transcript of Sara is analyzed.

Referent Specificity

In their discussion of discourse topic, Keenan and Schieffelin (1976) presented a dynamic model that included a sequence of steps for establishing a discourse topic in a conversation. This model is based on the assumption that speakers accomplish each step, and receive positive feedback from listeners that they have done so, before continuing the conversation. The four steps are that the speaker (1) elicits the listener's attention, (2) speaks clearly enough for the listener to hear the utterance, (3) identifies the referent in the topic, and (4) identifies the surrounding semantic relations of the referent in the topic. Keenan and Schieffelin posited that all four steps may be accomplished in a single utterance or in a separate utterance for each step. While all four steps are necessary to establish a discourse topic, each step could be applied to a successful single utterance.

It is the third step that we use in the first judgment of appropriateness. Keenan and Schieffelin (1976) reported that the process of identifying a topic's referent for the listener involves directing the listener to locate the referent in either "physical space" or "memory space." Young children initially rely on the listener's ability to locate the referent in physical space, and only later do they rely on the listener's ability to locate the referent in memory. In either case, young children presume the listener will do the locating with minimal assistance provided for the listener in the form of nonverbal behaviors, such as looking at, pointing to, and holding up the referent. Later, children begin to use verbal means to identify referents in physical space for their listeners, including the use of notice verbs (e.g., *look, see*), deictic particles (e.g., *these, this*), and interrogative forms (e.g., "What's this?").

Keenan and Schieffelin (1976) contended that children at the one-word stage can repair misunderstandings as a result of their attempts to specify referents located in physical space. Specifying the referent in memory space and/or repairing the situation when the listener fails to locate the referent in memory space is much more difficult for children. In fact, Keenan and Schieffelin reported that before age 3, children experience enormous difficulty in specifying nonsituated referents, or referents that are not present in the immediate situation, and they provide a variety of semantic, syntactic, and pragmatic reasons for this. Semantically, children do not use the previously mentioned notice verbs to assist the listener in locating the referent in memory space. Also, the notice verbs for locating referents in memory space (e.g., *remember, recall*) are not yet available to young children. Syntactically, children are not yet using tense markers consistently. Use of these and other syntactic structures (e.g., anaphoric pronouns, definite articles) would indicate to the listener that the referent is not present in the immediate context. Pragmatically, children continue to rely on nonverbal cues to locate referents for listeners, and this strategy is not useful for referents located in memory space.

This discussion should be helpful in identifying instances in which children fail to specify the referent of the topic for the listener. In adult–child conversation, the adult typically indicates to the child that the referent is not clear. The adult may do this explicitly (e.g., "I don't know what you're talking about") or indirectly, through the use of repairs (e.g., "What?" or "Huh?"). As in conversational moves analysis, identifying instances of a lack of specificity requires examination of a sequence of utterances. It would be very difficult to provide a series of examples for practice, so Example 4.3 should suffice.

In this exchange, it would be important to indicate on the Conversational Moves and Appropriateness Judgments Analysis form under the Referent Specificity column that a sequence of four child utterances lacked sufficient specificity. This would be indicated on the grid by putting a minus sign (–) in the Referent Specificity column in the rows corresponding to the utterance numbers. The fifth child utterance in this example would be marked with a check mark (✔) because the referent was specific enough to be identified.

Obviously, it is impossible to consider each utterance in isolation. The most effective method is to examine a sequence of utterances while looking for clues from the other speaker that an utterance has not been specific enough; then, backtrack and identify the child utterance that is the source of the problem. The child utterance that has caused the breakdown can then be marked with a minus sign, as would the utterances subsequent to the problem utterance. Once shared content is reestablished, checkmarks can be used again.

When the child repeats part or all of the preceding adult utterances, use N/A (Not Applicable). Judgments about specificity and conciseness are not applicable in that case. When there is not a follow-up adult utterance or action, use NK (Not Known).

Turn to Sara's transcript (Appendix E) and examine mother and child utterances for a lack of specificity. Keep in mind that an adult may choose to ignore child utterances that lack specificity; however, adults typically do attempt to repair the situation. Progress through the transcript, indicating on the Conversational Moves and Appropriateness Judgments Analysis form whether each utterance is sufficiently specific to allow the listener to identify the referent (✔) or whether an utterance lacks specificity (–). When the analysis is complete, compare your results with Form 4.5.

EXAMPLE 4.3

CODING FOR REFERENT SPECIFICITY

(M and C are reading books; C points to picture of cow and says)		
C:	baby cow/	
M:	That's not a baby cow/	Referent not identified
C:	no! a baby cow/	Repair attempted
M:	But that's not a baby calf/	Referent not identified
C:	calf/	Repair attempted
M:	Let's find a baby calf/	
C:	no! Grandma baby/	Repair attempted
M:	Grandma baby? Oh Grandma has a baby calf?	Referent identified
C:	yeah baby calf/	Referent confirmed

FORM 4.5   Name of Child: Sara

CONVERSATIONAL MOVES AND APPROPRIATENESS JUDGMENTS ANALYSIS

ADULT

UTT#	Initiating Moves	Responding Moves	Referent Specificity	Contributional Conciseness	Communication Style
1	N		✔		
2	E		✔		
3	E		✔		
4	E		✔		
5	E		✔		
6	E		✔		
7	E		✔		
8	E		✔		
9	E		✔		
10	E		✔		
11	E		✔		
12	E		✔		
13	E		✔		
14	E		✔		
15		E	✔		
16	E		✔		
17	E		✔		
18	E		✔		
19	E		✔		
20		E	✔		
21	E		✔		
22	E		✔		
23		E	✔		
24	E		✔		
25	E		✔		

CHILD

UTT#	Initiating Moves	Responding Moves	Referent Specificity	Contributional Conciseness	Communication Style
1		O	✔		
2		E	✔		
3		R	N/A		
4		E	✔		
5		E	✔		
6		E	✔		
7		E	✔		
8		O	✔		
9		E	✔		
10		R	N/A		
11		E	✔		
12		O	✔		
13		O	✔		
14		E	✔		
15	N		✔		
16		E	✔		
17		E	✔		
18		O	✔		
19		E	✔		
20		E	✔		
21		E	✔		
22		E	✔		
23		E	✔		
24		E	✔		
25		R	N/A		

FORM 4.5

CONVERSATIONAL MOVES AND APPROPRIATENESS JUDGMENTS ANALYSIS (continued)

ADULT

UTT#	Initiating Moves	Responding Moves	Referent Specificity	Contributional Conciseness	Communication Style
26	E		✔		
27		R	N/A		
28		A	✔		
29	E		✔		
30	E		✔		
31	E		✔		
32		E	✔		
33	E		✔		
34		A	✔		
35		E	✔		
36	E		✔		
37	E		✔		
38	E		✔		
39	E		✔		
40		A	✔		
41		A	✔		
42	E		✔		
43	E		✔		
44	E		✔		
45	E		✔		
46	E		✔		
47	E		✔		
48		E	✔		
49		Y	✔		
50	E		✔		

CHILD

UTT#	Initiating Moves	Responding Moves	Referent Specificity	Contributional Conciseness	Communication Style
26		E	✔		
27		R	N/A		
28		O	✔		
29		E	✔		
30	E		✔		
31		O	✔		
32		E	✔		
33		O	✔		
34		E	✔		
35		O	✔		
36	N		✔		
37	N		—		
38		Y	✔		
39	E		✔		
40		O	✔		
41		O	✔		
42		Y	✔		
43		O	✔		
44		E	✔		
45		O	✔		
46		E	✔		
47	E		✔		
48		O	✔		
49		O	✔		
50		E	✔		

(continues)

FORM 4.5

CONVERSATIONAL MOVES AND APPROPRIATENESS JUDGMENTS ANALYSIS (continued)

	ADULT						CHILD				
	Conversational Moves		Appropriateness Judgments				Conversational Moves		Appropriateness Judgments		
UTT#	Initiating Moves	Responding Moves	Referent Specificity	Contributional Conciseness	Communication Style	UTT#	Initiating Moves	Responding Moves	Referent Specificity	Contributional Conciseness	Communication Style
51	E		✓			51		O	✓		
52	E		✓			52		E	✓		
53	E		✓			53	N		—		
54		A	✓			54		E	✓		
55	E		✓			55		E	—		
56	E		✓			56		S	—		
57		E	✓			57		E	✓		
58	E		✓			58		E	✓		
59	E		✓			59		O	✓		
60	E		✓			60		E	✓		
61	E		✓			61		Y	✓		
62	E		✓			62	E		✓		
63	E		✓			63		E	—		
64		E	✓			64		S	—		
65	E		✓			65		Y	✓		
66	E		✓			66		E	—		
67		S	✓			67		E	✓		
68	E		✓			68		E	—		
69	E		✓			69		E	✓		
70	E		✓			70		E	✓		
71	E		✓			71		O	✓		
72		E	✓			72		E	✓		
73	E		✓			73		E	✓		
74	E		✓			74		R	N/A		
75	E		✓			75		E	✓		

FORM 4.5

CONVERSATIONAL MOVES AND APPROPRIATENESS JUDGMENTS ANALYSIS (continued)

	ADULT						CHILD				
	Conversational Moves		Appropriateness Judgments				Conversational Moves		Appropriateness Judgments		
UTT#	Initiating Moves	Responding Moves	Referent Specificity	Contributional Conciseness	Communication Style	UTT#	Initiating Moves	Responding Moves	Referent Specificity	Contributional Conciseness	Communication Style
76	E		✓			76		E	✓		
77	E		✓			77		E	✓		
78	E		✓			78		O	✓		
79	E		✓			79		E	✓		
80	E		✓			80	R		✓		
81	E		✓			81		E	—		
82	E		✓			82		S	✓		
83	E		✓			83	N		—		
84		R	N/A			84		Y	✓		
85		E	✓			85		O	✓		
86	E		✓			86		E	✓		
87	E		✓			87		O	—		
88	E		✓			88		Y	✓		
89	E		✓			89		E	✓		
90	E		✓			90		E	—		
91	E		✓			91		E	✓		
92	E		✓			92		E	✓		
93	E		✓			93		E	✓		
94	E		✓			94		O	✓		
95		A	✓			95		O	✓		
96	E		✓			96		O	✓		
97		A	✓			97		E	✓		
98	E		✓			98	E		✓		
99	E		✓			99		E	✓		
100		E	✓			100		O	NK		

FORM 4.5

CONVERSATIONAL MOVES AND APPROPRIATENESS JUDGMENTS ANALYSIS (continued)

	ADULT						CHILD				
	Conversational Moves		Appropriateness Judgments				Conversational Moves		Appropriateness Judgments		
UTT#	Initiating Moves	Responding Moves	Referent Specificity	Contributional Conciseness	Communication Style	UTT#	Initiating Moves	Responding Moves	Referent Specificity	Contributional Conciseness	Communication Style
101		S	✔								
102	E		✔								
103		A	✔								
104	E		✔								
105	E		✔								
106	N		✔								
107	E		✔								
108	E		✔								
109	E		✔								
110	E		✔								
111	E		✔								
112	E		✔								
113	E		✔								
114	E		NK								

As a result of the analysis of referent specificity, 12 utterance sequences should have been identified in which Sara was not specific enough in identifying the referent of her utterance so that her mother could locate it in either physical space or memory space. Five of the 12 instances are explained further to help you understand the type of exchange that would warrant such codings. The first exchange in which Sara's utterance lacks specificity begins at utterance #37, when Sara refers to some girl with no apparent contextual support and her mother is not quite sure to whom Sara is referring. Sara's mother's query clarifies the situation. Another exchange lacking specificity begins at utterance #63, when Sara refers to "cow people." It takes three repairs from her mother to establish the referent. Another exchange lacking specificity begins at utterance #66. In spite of three repairs on the part of the mother, it is not clear whether the referent is eventually identified. Another exchange lacking specificity begins at utterance #83, when Sara comments on the resemblance of a scoop to a bunny ear. Sara's mother is not quite sure what Sara means and seeks verification by examining the scoop herself. Once she does this, Sara's statement becomes clear. Another exchange lacking specificity begins at utterance #90, when Sara identifies a plate as a cover for the pot. Again, Sara's mother attempts to repair the lack of specificity, but Sara continues with her next utterance. No instances or utterance sequences lacking referent specificity were identified for Sara's mother.

What can be concluded from the analysis of referent specificity? Sara did not adequately specify her referent in every utterance to permit her mother to locate those referents without clarification. However, we should not necessarily expect a child of Sara's age and/or language level be expected to be specific enough in every exchange to ensure listener comprehension. Recall that Keenan and Schieffelin (1976) reported that children 3 years of age have considerable difficulty specifying referents that are not present. But before it can be concluded that Sara's lack of specificity is within normal limits, her productions need to be analyzed under other conversational conditions. Two other language samples in another setting and with another familiar adult world need to be obtained to determine whether referent specificity is a persistent problem for Sara.

Contributional Conciseness

The next variable that we consider has to do with the amount of conversational space taken up by a single utterance and the appropriateness of the detail provided in a particular contribution. The examination of this variable is based on one of a set of four conversational principles proposed by Grice (1975)—namely, the

EXAMPLE 4.4

CODING FOR CONTRIBUTIONAL CONCISENESS		
(M and C are sitting in clinic observation area, observing a session)		
C:	you know the teddy what Aaron had?/	Referent not identified
M:	Yes	Identification confirmed
C:	the one what talked?/	
M:	Yes/	Identification reconfirmed
C:	Aaron's teddy bear?/	
M:	I know which one you mean/	Identification reconfirmed
C:	well Jason gots one too/	
M:	Oh I see/	

quantity of conversational contributions. Grice contended that speakers should make their contributions as informative as the situation requires, but no *more* informative than it requires.

Young children typically have greater difficulty providing their listeners with enough information than they do with providing too much information. It is the former that is considered in appropriateness judgments of referent specificity; it is the latter that is considered in appropriateness judgments of contributional conciseness. Think of an adult who provides the listener with so much information that the listener becomes bored or annoyed or thinks, "So what?" Children violate this principle as well. In fact, children as young as 4 years of age provide the listener with too much information, as Example 4.4 indicates.

In appropriateness judgments regarding contributional conciseness, a judgment will be made, as Prutting and Kirchner (1983) suggested, regardless of whether violation of the conciseness principle is penalizing to the child. In other words, an attempt will be made to determine whether providing too much information interferes with the continuation of conversation. In the preceding example, the mother is on the verge of being irritated with her child for failing to see that she has enough information to know the referent of the child's sequence of utterances. The conversation does continue though. Perhaps if this child had persisted in failing to be sufficiently concise, it would have had negative consequences. Without more of the conversation, we cannot be certain.

In analyzing Sara's transcript, sequences of utterances (as opposed to each utterance in isolation) are considered in an attempt to find instances of a lack of conciseness. Progress through the transcript and examine mother and child utterances in sequence, indicating with a check mark (✔) when the utterance is appropriately concise. (Follow the same coding procedure for N/A and NK as described previously for referent specificity.) If evidence is found of Sara providing so much information that her mother responds negatively, mark a minus sign (–) in the Contributional Conciseness column in the row corresponding to the appropriate utterance number on the Conversational Moves and Appropriateness Moves Analysis form. (The same procedure would be followed if Sara's mother provided so much information that Sara responded negatively.) Keep in mind that inappropriately providing too much information often occurs over more than one utterance. When the entire transcript has been examined, compare results with Form 4.6.

Analysis of Sara's transcript reveals no instances in which she provided so much information that it was penalizing to her as a speaker. There were several instances in which she seemed to provide irrelevant information (e.g., utterances #3 and #68), but these instances did not appear to penalize her as a speaker; thus, they were not judged as inappropriate. It could be concluded that for this listener, Sara's utterances were not judged as lacking conciseness. In addition, no utterances on the part of Sara's mother appeared to provide too much information.

FORM 4.6

Name of Child: Sara

CONVERSATIONAL MOVES AND APPROPRIATENESS JUDGMENTS ANALYSIS

ADULT

UTT#	Initiating Moves	Responding Moves	Referent Specificity	Contributional Conciseness	Communication Style
1	N		✔	✔	
2	E		✔	✔	
3	E		✔	✔	
4	E		✔	✔	
5	E		✔	✔	
6	E		✔	✔	
7	E		✔	✔	
8	E		✔	✔	
9	E		✔	✔	
10	E		✔	✔	
11	E		✔	✔	
12	E		✔	✔	
13	E		✔	✔	
14	E		✔	✔	
15		E	✔	✔	
16	E		✔	✔	
17	E		✔	✔	
18	E		✔	✔	
19	E		✔	✔	
20		E	✔	✔	
21	E		✔	✔	
22	E		✔	✔	
23		E	✔	✔	
24	E		✔	✔	
25	E		✔	✔	

CHILD

UTT#	Initiating Moves	Responding Moves	Referent Specificity	Contributional Conciseness	Communication Style
1		O	✔	✔	
2		E	✔	✔	
3		R	N/A	N/A	
4		E	✔	✔	
5		E	✔	✔	
6		E	✔	✔	
7		E	✔	✔	
8		O	✔	✔	
9		E	✔	✔	
10		R	N/A	N/A	
11		E	✔	✔	
12		O	✔	✔	
13		O	✔	✔	
14		E	✔	✔	
15	N		✔	✔	
16		E	✔	✔	
17		E	✔	✔	
18		O	✔	✔	
19		E	✔	✔	
20		E	✔	✔	
21		E	✔	✔	
22		E	✔	✔	
23		E	✔	✔	
24		E	✔	✔	
25		R	N/A	N/A	

FORM 4.6

CONVERSATIONAL MOVES AND APPROPRIATENESS JUDGMENTS ANALYSIS (continued)

ADULT

UTT#	Initiating Moves	Responding Moves	Referent Specificity	Contributional Conciseness	Communication Style
26	E		✔	✔	
27		R	N/A	N/A	
28		A	✔	✔	
29	E		✔	✔	
30	E		✔	✔	
31	E		✔	✔	
32		E	✔	✔	
33	E		✔	✔	
34		A	✔	✔	
35		E	✔	✔	
36	E		✔	✔	
37	E		✔	✔	
38	E		✔	✔	
39	E		✔	✔	
40		A	✔	✔	
41		A	✔	✔	
42	E		✔	✔	
43	E		✔	✔	
44	E		✔	✔	
45	E		✔	✔	
46	E		✔	✔	
47	E		✔	✔	
48		E	✔	✔	
49		Y	✔	✔	
50	E		✔	✔	

CHILD

UTT#	Initiating Moves	Responding Moves	Referent Specificity	Contributional Conciseness	Communication Style
26		E	✔	✔	
27		R	N/A	N/A	
28		O	✔	✔	
29		E	✔	✔	
30	E		✔	✔	
31		O	✔	✔	
32		E	✔	✔	
33		O	✔	✔	
34		E	✔	✔	
35		O	✔	✔	
36	N		✔	✔	
37	N		—	✔	
38		Y	✔	✔	
39	E		✔	✔	
40		O	✔	✔	
41		O	✔	✔	
42		Y	✔	✔	
43		O	✔	✔	
44		E	✔	✔	
45		O	✔	✔	
46		E	✔	✔	
47	E		✔	✔	
48		O	✔	✔	
49		O	✔	✔	
50		E	✔	✔	

(continues)

FORM 4.6

CONVERSATIONAL MOVES AND APPROPRIATENESS JUDGMENTS ANALYSIS (continued)

ADULT

UTT#	Initiating Moves	Responding Moves	Referent Specificity	Contributional Conciseness	Communication Style
51	E		✓	✓	
52	E		✓	✓	
53	E		✓	✓	
54		A	✓	✓	
55	E		✓	✓	
56	E		✓	✓	
57		E	✓	✓	
58	E		✓	✓	
59	E		✓	✓	
60	E		✓	✓	
61	E		✓	✓	
62	E		✓	✓	
63	E		✓	✓	
64		E	✓	✓	
65	E		✓	✓	
66	E		✓	✓	
67		S	✓	✓	
68	E		✓	✓	
69	E		✓	✓	
70	E		✓	✓	
71	E		✓	✓	
72		E	✓	✓	
73	E		✓	✓	
74	E		✓	✓	
75	E		✓	✓	

CHILD

UTT#	Initiating Moves	Responding Moves	Referent Specificity	Contributional Conciseness	Communication Style
51		O	✓	✓	
52		E	✓	✓	
53	N		—	✓	
54		E	✓	✓	
55		E	—	✓	
56		S	—	✓	
57		E	✓	✓	
58		E	✓	✓	
59		O	✓	✓	
60		E	✓	✓	
61		Y	✓	✓	
62	E		✓	✓	
63		E	—	✓	
64		S	—	✓	
65		Y	✓	✓	
66		E	—	✓	
67		E	✓	✓	
68		E	—	✓	
69		E	✓	✓	
70		E	✓	✓	
71		O	✓	✓	
72		E	✓	✓	
73		E	✓	✓	
74		R	N/A	N/A	
75		E	✓	✓	

FORM 4.6

CONVERSATIONAL MOVES AND APPROPRIATENESS JUDGMENTS ANALYSIS (continued)

ADULT

UTT#	Initiating Moves	Responding Moves	Referent Specificity	Contributional Conciseness	Communication Style
76	E		✓	✓	
77	E		✓	✓	
78	E		✓	✓	
79	E		✓	✓	
80	E		✓	✓	
81	E		✓	✓	
82	E		✓	✓	
83	E		✓	✓	
84		R	N/A	N/A	
85		E	✓	✓	
86	E		✓	✓	
87	E		✓	✓	
88	E		✓	✓	
89	E		✓	✓	
90	E		✓	✓	
91	E		✓	✓	
92	E		✓	✓	
93	E		✓	✓	
94	E		✓	✓	
95		A	✓	✓	
96	E		✓	✓	
97		A	✓	✓	
98	E		✓	✓	
99	E		✓	✓	
100		E	✓	✓	

CHILD

UTT#	Initiating Moves	Responding Moves	Referent Specificity	Contributional Conciseness	Communication Style
76		E	✓	✓	
77		E	✓	✓	
78		O	✓	✓	
79		E	✓	✓	
80	R		✓	✓	
81		E	—	✓	
82		S	✓	✓	
83	N		—	✓	
84		Y	✓	✓	
85		O	✓	✓	
86		E	✓	✓	
87		O	—	✓	
88		Y	✓	✓	
89		E	✓	✓	
90		E	—	✓	
91		E	✓	✓	
92		E	✓	✓	
93		E	✓	✓	
94		O	✓	✓	
95		O	✓	✓	
96		O	✓	✓	
97		E	✓	✓	
98	E		✓	✓	
99		E	✓	✓	
100		O	NK	NK	

FORM 4.6

CONVERSATIONAL MOVES AND APPROPRIATENESS JUDGMENTS ANALYSIS (continued)

	ADULT						CHILD				
	Conversational Moves		Appropriateness Judgments				Conversational Moves		Appropriateness Judgments		
UTT#	Initiating Moves	Responding Moves	Referent Specificity	Contributional Conciseness	Communication Style	UTT#	Initiating Moves	Responding Moves	Referent Specificity	Contributional Conciseness	Communication Style
101		S	✔	✔							
102	E		✔	✔							
103		A	✔	✔							
104	E		✔	✔							
105	E		✔	✔							
106	N		✔	✔							
107	E		✔	✔							
108	E		✔	✔							
109	E		✔	✔							
110	E		✔	✔							
111	E		✔	✔							
112	E		✔	✔							
113	E		✔	✔							
114	E		NK	NK							

Again, no normative data are available to which the results can be compared. Clinical judgment regarding a child's failure to be appropriately concise must be relied on when considering an individual child who is interacting with a variety of speakers. If the failure to be concise is penalizing to the child, intervention would be warranted. Explicit feedback would be provided to the child to increase awareness of listeners' reactions to providing too much information. Only then could the child be expected to make use of specific strategies for increasing the conciseness of contributions in appropriate situations. As always, two other language samples in another setting and with another familiar adult would need to be obtained to determine whether contributional conciseness is a persistent problem for Sara.

Communication Style

The final variable that we consider in making appropriateness judgments is that of communication style, or the ability to alter the style of a contribution based on the listener's characteristics. Shatz and Gelman (1973) were the first to provide evidence indicating that young children could alter the form of their contributions on the basis of language differences of their listeners. In their study, the language of 4-year-old children was compared when the children interacted with 2-year-old children and then with adults. Results indicated that by age 4, children could adjust length, complexity, and use of attention-holders in their language depending on the age and/or language abilities of conversational partners. Since this study, other studies have followed that indicated that children as young as 3 years of age can use various styles of interacting depending on whether they are assuming a role (as of a baby or a daddy), talking with a younger child, talking with a familiar adult, or talking with an unfamiliar adult (Berko Gleason, 1973; Sachs & Devin, 1976).

The analysis of the ability to use stylistic variations in communication is based on two assumptions. The first assumption is that the child's ability to make adjustments reflects an abstract knowledge of the appropriateness of speech to the listener (Sachs & Devin, 1976). This assumption implies an integration of the cognitive system and the linguistic system. The second assumption is that a child who does not make adjustments will be penalized in some way as a speaker. Prutting and Kirchner (1983) suggested that a failure to adjust even loudness level can have a negative impact on the reactions of strangers, classmates, and/or teachers regarding the child's communicative abilities. Both of these assumptions serve to justify the examination of a pragmatic variable that may occur infrequently.

In Example 4.5, the child uses a style of communication that is too informal for a school situation when adults are present. The mother reminds the child of the need to use a more polite form when addressing the teacher and the child immediately modifies the form of his request. The more polite form is a stylistic modification that would be noted when analyzing a transcript for appropriate or inappropriate use of communication style.

In making appropriateness judgments regarding communication style, identify the child's failure to make syntactic modifications, vocal quality modifications, and vocal intensity modifications as demanded by the situation. For example, if a young boy is interacting with a younger child and fails to shorten the length and/or reduce the complexity of his utterances, enter a minus sign (−) in the Communication Style column (on the Conversational Moves and Appropriateness Judgments Analysis form) corresponding to the utterances where those modifications would have been appropriate. If the child is role-playing and fails to make vocal-quality changes (e.g., lower voice for the daddy, higher voice for the baby) and/or syntactic changes (e.g., more imperatives for the daddy, babbling and/or one-word utterances for the baby) as a result of his role, enter a minus sign in the Communication Style column corresponding to the utterances where those modifications would have been appropriate. Or if the child fails to use politeness markers when interacting with unfamiliar adults and/or uses aggressive vocal intensity when interacting with peers or adults, put a minus sign in the Communication Style column. If either speaker made appropriate adjustments, put a plus sign (+) in the Communication Style column corresponding to the utterances where the adjustments were made. Use the NK coding feature as described earlier. All other boxes in the Communication Style column should be left blank.

Now turn to Sara's transcript and review sequences of utterances to determine whether there was a need for Sara or her mother to alter her communication style and whether the appropriate adjustments were made. The same procedure should be followed for the utterances of both Sara and her mother. When the entire transcript has been examined, compare your results with Form 4.7.

Analysis of Sara's transcript reveals that there were no instances in which she should have made adjustments in her communication style and did not make them. In fact, there were no instances in which she should have made adjustments and did. In addition, there were no instances in which Sara's mother should have made adjustments in her communication style and did not make them, nor were there instances in which she should not have made adjustments and did. This clearly points out the need to have samples of communicative interaction under a variety of conditions and with a variety of partners. Only then can it be concluded that a child does or does not make adjustments in his or her communication style.

EXAMPLE 4.5

CODING FOR COMMUNICATION STYLE

(M, C, and teacher are at table; C reaches for crayon near teacher)	
C: gimme that/	Child fails to modify language to include polite forms.
M: Excuse me?	
C: can I have that crayon please?/	When prompted by mother, child uses more appropriate style.

FORM 4.7

CONVERSATIONAL MOVES AND APPROPRIATENESS JUDGMENTS ANALYSIS

Name of Child: Sara

ADULT

UTT#	Conversational Moves		Appropriateness Judgments		
	Initiating Moves	Responding Moves	Referent Specificity	Contributional Conciseness	Communication Style
1	N		✔	✔	
2	E		✔	✔	
3	E		✔	✔	
4	E		✔	✔	
5	E		✔	✔	
6	E		✔	✔	
7	E		✔	✔	
8	E		✔	✔	
9	E		✔	✔	
10	E		✔	✔	
11	E		✔	✔	
12	E		✔	✔	
13	E		✔	✔	
14	E		✔	✔	
15		E	✔	✔	
16	E		✔	✔	
17	E		✔	✔	
18	E		✔	✔	
19	E		✔	✔	
20		E	✔	✔	
21	E		✔	✔	
22	E		✔	✔	
23		E	✔	✔	
24	E		✔	✔	
25	E		✔	✔	

CHILD

UTT#	Conversational Moves		Appropriateness Judgments		
	Initiating Moves	Responding Moves	Referent Specificity	Contributional Conciseness	Communication Style
1		O	✔	✔	
2		E	✔	✔	
3		R	N/A	N/A	
4		E	✔	✔	
5		E	✔	✔	
6		E	✔	✔	
7		E	✔	✔	
8		O	✔	✔	
9		E	✔	✔	
10		R	N/A	N/A	
11		E	✔	✔	
12		O	✔	✔	
13		O	✔	✔	
14		E	✔	✔	
15	N		✔	✔	
16		E	✔	✔	
17		E	✔	✔	
18		O	✔	✔	
19		E	✔	✔	
20		E	✔	✔	
21		E	✔	✔	
22		E	✔	✔	
23		E	✔	✔	
24		E	✔	✔	
25		R	N/A	N/A	

FORM 4.7

CONVERSATIONAL MOVES AND APPROPRIATENESS JUDGMENTS ANALYSIS (continued)

ADULT

UTT#	Conversational Moves		Appropriateness Judgments		
	Initiating Moves	Responding Moves	Referent Specificity	Contributional Conciseness	Communication Style
26	E		✔	✔	
27		R	N/A	N/A	
28		A	✔	✔	
29	E		✔	✔	
30	E		✔	✔	
31	E		✔	✔	
32		E	✔	✔	
33	E		✔	✔	
34		A	✔	✔	
35		E	✔	✔	
36	E		✔	✔	
37	E		✔	✔	
38	E		✔	✔	
39	E		✔	✔	
40		A	✔	✔	
41		A	✔	✔	
42	E		✔	✔	
43	E		✔	✔	
44	E		✔	✔	
45	E		✔	✔	
46	E		✔	✔	
47	E		✔	✔	
48		E	✔	✔	
49		Y	✔	✔	
50	E		✔	✔	

CHILD

UTT#	Conversational Moves		Appropriateness Judgments		
	Initiating Moves	Responding Moves	Referent Specificity	Contributional Conciseness	Communication Style
26		E	✔	✔	
27		R	N/A	N/A	
28		O	✔	✔	
29		E	✔	✔	
30	E		✔	✔	
31		O	✔	✔	
32		E	✔	✔	
33		O	✔	✔	
34		E	✔	✔	
35		O	✔	✔	
36	N		✔	✔	
37	N		—	✔	
38		Y	✔	✔	
39	E		✔	✔	
40		O	✔	✔	
41		O	✔	✔	
42		Y	✔	✔	
43		O	✔	✔	
44		E	✔	✔	
45		O	✔	✔	
46		E	✔	✔	
47	E		✔	✔	
48		O	✔	✔	
49		O	✔	✔	
50		E	✔	✔	

(continues)

Guide to Analysis of Language Transcripts

FORM 4.7

CONVERSATIONAL MOVES AND APPROPRIATENESS JUDGMENTS ANALYSIS (continued)

ADULT

UTT#	Initiating Moves	Responding Moves	Referent Specificity	Contributional Conciseness	Communication Style
51	E		✔	✔	
52	E		✔	✔	
53	E		✔	✔	
54		A	✔	✔	
55	E		✔	✔	
56	E		✔	✔	
57		E	✔	✔	
58	E		✔	✔	
59	E		✔	✔	
60	E		✔	✔	
61	E		✔	✔	
62	E		✔	✔	
63	E		✔	✔	
64		E	✔	✔	
65	E		✔	✔	
66	E		✔	✔	
67		S	✔	✔	
68	E		✔	✔	
69	E		✔	✔	
70	E		✔	✔	
71	E		✔	✔	
72		E	✔	✔	
73	E		✔	✔	
74	E		✔	✔	
75	E		✔	✔	

CHILD

UTT#	Initiating Moves	Responding Moves	Referent Specificity	Contributional Conciseness	Communication Style
51		O	✔	✔	
52		E	✔	✔	
53	N		—	✔	
54		E	✔	✔	
55		E	—	✔	
56		S	—	✔	
57		E	✔	✔	
58		E	✔	✔	
59		O	✔	✔	
60		E	✔	✔	
61		Y	✔	✔	
62	E		✔	✔	
63		E	—	✔	
64		S	—	✔	
65		Y	✔	✔	
66		E	—	✔	
67		E	✔	✔	
68		E	—	✔	
69		E	✔	✔	
70		E	✔	✔	
71		O	✔	✔	
72		E	✔	✔	
73		E	✔	✔	
74		R	N/A	N/A	
75		E	✔	✔	

FORM 4.7

CONVERSATIONAL MOVES AND APPROPRIATENESS JUDGMENTS ANALYSIS (continued)

ADULT

UTT#	Initiating Moves	Responding Moves	Referent Specificity	Contributional Conciseness	Communication Style
76	E		✔	✔	
77	E		✔	✔	
78	E		✔	✔	
79	E		✔	✔	
80	E		✔	✔	
81	E		✔	✔	
82	E		✔	✔	
83	E		✔	✔	
84		R	N/A	N/A	
85		E	✔	✔	
86	E		✔	✔	
87	E		✔	✔	
88	E		✔	✔	
89	E		✔	✔	
90	E		✔	✔	
91	E		✔	✔	
92	E		✔	✔	
93	E		✔	✔	
94	E		✔	✔	
95		A	✔	✔	
96	E		✔	✔	
97		A	✔	✔	
98	E		✔	✔	
99	E		✔	✔	
100		E	✔		

CHILD

UTT#	Initiating Moves	Responding Moves	Referent Specificity	Contributional Conciseness	Communication Style
76		E	✔	✔	
77		E	✔	✔	
78		O	✔	✔	
79		E	✔	✔	
80	R		✔	✔	
81		E	—	✔	
82		S	✔	✔	
83	N		—	✔	
84		Y	✔	✔	
85		O	✔	✔	
86		E	✔	✔	
87		O	—	✔	
88		Y	✔	✔	
89		E	✔	✔	
90		E	—	✔	
91		E	✔	✔	
92		E	✔	✔	
93		E	✔	✔	
94		O	✔	✔	
95		O	✔	✔	
96		O	✔	✔	
97		E	✔	✔	
98	E		✔	✔	
99		E	✔	✔	
100		O	NK	NK	NK

FORM 4.7

CONVERSATIONAL MOVES AND APPROPRIATENESS JUDGMENTS ANALYSIS (continued)

	ADULT						CHILD				
	Conversational Moves		Appropriateness Judgments				Conversational Moves		Appropriateness Judgments		
UTT#	Initiating Moves	Responding Moves	Referent Specificity	Contributional Conciseness	Communication Style	UTT#	Initiating Moves	Responding Moves	Referent Specificity	Contributional Conciseness	Communication Style
101		S	✔	✔							
102	E		✔	✔							
103		A	✔	✔							
104	E		✔	✔							
105	E		✔	✔							
106	N		✔	✔							
107	E		✔	✔							
108	E		✔	✔							
109	E		✔	✔							
110	E		✔	✔							
111	E		✔	✔							
112	E		✔	✔							
113	E		✔	✔							
114	E		NK	NK	NK						

And what should be done if a child does not make adjustments in communication style as situations demand? It is possible to teach the child to make the appropriate syntactic and vocal adjustments and to recognize when these adjustments are necessary. Because the ability to vary communication style is a reflection of the integration of the child's cognitive, semantic, syntactic, and pragmatic systems, this appropriateness variable is important in determining a child's overall communicative abilities. In Sara's case, two other language samples in another setting and with another familiar adult would need to be obtained to determine whether communication style is a persistent problem.

Implications for Intervention

Completion of each of the appropriate pragmatic analyses should be followed by a synthesis of results. The Conversational Moves and Appropriateness Judgments Summary form (available in Appendix D, online) can be used for this synthesis. Form 4.8 is a completed summary form for Sara's transcript.

While problems with any one of the areas analyzed may not be related to problems in another area, results of each analysis procedure completed must be reviewed to develop comprehensive goals and objectives for intervention. The sequence of normal development is not as detailed for pragmatic milestones as it is for semantic and syntactic behaviors; however, judgments about what to target in treatment for identified pragmatic problems continue to be based on what is known about normal language acquisition. Norms are not readily available, but knowledgeable judgments can be made. As in previous chapters, the suggestions provided here should be considered general guidelines, not hard-and-fast rules, for developing intervention goals and objectives.

Data obtained from frequency-of-occurrence analysis of various pragmatic categories (e.g., Dore's primitive speech acts [1974]; Dore's conversational acts [1978]; or Martlew's conversational moves [1980]) that indicate use of a limited range of categories can provide the foundation for developing objectives that target use of a wider variety of categories. For example, if a child's language abilities are at a one-word level overall

FORM 4.8 Name of Child **Sara**

CONVERSATIONAL MOVES AND APPROPRIATENESS JUDGMENTS SUMMARY

Child's Total Utterances ___100___

CONVERSATIONAL MOVES

INITIATING MOVES	5	New Topic Introduction	=	5	% of Total Utterances
	1	Restarting Old Topic	=	1	% of Total Utterances
	5	Eliciting Verbal Response	=	5	% of Total Utterances
	0	Intruding	=	0	% of Total Utterances
RESPONDING MOVES	0	Acknowledging	=	0	% of Total Utterances
	6	Yes/No Responses	=	6	% of Total Utterances
	25	One-Word Answers	=	25	% of Total Utterances
	5	Repeating	=	5	% of Total Utterances
	3	Sustaining Topic	=	3	% of Total Utterances
	50	Extending Topic	=	50	% of Total Utterances
FALSE STARTS	0		=	—	% of Total Utterances

APPROPRIATENESS JUDGMENTS

Referent Specificity	12	Lacked Specificity	=	12	% of Total Utterances
Contributional Conciseness	0	Lacked Conciseness	=	—	% of Total Utterances
Communication Style	0	Lacked Stylistic Variation	=	—	% of Total Utterances

Adult's Total Utterances ___114___

CONVERSATIONAL MOVES

INITIATING MOVES	2	New Topic Introduction	=	1.8	% of Total Utterances
	0	Restarting Old Topic	=	—	% of Total Utterances
	88	Eliciting Verbal Response	=	77.2	% of Total Utterances
	0	Intruding	=	—	% of Total Utterances
RESPONDING MOVES	8	Acknowledging	=	7	% of Total Utterances
	1	Yes/No Responses	=	.9	% of Total Utterances
	0	One-Word Answers	=	—	% of Total Utterances
	2	Repeating	=	1.8	% of Total Utterances
	2	Sustaining Topic	=	1.8	% of Total Utterances
	11	Extending Topic	=	9.6	% of Total Utterances
FALSE STARTS	0		=	—	% of Total Utterances

APPROPRIATENESS JUDGMENTS

Referent Specificity	0	Lacked Specificity	=	—	% of Total Utterances
Contributional Conciseness	0	Lacked Conciseness	=	—	% of Total Utterances
Communication Style	0	Lacked Stylistic Variation	=	—	% of Total Utterances

and he or she is using a limited number of types of primitive speech acts, it would be appropriate to provide the child with opportunities to use a broader range of primitive speech acts.

When working with very young children with ASD, speech–language pathologists should pay careful attention to the communicative functions that are being produced by the child. For very minimal communicators, communication for the purpose of behavioral regulation (**requesting action, protest**) may need to be the initial focus of intervention, as this communicative function appears to be the most easily mastered by children with ASD. However, as the child becomes a successful communicator, the categories of **labeling**, **answering**, and **requesting answer** should be considered as intervention targets. When the child uses these functions while clearly addressing an adult, these utterances fall under the broader category of joint attention. This is a distinct area of challenge for children with ASD and, thus, will need to be a specific focus of intervention for this population. Speech–language pathologists may choose to initially target use of gestures for intentional communication across a variety of communicative functions because the use of gestures may lead to later linguistic developments. Further, a limited use of gestures to initiate joint attention is correlated with impaired language development; addressing the use of communication for the purpose of establishing joint attention may help to mitigate these language delays (Landra, Holman, & Garrett-Mayer, 2007).

If the child's language abilities are typical of children with normal language skills between 2 and 5 years of age and the child is using a limited number of conversational acts, it would be appropriate to provide the child with opportunities to use additional conversational acts. In either case, it would be crucial to consider the role that the conversational co-participant may play in the opportunities for expressing a variety of communicative functions, such as those specified in Dore's primitive speech acts and conversational acts analyses.

Examination of the roles expressed by Sara's mother raised questions regarding the opportunities Sara may have had for expressing various conversational roles. Dore (1978) concluded that variations in setting (e.g., preschool classroom vs. supermarket) and in situation or condition (e.g., group vs. dyad; question asking vs. free play) may result in different distributions of types of conversational acts. Consequently, targeting an increase in use of particular functions or acts in an intervention goal can be accomplished only by varying the child's opportunity to engage in conversation with different partners, in different settings, and under different conditions. Results of analysis using Martlew's (1980) conversational moves that reveal a distribution of **initiating moves** and **responding moves** substantially different from results obtained by Martlew may indicate a need to teach the child additional means of initiating or responding. In other words, for a child whose **initiating moves** constitute substantially less than 30% of his speaking turns, Martlew's types of **initiating moves** could be taught in the context of a variety of conversational settings and situations with a variety of conversational partners. For a child whose **initiating moves** constitute substantially more than 30% of his speaking turns, it would be productive to teach the child to use various types of **responding moves** by paying attention to the contributions of his conversational co-participant and by using more diverse types of Martlew's **responding moves**. For example, children with ASD or those who are at risk of this diagnosis may present with higher **initiating moves** and fewer **responding moves** due to a tendency to use fewer contingent utterances. Research suggests that intervention can, and should, specifically address the extinction of these noncontingent utterances (Hale & Tager-Flusberg 2005). Work on increasing a child's use of **responding moves** may be prove essential in improving overall communicative competence.

Again, attention to the setting, situation, and partner is very important when targeting discourse aspects of communication. Various accounts of proposed intervention formats targeting turn taking, conversational contributions, and other discourse variables continue to appear in the literature (Adams, Lockton, Gaile, Earl, & Freed, 2012; Anderson-Wood & Smith, 1997; Bedrosian, 1985; Beveridge & Conti-Ramsden, 1987; Brinton, Robinson, & Fujiki, 2004; Cross, 1984; Dotson, Leaf, Sheldon, & Sherman, 2010; Fey, 1986; Fujiki, Brinton, McCleave, Anderson, & Chamberlain, 2013; Gallagher, 1991; Gerber, Brice, Capone, Fujiki, & Timler, 2012; Leinonen & Smith, 1994; Leonard & Fey, 1991; McTear, 1985; McTear & Conti-Ramsden, 1991; Merrison & Merrison, 2005; Muller, Cannon, Kornblum, Clark, & Powers, 2016; Norris & Damico, 1990; Owens, 2014; Smedley, 1989; Smith & Leinonen, 1992). Consideration of each of these discourse variables will be helpful in developing intervention goals, objectives, and techniques.

Data obtained from analysis of discourse variables that result in appropriateness judgments can be used to target behaviors that would increase the appropriateness of each variable. For example, if a child lacks specificity in referent identification, he can be taught to respond to explicit feedback from the conversational co-participant in order to be more specific. While the child's ability to respond to decreasing explicitness in requests for revision increases with age, children as young as 2 years can respond to requests for revision. In addition, the types of revisions that children make change developmentally. Therefore, the expectations for adding specificity must be developmentally appropriate and based on what is known about normal language acquisition. These guidelines also hold for the child who is too informative. This child can be taught to respond to feedback from the conversational co-participant, indicating that the amount of information provided is inappropriately high, resulting in the judgment of a lack of conciseness. The child can be taught various syntactic conventions for increasing conciseness (e.g., use of pronouns, ellipsis), and he can be taught to decrease the number of speaking turns used to establish his referent. Again, the behaviors targeted must be developmentally appropriate and based on normal language acquisition information. In addition, as with all preceding pragmatic variables, it is crucial to consider the impact that setting, situation, and conversational co-participant have on the child's ability to make modifications that could lead to judgments of appropriate referent specificity and contributional conciseness.

Finally, the child who does not vary his communication style depending on the setting and/or conversational co-participant can be taught to recognize such a need and then to vary his style. The ability to recognize a need to vary communication style will change developmentally, as will the conventions available to vary that style. Judgments about what behaviors to target must be based on what is known about normal language development in relation to the child's overall language production.

In general, analysis of communicative functions and discourse relations yields quantitative and qualitative data that can be used to identify children with problems in the pragmatic area of language production. These data also can be used to develop intervention goals and objectives. The suggestions and the information on the typical language acquisition sequence provided in this chapter (e.g., primitive versus conversational acts) can lead to the appropriate development of productive goals and objectives. In addition, the variables to consider in developing goals and objectives can be used in diagnostic therapy to ensure accurate judgments of pragmatic performance.

APPENDIX E SARA'S TRANSCRIPT AND ANALYSES

The following analyses were performed on Sara's transcript and appear on the pages indicated. Her transcript was not subjected to Bloom's (1973) One-Word Utterance Types, Nelson's (1973) One-Word Utterance Types, or Dore's (1974) Primitive Speech Acts analyses, because Sara's utterances were too long and complex for such analyses.

TRANSCRIPT 160

SEMANTIC ANALYSIS 169

    Semantic Roles Coding. 169

    Total Use of 20 Semantic Roles 173

    Meaning Relationships in One-Word and Multiword Utterances 174

    Semantic Roles Summary 176

    Brown's Prevalent Semantic Relations 177

    Brown's Prevalent Semantic Relations Summary 178

    Templin's Type-Token Ratio Analysis 179

SYNTACTIC ANALYSIS 181

    Structural Stage Analysis. 181

    Length Distribution Analysis 183

    Grammatical Morphemes Analysis 184

    Production Characteristics Summary 185

    Data Summary and Interpretation. 186

PRAGMATIC ANALYSIS. 187

    Dore's Conversational Acts Analysis 187

    Conversational Moves and Appropriateness Judgments Analysis 188

    Conversational Moves and Appropriateness Judgments Summary 193

TRANSCRIPT (SARA)

Name of Child **Sara**	Chronological Age **4-10**
Type of Situation **free play in playroom of preschool**	Date **10-6**
Length of Recording **45 min** Length of Transcript **100 utterances**	Time of Day **2 pm**

Materials Present **playground set, bendable people, toy dishes**

People Present **S=Sara; M=Mother**

ADULT	CONTEXT	CHILD	
1 What do you have huh?			
		toys/	1
2 Toys?			
3 What is that?	(M pointing to swing set)		
4 What does it look like to you?			
	(S shrugs shoulders)		
5 What is it?			
6 What does it look like?			
7 Where would you go to play with toys like this?			
		XXX/	
8 If we said we were going somewhere • to play with toys like this where would you play with these?			
		at the park!/	2
9 It looks like a park doesn't it?			
		a park/	3
10 What's that?			
	(S touches slide)		
		it's a swing set/	4
	(M touches slide)		
11 This is?			
		no that a slide/	5
	(S pointing to swing set)	there's the swing set/	6
12 What do you do with it?			
	(S climbs slide with fingers)		
	(S using finger to slide down)	climb up and wee/	7
13 Why don't you take one of the people and show me what you do?			

	(S picks up doll)		
14 Who's that?			
		Mama/	8
15 Show me how she does it/			
	(S slides doll down slide)		
		she can't go/	9
		she can't go down/	10
16 How come?			
		'cuz she's stuck there/	11
	(M points to sandbox)		
17 What's that?			
		sandbox/	12
18 What do you do with a sandbox?			
	(S picks up cup and puts it up to her mouth)		
19 What are you doing?			
		drinking/	13
	(S picks up sand spilled on floor)		
		uh-oh/	14
	(S puts cup in sandbox)		
		I make coffee/	15
20 Okay we'll make coffee/			
	(M pulls picnic table toward herself)		
21 What's this?			
		that's a picnic table/	16
		and that's a swing set/	17
22 What do you do on a swing set?			
		swing/	18
	(S pours sand into cup)		
23 Let's hold it over here/			
	(S stirs sand in cup with spoon)		
24 Now what are you doing?			
		um I mix it up/	19
25 Then what?			
	(S covers top of cup with hand)		
		then you • shake it/	20
	(S shakes cup)		

ADULT	CONTEXT	CHILD	
26 Who should we pretend that we are?			
		not done yet/	21
27 Oh not done yet/			
		now it's done/	22
	(S pours into another cup)		
28 Okay/			
	(S picking up spoon and stirring in cup)	I use a spoon/	23
29 What are you doing?			
30 Mixing it up?		I mixing/	24
		mixing it up/	25
		now put it in the cup/	26
31 What's that?	(M pointing to picnic table)		
		XXX/	
	(S drops cup in sandbox, which spills sand)		
32 Oops/			
		oops/	27
33 What is that over there?			
		table/	28
34 Okay/			
35 That looks like a picnic table/			
36 What do you do at a picnic table?			
		sit on it/	29
	(S picks up girl doll)		
37 Put them over there?			
38 Can you put them over there?			
	(S tries to bend doll's legs)		
		how do you do this?/	30
39 What do you want her to do?			
		sit down/	31
40 Okay/			
	(S looks at M)		
		also she lays down/	32

41	She can/		
		(S sits dolls at picnic table)	
42	What are they doing?		
			sitting/ 33
43	What are they gonna do now?		
			they are um gonna eat/ 34
44	They are?		
45	What are they gonna eat?		
			pancakes/ 35
		(S takes another doll off swing set and puts it at table)	
			it's time to go/ 36
46	Oh?		
		(S looking at camera)	where's that um girl?/ 37
47	Beret?		
			yeah Beret/ 38
48	She's in the other room/		
			'cuz she isn't playing↑/ 39
49	Um-hmm/		
50	Now what are the people eating?		
			pancakes/ 40
51	And what else?		
		(S straightens doll)	
			milk/ 41
52	That's all they need?		
			yeah/ 42
53	Who made the meal • who made the pancakes?		
			Mama/ 43
		(S picks up man doll)	
			and this is the daddy/ 44
54	Okay/		
55	Who are these two?	(M pointing to dolls at table)	
			children/ 45
56	Do you want to give them names?		
			Mark • Kristen • Pete/ 46
		(S picks up woman doll)	
			who's this?/ 47

ADULT	CONTEXT	CHILD	
57 That's the mommy/			
	(M points to swing set)		
58 What's this thing?			
		swing set/	48
59 And what do you do on a swing set?			
		swing/	49
	(S puts woman doll down and picks up man doll)		
		now he's gonna go on/	50
60 What's this?	(M pointing to teeter-totter)		
	(S shrugs shoulders)		
61 What is this one?			
		teetotter/	51
62 What do you do on it?			
	(S puts doll on one end and goes up and down)		
		teetot • teetot/ (sg)	52
	(S sifts "sand" in sandbox)		
		this is birdseed/	53
63 It is?			
		yeah but it also's sand/	54
64 Um-hmm • we're pretending it's sand though/			
65 Now how does a teeter-totter work?			
	(M and S each hold doll on the ends of teeter-totter)		
		teetot • teetot/ (sg)	55
66 Tell me how it works/			
		teetot • teetot/ (sg)	56
67 Tell me/			
		I don't know/	57
68 Well can it put s/c can one person do the teeter-totter?			
	(S slides doll down teeter-totter)		
		put it down here/	58
69 How many does it take?			
		two • two • two/	59
	(M points to shelter)		

ADULT	CONTEXT	CHILD	
70 What's this for?			
		that's a house/	60
71 Do you know what this is called?			
		no/	61
		what?/	62
72 This is called a shelter/			
73 What do you think they would use that for?			
		for cow people/	63
74 Cow people?			
		for cow people/	64
75 What does that mean?			
	(S shrugs shoulders)		
		that means _____ /	
76 Cowboys?			
		yeah/	65
77 What if you saw one of these at the park?			
78 What do you think it's for?			
	(S picks up doll)		
		for he-mans/	66
79 He-mans?			
	(S dances doll on roof of shelter)		
		this goes like this/	67
		he-mans • he-mans • he-mans/ (sg)	68
80 Where did you learn about that?			
		at Kristi's house/	69
81 At Kristi's house?			
82 What would happen if it started to rain?			
	(S shrugging shoulders)	go in the house/	70
83 What's this called?	(M pointing to shelter)		
		shelter house/	71
84 Shelter house/			
85 Let's pretend it's raining/			
86 What would you do?			
		play with kids inside the shelter/	72

ADULT	CONTEXT	CHILD	
	(S singing and dancing dolls into house)	inside we go go go go/ (sg)	73
	(S picks up another doll)		
		inside we go/	74
87 What if they want to eat lunch now?			
		they can/	75
		it stopped raining/	76
88 Okay what should they do now?			
	(S taking doll out of house)	go outside/	77
89 What do you think they would like to play on?			
	(S pointing to trapeze)	that/	78
90 Okay what is that?			
	(S shrugs shoulders)		
91 It looks like a trapeze doesn't it?			
	(S puts doll's feet through trapeze rings)		
92 Now what are they gonna play with?			
		in the sandbox/	79
	(S makes doll fly to sandbox)		
	(S getting dishes out of box)	I fixed supper already/	80
93 Can you put the dishes on the table?			
	(S spoons sand into cups)		
94 What are you doing?			
		making popcorn/	81
95 Okay/			
96 What are you fixing for supper tonight?			
		I said popcorn/	82
97 Oh okay/			
98 What else?			
	(S picking up scoop)	hey this looks like a bunny ear/	83
99 A bunny ear?			
		yeah/	84
100 Let me see/	(M reaching for scoop)		
101 Oh it does look like a bunny's ear/			

ADULT	CONTEXT	CHILD	
102 How many ears does a bunny have?			
		two/	85
	(S turns scoop over)		
		and it almost like a ear/	86
103 Um-hmm/			
	(M picks up another scoop and turns it over)		
104 What does this one look like?			
	(S leaning over)	a shell/	87
105 A shell?			
	(S takes scoop)		
		um-hmm/	88
	(cup of sand falls off picnic table)		
106 Oop • I'll clean it up			
107 You set the rest of the table okay?			
	(M brushes sand into hand; S puts plates on table)		
108 What are you doing?			
		putting the plates on/	89
	(S turns plate over in hand)		
		this is the cover for the pot/	90
109 The cover for the pot?			
	(S puts spoons in cups)		
		in the cups/	91
		that goes on there/	92
	(S puts knife on table)		
110 What are those?			
		knife and spoon/	93
		knife and spoon/	
111 How many plates are there?			
	(S pointing to each plate)	one↑/	94
		two↑/	95
		three↑/	96
		there's not enough/	97
	(S looks in box)		
		how 'bout for the children?/	98

ADULT	CONTEXT	CHILD
112 How 'bout for the children?		
113 Oh I think there's s/c how many do we need?		
	(S pointing to each plate)	one two three/ 99
114 How many people are there?		
	(S points to each doll)	
		four/ 100

Name of Child: Sara

SEMANTIC ROLES CODING

Utterance Number	Semantic Coding	Question
1	One-Term Entity	
2	Locative	
3	One-Term Entity	
4	"No" → Experiencer-State-Multiterm Entity	
5	(CD Yes/No Response) Demonstrative-Multiterm Entity	
6	Demonstrative-State-Multiterm Entity	
7	COMPLEX	
8	One-Term Entity	
9	Agent-Negation-Action	
10	Agent-Negation-Action-Locative	
11	COMPLEX	
12	One-Term Entity	
13	Action	
14	CR (Sounds Accompanying)	
15	Agent-Action-Created Object	
16	Demonstrative-State-Attribute-Multiterm Entity	
17	COMPLEX	
18	Action	
19	(CD Interjection) Agent-Action-Object	
20	COMPLEX	
21	Negation-State-Adverbial	
22	Adverbial-Experiencer-State-Adverbial	
23	Agent-Action-Instrument	
24	Agent-Action	
25	Action-Object	

Notes:
- "Swing set" is considered one word.
- In "go down," "down" distinctly refers to location.

(continues)

SEMANTIC ROLES CODING (continued)

Utterance Number	Semantic Coding	Question
26	Adverbial-Action-Object-Locative	
27	(CR) Sounds Accompanying	
28	One-Term Entity	
29	Action-Object	
30	Adverbial-Agent-Action-Object	✔
31	Action	
32	COMPLEX	
33	Action	
34	Agent (CD Interjection) Action	
35	One-Term Entity	
36	COMPLEX	
37	Locative-State-Demonstrative (CD Interjection) Experiencer	✔
38	(CD Yes/No Response) One-Term Entity	
39	COMPLEX	
40	One-Term Entity	
41	One-Term Entity	
42	CD (Yes/No Response)	
43	One-Term Entity	
44	COMPLEX	
45	One-Term Entity	
46	OTHER	
47	Multiterm Entity-State-Demonstrative	✔
48	One-Term Entity	
49	Action	
50	Adverbial-Agent-Action	

Note on utterance 30: Although "this" is a demonstrative pronoun, it serves as the object of the action, and thus that semantic role takes precedence over the demonstrative role.

SEMANTIC ROLES CODING (continued)

Utterance Number	Semantic Coding	Question
51	One-Term Entity	
52	CR (Sounds Accompanying)	
53	Demonstrative-State-Multiterm Entity	
54	COMPLEX	
55	CR (Sounds Accompanying)	
56	CR (Sounds Accompanying)	
57	Agent-Negation-Action	
58	Action-Object-Locative	
59	Quantifier	
60	Demonstrative-State-Multiterm Entity	
61	Negation	
62	One-Term Entity	✔
63	Beneficiary	
64	Beneficiary	
65	CD (Yes/No Response)	
66	Beneficiary	
67	Agent-Action-Adverbial	
68	CR (Sounds Accompanying)	
69	Locative	
70	Action-Locative	
71	Attribute-Multiterm Entity	
72	Action-Comitative-Locative	
73	Locative-Agent-Action CR (Sounds Accompanying)	
74	Locative-Agent-Action	
75	Agent-Action	

Although "this" is a demonstrative pronoun, because of the action verb, it's clear that the pronoun serves as the agent of the action.

(continues)

SEMANTIC ROLES CODING (continued)

Utterance Number	Semantic Coding	Question
76	COMPLEX	
77	Action-Locative	
78	Demonstrative	
79	Locative	
80	Agent-Action-Created Object-Adverbial	
81	Action-Created Object	
82	Agent-Action-Object	
83	(CD Interjection) Demonstrative-State-Attribute-Multiterm Entity	
84	CD (Yes/No Response)	
85	Quantifier	
86	COMPLEX	
87	One-Term Entity	
88	CD (Yes/No Response)	
89	Action-Object	
90	Demonstrative-State-Multiterm Entity-Possessor	
91	Locative	
92	Demonstrative-State-Locative	
93	COMPLEX	
94	One-Term Entity	
95	One-Term Entity	
96	One-Term Entity	
97	Demonstrative-State-Negation-Quantifier	
98	Adverbial-Beneficiary	✓
99	One-Term Entity	
100	One-Term Entity	

"Put on" is considered a two-part verb. (note attached to utterance 89)

Name of Child: Sara

TOTAL USE OF 20 SEMANTIC ROLES

Role	Tally	#	%
Action	~~IIII~~ ~~IIII~~ ~~IIII~~ ~~IIII~~ ~~IIII~~ ~~IIII~~	30	19.1
Locative	~~IIII~~ ~~IIII~~ IIII	14	8.9
Agent	~~IIII~~ ~~IIII~~ ~~IIII~~ I	16	10.2
Object	~~IIII~~ III	8	5.1
Demonstrative	~~IIII~~ ~~IIII~~ II	12	7.6
Recurrence		0	—
Possessor	I	1	0.6
Quantifier	III	3	2.0
Experiencer	III	3	2.0
Recipient		0	—
Beneficiary	IIII	4	2.5
Comitative	I	1	0.6
Created Object	III	3	2.0
Instrument	I	1	0.6
State	~~IIII~~ ~~IIII~~ III	13	8.3
Entity (one-term)	~~IIII~~ ~~IIII~~ ~~IIII~~ ~~IIII~~	20	12.7
Multiterm Entity	~~IIII~~ ~~IIII~~	10	6.4
Negation	~~IIII~~ I	6	3.8
Attribute	III	3	2.0
Adverbial	~~IIII~~ IIII	9	5.7
	Total	157	100.1

Guide to Analysis of Language Transcripts

Name of Child: **Sara**

MEANING RELATIONSHIPS IN ONE-WORD AND MULTIWORD UTTERANCES

Utterance Number	One Term	Two Term	Three Term	Four Term Plus	Conversational Device	Communication Routine	Complex	Other
1	✓							
2	✓							
3	✓							
4			✓					
5		✓						
6			✓					
7							✓	
8	✓							
9			✓					
10				✓				
11							✓	
12	✓							
13	✓							
14						✓		
15			✓					
16				✓				
17							✓	
18	✓							
19			✓					
20							✓	
21			✓					
22				✓				
23			✓					
24		✓						
25		✓						
26				✓				
27						✓		
28	✓							
29		✓						
30				✓				
31	✓							
32							✓	
33	✓							
34		✓						
35	✓							
36							✓	
37				✓				
38	✓							
39							✓	
40	✓							
41	✓							
42					✓			
43	✓							
44							✓	
45	✓							
46								✓
47			✓					
48	✓							
49	✓							
50			✓					

MEANING RELATIONSHIPS IN ONE-WORD AND MULTIWORD UTTERANCES (continued)

Utterance Number	One Term	Two Term	Three Term	Four Term Plus	Conversational Device	Communication Routine	Complex	Other
51	✔							
52						✔		
53		✔						
54							✔	
55						✔		
56						✔		
57			✔					
58			✔					
59	✔							
60			✔					
61	✔							
62	✔							
63	✔							
64	✔							
65					✔			
66	✔							
67			✔					
68						✔		
69	✔							
70		✔						
71		✔						
72			✔					
73			✔					
74			✔					
75		✔						
76							✔	
77		✔						
78	✔							
79	✔							
80				✔				
81		✔						
82		✔						
83				✔				
84					✔			
85	✔							
86							✔	
87	✔							
88					✔			
89		✔						
90				✔				
91	✔							
92			✔					
93							✔	
94	✔							
95	✔							
96	✔							
97				✔				
98		✔						
99	✔							
100	✔							
Total	36	12	19	10	4	6	12	1

Name of Child: Sara

SEMANTIC ROLES SUMMARY

Total Number of Semantically Coded Utterances = __77__ = __77.0__ % of Total Utterances

Percentage of Total Semantic Roles Accounted For By Each Semantic Role:

- Action = __19.1__ %
- Locative = __8.9__ %
- Agent = __10.2__ %
- Object = __5.1__ %
- Demonstrative = __7.6__ %
- Recurrence = __—__ %
- Possessor = __0.6__ %
- Quantifier = __2.0__ %
- Experiencer = __2.0__ %
- Recipient = __—__ %
- Benenficiary = __2.5__ %
- Comitative = __0.6__ %
- Created Object = __2.0__ %
- Instrument = __0.6__ %
- State = __8.3__ %
- Entity (one-term) = __12.7__ %
- Multiterm Entity = __6.4__ %
- Negation = __3.8__ %
- Attribute = __2.0__ %
- Adverbial = __5.7__ %

Total Number of Utterances Coded **Conversational Device** __4__ = __4.0__ % of Total Utterances

Total Number of Utterances Coded **Communication Routine** __6__ = __6.0__ % of Total Utterances

Total Number of Utterances Coded **Complex** __12__ — __12.0__ % of Total Utterances

Total Number of Utterances Coded **Other** __1__ = __1.0__ % of Total Utterances

Name of Child: Sara

BROWN'S PREVALENT SEMANTIC RELATIONS

		Utterance Number	Demonstrative	Attributive	Possessive
Two Term	**Agent**-Action	24, 34, 75			
	Action-**Object**	25, 29, 89			
	Agent-Object		✕	✕	✕
	Demonstrative-**Entity**	5		✕	✕
	Entity-Locative				
	Action-Locative	70, 77	✕	✕	✕
	(–Entity)* **Possessor**-Possession				
	(Recurrence–)* Attribute-Entity	71			
Three Term	Agent-Action-Object	19, 82			
	Agent-Action-Locative	73, 74			
	Action-Object-Locative	58			

*Per Retherford et al. (1981)

Note. Bolded terms show the most common relations.

Guide to Analysis of Language Transcripts

Name of Child __Sara__

BROWN'S PREVALENT SEMANTIC RELATIONS SUMMARY

Two-Term Prevalent Semantic Relations   **Expansions**

__3__ **Agent**-Action   __0__ Dem   __0__ Att   __0__ Poss.   = __0__

__3__ Action-**Object**   __0__ Dem   __0__ Att   __0__ Poss.   = __0__

__0__ Agent-Object

__1__ Demonstrative-**Entity**   __0__ Att   __0__ Poss.   = __0__

__0__ **Entity**-Locative   __0__ Dem   __0__ Att   __0__ Poss.   = __0__

__2__ Action-Locative

__0__ **Possessor**-Possession   __0__ Dem   __0__ Att   = __0__

__1__ Attribute-Entity   = __0__ Total Expansions

__10__ Total Two-Term Utterances

Three-Term Prevalent Semantic Relations

__2__ Agent-Action-Object

__2__ Agent-Action-Locative

__1__ Action-Object-Locative

__5__ Total Three-Term Utterances

__10__ Two-Term Utterances ÷ __41__ Multiterm Utterances = __24.4__ % of Multiterm Utterances Accounted For by Brown's Two-Term Semantic Relations

__10__ Two-Term Utterances ÷ __77__ Semantically Coded Utterances = __13.0__ % of Semantically Coded Utterances Accounted For by Brown's Two-Term Semantic Relations

__0__ Total Expansions ÷ __41__ Multiterm Utterances = __0__ % of Semantically Coded Utterances Accounted For by Expansions of Brown's Prevalent Semantic Relations

__5__ Three-Term Utterances ÷ __41__ Multiterm Utterances = __12.2__ % of Multiterm Utterances Accounted For by Brown's Three-Term Semantic Relations

__5__ Three-Term Utterances ÷ __77__ Semantically Coded Utterances = __6.5__ % of Semantically Coded Utterances Accounted For by Brown's Three-Term Relations

Name of Child: Sara

TEMPLIN'S TYPE-TOKEN RATIO ANALYSIS

Nouns	Verbs	Adjectives	Adverbs	Prepositions
cup	put I	swing I	now I	in I
table	sit I	two	down II	on I
pancakes I	do I	shelter I	time	to
girl	lays		here	for II
Beret	sitting		like	at
milk	are		inside II	with
Mama	gonna I			
daddy	eat			
children	's IIII			
Mark	go IIII			
Kristen	isn't			
Pete	playing			
set	is I			
teetotter	don't			
teetot II	know			
birdseed	goes			
sand	play			
house III	can			6 10
cow I				**Others**
people I				oops
he-mans I				um I
Kristi's				
kids				
23 32	18 32	3 5	6 11	2 3

"Swing set" is counted as two words in this analysis per Templin's rules.

(continues)

TEMPLIN'S TYPE-TOKEN RATIO ANALYSIS (continued)

Pronouns	Conjunctions	Negatives/ Affirmatives	Articles	Wh- Words
it IIII	'cuz	yeah III	the III	how
you	and	no	a	where
this HH	but			who
she I	also I			what
they I				
that I				
he				
I				
we I				
9 22	4 5	2 5	2 5	4 4

Total Number of Different:

Nouns ___23___
Verbs ___18___
Adjectives ___3___
Adverbs ___6___
Prepositions ___6___
Others ___2___
Pronouns ___9___
Conjunctions ___4___
Negatives/Affirmatives ___2___
Articles ___2___
Wh- Words ___4___

Total Number of Different Words: ___79___

$\frac{79 - 120.4}{27.6} = -1.5$

Total Number of:

Nouns ___32___
Verbs ___32___
Adjectives ___5___
Adverbs ___11___
Prepositions ___10___
Others ___3___
Pronouns ___22___
Conjunctions ___5___
Negatives/Affirmatives ___5___
Articles ___5___
Wh- Words ___4___

Total Number of Words: ___134___

$\frac{134 - 268.8}{72.6} = -1.86$

$$\frac{\text{Total Number of Different Words}}{\text{Total Number of Words}} \quad \frac{79}{134} = .5895 = \underline{.59} \quad \text{Type-Token Ratio (TTR)}$$

STRUCTURAL STAGE ANALYSIS

Name of Child: Sara

Annotations:
- "Swingset" considered one morpheme (utterances 3, 6)
- Response to yes/no question (utterance 5)
- Article in prep phrase (utterance 26)
- The dummy "do" does not make a complex sentence. (utterance 33)
- This sentence contains "and," but it does not conjoin two sentences. (utterance 50)

Utterance Number	Number of Morphemes	Negation	Yes/No Question	Wh- Question	Noun Phrase	Verb Phrase	Complex Sentence
1	2	—	—	—	I-II	—	—
2	3	—	—	—	III	—	—
3	2	—	—	—	III	—	—
4	4	—	—	—	LIV/EV	LV	—
5	4	—	—	—	III	—	—
6	4	—	—	—	III	LV	—
7	4	—	—	—	—	III	EIV
8	1	—	—	—	I-II	—	—
9	4	EIV-LIV/EV	—	—	LIV/EV	III	—
10	5	EIV-LIV/EV	—	—	LIV/EV	III	—
11	5	—	—	—	LIV/EV	LV	V+
12	1	—	—	—	I-II	—	—
13	2	—	—	—	—	I-II	—
14	1	—	—	—	—	—	—
15	3	—	—	—	LIV/EV	III	—
16	5	—	—	—	III	LV	—
17	5	—	—	—	III	LV	—
18	1	—	—	—	—	I-II	—
19	4	—	—	—	LIV/EV	III	—
20	4	—	—	—	LIV/EV	III	—
21	3	EIV-LIV/EV	—	—	—	—	—
22	4	—	—	—	III	LV	—
23	4	—	—	—	LIV/EV	III	—
24	3	—	—	—	LIV/EV	I-II	—
25	4	—	—	—	II	I-II	—
26	6	—	—	—	III	I-II	—
27	1	—	—	—	—	—	—
28	1	—	—	—	I-II	—	—
29	3	—	—	—	II	I-II	—
30	5	—	—	EIV	LIV/EV	III	—
31	2	—	—	—	—	I-II	—
32	5	—	—	—	LIV/EV	LV	—
33	2	—	—	—	—	I-II	II
34	4	—	—	—	LIV/EV	V+	II
35	2	—	—	—	I-II	—	—
36	5	—	—	—	LIV/EV	LV	EIV
37	4	—	—	EIV	III	LV	—
38	2	—	—	—	I-II	—	—
39	6	EIV-LIV/EV	EI-III	—	LIV/EV	LIV/EV	V+
40	2	—	—	—	I-II	—	—
41	1	—	—	—	I-II	—	—
42	1	—	—	—	—	—	—
43	1	—	—	—	I-II	—	—
44	5	—	—	—	III	V+	—
45	1	—	—	—	I-II	—	—
46	3	—	—	III	I-II	—	—
47	3	—	—	—	III	LV	—
48	1	—	—	—	I-II	—	—
49	1	—	—	—	—	I-II	—
50	6	—	—	—	LIV/EV	V+	II
Subtotal 1	155						

STRUCTURAL STAGE ANALYSIS (continued)

Annotations:
- Utterances 52, 55, 56, 68: Singsong fillers
- Utterance 54 Complex Sentence (LIV/EV): "The elliptical 'yeah [it is]' is conjoined to the next sentence with 'but.'"
- Utterance 86 Complex Sentence: "There is no verb, so the utterance cannot be complex."

Utterance Number	Number of Morphemes	Negation	Yes/No Question	Wh- Question	Noun Phrase	Verb Phrase	Complex Sentence
51	1	—	—	—	I–II	—	—
52	—	—	—	—	—	—	—
53	3	—	—	—	III	V+	—
54	6	—	—	—	LIV/EV	LV	LIV/EV
55	—	—	—	—	—	—	—
56	—	—	—	—	—	—	—
57	4	EIV–LIV/EV	—	—	LIV/EV	III	—
58	4	—	—	—	II	I–II	—
59	1	—	—	—	—	—	—
60	4	—	—	—	III	LV	—
61	1	—	—	—	—	—	—
62	1	—	—	—	—	—	—
63	3	—	—	—	I–II	—	—
64	3	—	—	—	I–II	—	—
65	1	—	—	—	—	—	—
66	3	—	—	—	I–II	—	—
67	5	—	—	—	III	LV	—
68	—	—	—	—	—	—	—
69	4	—	—	—	LIV/EV	—	—
70	4	—	—	—	III	I–II	—
71	2	—	—	—	I–II	—	—
72	7	—	—	—	III	III	—
73	3	—	—	—	LIV/EV	III	—
74	3	—	—	—	LIV/EV	III	—
75	2	—	—	—	LIV/EV	III	—
76	5	—	—	—	LIV/EV	LV	V+
77	2	—	—	—	—	I–II	—
78	1	—	—	—	I–II	—	—
79	3	—	—	—	III	—	—
80	5	—	—	—	LIV/EV	LV	—
81	3	—	—	—	II	I–II	—
82	3	—	—	—	LIV/EV	LV	—
83	7	—	—	—	III	LV	—
84	1	—	—	—	—	—	—
85	1	—	—	—	—	—	—
86	6	—	—	—	LIV/EV	—	—
87	2	—	—	—	III	—	—
88	1	—	—	—	—	—	—
89	6	—	—	—	III	I–II	—
90	7	—	—	—	LIV/EV	V+	—
91	4	—	—	—	III	—	—
92	5	—	—	—	III	LV	—
93	3	—	—	—	I–II	—	—
94	1	—	—	—	—	—	—
95	1	—	—	—	—	—	—
96	1	—	—	—	—	—	—
97	4	EIV–LIV/EV	—	—	III	LV	—
98	5	—	—	EIV	III	—	—
99	3	—	—	—	—	—	—
100	1	—	—	—	—	—	—
Subtotal 2	146						

[155] + [146] = 301
No. of Morphemes (Subtotal 1) + No. of Morphemes (Subtotal 2) = Total No. of Morphemes

$$\frac{\text{Total No. of Morphemes}}{\text{Total No. of Utterances}} = \frac{[301]}{[96]} = 3.14 \text{ MLU}$$

Annotation on denominator (96): 4–0 morphemes (fillers)

Name of Child __Sara__

LENGTH DISTRIBUTION ANALYSIS

Length in Morphemes	Tally	Total
1	ЖЖ ЖЖ ЖЖ ЖЖ ЖЖ	25
2	ЖЖ ЖЖ II	12
3	ЖЖ ЖЖ ЖЖ III	18
4	ЖЖ ЖЖ ЖЖ IIII	19
5	ЖЖ ЖЖ III	13
6	ЖЖ I	6
7	III	3
8		0
9		0
10		0
11		0
12		0
13		0
14		0
15		0

Upper Bound Length = __7__ morpheme(s)

Lower Bound Length = __1__ morpheme(s)

4-0 morphemes (fillers)

Name of Child: Sara

GRAMMATICAL MORPHEMES ANALYSIS

Grammatical Morpheme	Obligatory Context	Use	% Correct Use in Obligatory Contexts
1. -ing	13, 15, 19, 24, 25, 33, 39, 81, 89	13, 24, 25, 33, 39, 81, 89	78
2. plural -s	1, 35, 40, 72, 89, 91	1, 35, 40, 72, 89, 91	100
3. in	26, 70, 79, 91	26, 70, 79, 91	100
4. on	29, 50, 89, 92	29, 50, 89, 92	100
5. possessive -s	69	69	100
6. regular past tense -ed	76, 80	76, 80	100
7. irregular past tense	82	82	100
8. regular third-person singular present tense -s	32, 67, 83, 92	32, 67, 83, 92	100
9. articles a, an, the	2, 3, 4, 5, 6, 16, 17, 23, 26, 44, 60, 70, 72, 79, 83, 86, 87, 89, 90, 91, 98	2, 3, 4, 5, 6, 16, 17, 23, 26, 44, 60, 70, 72, 79, 83, 86, 87, 89, 90, 91, 98	100
10. contractible copula	4, 5, 6, 11, 16, 17, 22, 36, 37, 47, 54, 60, 86, 97	4, 6, 11, 16, 17, 22, 36, 37, 47, 54, 60, 97	86
11. contractible auxiliary	15, 19, 24, 34, 50	34, 50	40
12. uncontractible copula	44, 53, 90	44, 53, 90	100
13. uncontractible auxiliary	39	39	—
14. irregular third-person singular present tense	—	—	—

Name of Child: Sara

PRODUCTION CHARACTERISTICS SUMMARY

Stage	Grammatical Morphemes	Negation	Yes/No Questions	Wh- Questions	Complex Sentences	Stage	Noun Phrase	Verb Phrase
Early I			↓			I	↓	↓
Late I/ Early II		↓		↓		II	|||| |||| |||| |||| ||||	|||| ||||
II	1. 78% 2. 100% 3. 100%	|		||||	||	III	|||| |||| |||| |||| ||||	|||| |||| |||
III	4. 100% 5. 100%		|	|			✕	✕
Early IV		↓		|||	|||			
Late IV/ Early V		||||			|		|||| |||| |||| |||| |||| |	|
Late V	6. 100% 7. 100% 8. 100% 9. 100% 10. 86%							|||| |||| |||| ||||
V+	11. 40% 12. 100% 13. 100% 14. —				|||			||||
V++								

Name of Child __Sara__

DATA SUMMARY AND INTERPRETATION

Mean Length of Utterance in Morphemes (MLU)

_____3.14_____ morphemes

Structural Stage by MLU: Stage _____EIV_____

Upper Bound Length: _____7_____ morpheme(s)

Lower Bound Length: _____1_____ morpheme(s)

CA=58 mos.
use 57 mos. figures
3.14−5.32 = −1.94
*   1.125*

	Most Typical Stage	Most Advanced Stage
Grammatical Morphemes:	Stage LV	Stage V+
Negation:	Stage EIV-LIV/EV	Stage EIV-LIV/EV
Yes/No Questions:	Stage EI-III	Stage EI-III
Wh- Questions:	Stage EIV	Stage EIV
Noun Phrase:	Stage LIV/EV	Stage LIV/EV
Verb Phrase:	Stage LV	Stage V+
Complex Sentences:	Stage EIV, V+	Stage V+

Comments: _MLU stage is higher than Most Typical Stage for Yes/No Questions; commensurate with Negation and Wh- Questions; lower than Grammatical Morphemes, Noun Phrase and Verb Phrase; and split for Complex Sentences. Gaps between the Most Typical and the Most Advanced Stage for Grammatical Morphemes and Verb Phrases. No gap for all others. MLU almost 2 standard deviations below mean._

Name of Child __Sara__

DORE'S CONVERSATIONAL ACTS ANALYSIS

Total	%	Adult Utterance Number	Act	Child Utterance Number	Total	%
91	79.8	1, 2, 3, 4, 5, 6, 7, 8, 9, 10, 11, 12, 13, 14, 15, 16, 17, 18, 19, 21, 22, 24, 25, 26, 29, 30, 31, 33, 36, 37, 38, 39, 42, 43, 44, 45, 47, 50, 51, 52, 53, 55, 56, 58, 59, 60, 61, 62, 63, 65, 66, 67, 68, 69, 70, 71, 73, 74, 75, 76, 77, 78, 79, 80, 81, 82, 83, 86, 87, 88, 89, 90, 91, 92, 93, 94, 96, 98, 99, 100, 102, 104, 105, 107, 108, 109, 110, 111, 112, 113, 114	Request	30, 37, 39, 47, 58, 62, 98	7	7
4	3.5	48, 49, 57, 72	Response to Request	1, 2, 3, 4, 5, 7, 8, 9, 11, 12, 13, 16, 18, 19, 20, 21, 24, 25, 28, 29, 31, 33, 34, 35, 38, 40, 41, 42, 43, 45, 46, 48, 49, 51, 52, 54, 55, 56, 57, 59, 60, 61, 63, 64, 65, 66, 69, 70, 71, 72, 75, 77, 78, 79, 81, 82, 84, 85, 87, 88, 89, 93, 94, 95, 96, 99, 100	67	67
0	0		Description	6, 15, 17, 23, 44, 53, 73, 74, 76, 80, 91, 97	12	12
8	7	20, 23, 35, 41, 64, 85, 101, 106	Statement	10, 22, 26, 32, 36, 50, 67, 83, 86, 90, 92	11	11
9	7.9	27, 28, 34, 40, 54, 84, 95, 97, 103	Acknowledgment		0	0
1	.9	46	Organizational Device		0	0
0	0		Performative	14, 68	2	2
1	.9	32	Miscellaneous	27	1	1

CONVERSATIONAL MOVES AND APPROPRIATENESS JUDGMENTS ANALYSIS

Name of Child: Sara

ADULT

UTT#	Conversational Moves		Appropriateness Judgments		
	Initiating Moves	Responding Moves	Referent Specificity	Contributional Conciseness	Communication Style
1	N		✓	✓	
2	E		✓	✓	
3	E		✓	✓	
4	E		✓	✓	
5	E		✓	✓	
6	E		✓	✓	
7	E		✓	✓	
8	E		✓	✓	
9	E		✓	✓	
10	E		✓	✓	
11	E		✓	✓	
12	E		✓	✓	
13	E		✓	✓	
14	E		✓	✓	
15		E	✓	✓	
16	E		✓	✓	
17	E		✓	✓	
18	E		✓	✓	
19	E		✓	✓	
20		E	✓	✓	
21	E		✓	✓	
22	E		✓	✓	
23		E	✓	✓	
24	E		✓	✓	
25	E		✓	✓	

CHILD

UTT#	Conversational Moves		Appropriateness Judgments		
	Initiating Moves	Responding Moves	Referent Specificity	Contributional Conciseness	Communication Style
1		O	✓	✓	
2		E	✓	✓	
3		R	N/A	N/A	
4		E	✓	✓	
5		E	✓	✓	
6		E	✓	✓	
7		O	✓	✓	
8		E	✓	✓	
9		R	N/A	N/A	
10		E	✓	✓	
11		O	✓	✓	
12		O	✓	✓	
13		E	✓	✓	
14	N				
15		E	✓	✓	
16		E	✓	✓	
17		O	✓	✓	
18		E	✓	✓	
19		E	✓	✓	
20		E	✓	✓	
21		E	✓	✓	
22		E	✓	✓	
23		E	✓	✓	
24		R	N/A	N/A	

CONVERSATIONAL MOVES AND APPROPRIATENESS JUDGMENTS ANALYSIS (continued)

ADULT

UTT#	Conversational Moves		Appropriateness Judgments		
	Initiating Moves	Responding Moves	Referent Specificity	Contributional Conciseness	Communication Style
26	E		✓	✓	
27		R	N/A	N/A	
28		A	✓	✓	
29	E		✓	✓	
30	E		✓	✓	
31			✓	✓	
32	E	E	✓	✓	
33			✓	✓	
34		A	✓	✓	
35		E	✓	✓	
36	E		✓	✓	
37	E		✓	✓	
38	E		✓	✓	
39	E		✓	✓	
40		A	✓	✓	
41		A	✓	✓	
42	E		✓	✓	
43	E		✓	✓	
44	E		✓	✓	
45	E		✓	✓	
46	E		✓	✓	
47	E		✓	✓	
48		E	✓	✓	
49		Y	✓	✓	
50	E		✓	✓	

CHILD

UTT#	Conversational Moves		Appropriateness Judgments		
	Initiating Moves	Responding Moves	Referent Specificity	Contributional Conciseness	Communication Style
26		E	✓	✓	
27		R	N/A	N/A	
28		O	✓	✓	
29		E	✓	✓	
30	E		✓	✓	
31		O	✓	✓	
32		E	✓	✓	
33		O	✓	✓	
34		E	✓	✓	
35		O	✓	✓	
36	N		✓	✓	
37	N		—	✓	
38		Y	✓	✓	
39	E		✓	✓	
40		O	✓	✓	
41		O	✓	✓	
42		Y	✓	✓	
43		O	✓	✓	
44		E	✓	✓	
45		O	✓	✓	
46		E	✓	✓	
47	E		✓	✓	
48		O	✓	✓	
49		O	✓	✓	
50		E	✓	✓	

CONVERSATIONAL MOVES AND APPROPRIATENESS JUDGMENTS ANALYSIS (continued)

ADULT

UTT#	Conversational Moves		Appropriateness Judgments		
	Initiating Moves	Responding Moves	Referent Specificity	Contributional Conciseness	Communication Style
51	E		✓	✓	
52	E		✓	✓	
53	E		✓	✓	
54		A	✓	✓	
55	E		✓	✓	
56	E		✓	✓	
57		E	✓	✓	
58	E		✓	✓	
59	E		✓	✓	
60	E		✓	✓	
61	E		✓	✓	
62	E		✓	✓	
63	E		✓	✓	
64		E	✓	✓	
65	E		✓	✓	
66	E		✓	✓	
67		S	✓	✓	
68	E		✓	✓	
69	E		✓	✓	
70	E		✓	✓	
71	E		✓	✓	
72		E	✓	✓	
73	E		✓	✓	
74	E		✓	✓	
75	E		✓	✓	

CHILD

UTT#	Conversational Moves		Appropriateness Judgments		
	Initiating Moves	Responding Moves	Referent Specificity	Contributional Conciseness	Communication Style
51		O	✓	✓	
52		E	✓	✓	
53	N		—	✓	
54		E	✓	✓	
55		E	—	✓	
56		S	—	✓	
57		E	✓	✓	
58		E	✓	✓	
59		O	✓	✓	
60		E	✓	✓	
61		Y	—	✓	
62	E		—	✓	
63		E	✓	✓	
64		S	—	✓	
65		Y	—	✓	
66		E	✓	✓	
67		E	—	✓	
68		E	✓	✓	
69		E	✓	✓	
70		O	✓	✓	
71		E	✓	✓	
72		E	✓	✓	
73		E	✓	✓	
74		R	N/A	N/A	
75		E	✓	✓	

CONVERSATIONAL MOVES AND APPROPRIATENESS JUDGMENTS ANALYSIS (continued)

ADULT

UTT#	Conversational Moves		Appropriateness Judgments		
	Initiating Moves	Responding Moves	Referent Specificity	Contributional Conciseness	Communication Style
76	E		✓	✓	
77	E		✓	✓	
78	E		✓	✓	
79	E		✓	✓	
80	E		✓	✓	
81	E		✓	✓	
82	E		✓	✓	
83	E		✓	✓	
84		R	N/A	N/A	
85		E	✓	✓	
86	E		✓	✓	
87	E		✓	✓	
88	E		✓	✓	
89	E		✓	✓	
90	E		✓	✓	
91	E		✓	✓	
92	E		✓	✓	
93	E		✓	✓	
94	E		✓	✓	
95		A	✓	✓	
96	E		✓	✓	
97		A	✓	✓	
98	E		✓	✓	
99	E		✓	✓	
100		E	✓	✓	

CHILD

UTT#	Conversational Moves		Appropriateness Judgments		
	Initiating Moves	Responding Moves	Referent Specificity	Contributional Conciseness	Communication Style
76		E	✓	✓	
77		E	✓	✓	
78		O	✓	✓	
79		E	✓	✓	
80	R		✓	✓	
81		E	—	✓	
82		S	✓	✓	
83	N		—	✓	
84		Y	✓	✓	
85		O	✓	✓	
86		E	✓	✓	
87		O	—	✓	
88		Y	✓	✓	
89		E	✓	✓	
90		E	—	✓	
91		E	✓	✓	
92		E	✓	✓	
93		E	✓	✓	
94		O	✓	✓	
95		O	✓	✓	
96		O	✓	✓	
97		E	✓	✓	
98	E		✓	✓	
99		E	✓	✓	
100		O	NK	NK	NK

CONVERSATIONAL MOVES AND APPROPRIATENESS JUDGMENTS ANALYSIS (continued)

ADULT

UTT#	Conversational Moves		Appropriateness Judgments		
	Initiating Moves	Responding Moves	Referent Specificity	Contributional Conciseness	Communication Style
101		S			
102	E		✓	✓	
103		A	✓	✓	
104	E		✓	✓	
105	E		✓	✓	
106	N		✓	✓	
107	E		✓	✓	
108	E		✓	✓	
109	E		✓	✓	
110	E		✓	✓	
111	E		✓	✓	
112	E		✓	✓	
113	E		NK	NK	NK
114	E				

CHILD

UTT#	Conversational Moves		Appropriateness Judgments		
	Initiating Moves	Responding Moves	Referent Specificity	Contributional Conciseness	Communication Style

Name of Child: Sara

CONVERSATIONAL MOVES AND APPROPRIATENESS JUDGMENTS SUMMARY

Child's Total Utterances 100

CONVERSATIONAL MOVES

INITIATING MOVES	5	New Topic Introduction	=	5	% of Total Utterances
	1	Restarting Old Topic	=	1	% of Total Utterances
	5	Eliciting Verbal Response	=	5	% of Total Utterances
	0	Intruding	=	—	% of Total Utterances
RESPONDING MOVES	0	Acknowledging	=	—	% of Total Utterances
	6	Yes/No Responses	=	6	% of Total Utterances
	25	One-Word Answers	=	25	% of Total Utterances
	5	Repeating	=	5	% of Total Utterances
	3	Sustaining Topic	=	3	% of Total Utterances
	50	Extending Topic	=	50	% of Total Utterances
FALSE STARTS	0		=	—	% of Total Utterances

APPROPRIATENESS JUDGMENTS

Referent Specificity	12	Lacked Specificity	=	12	% of Total Utterances
Contributional Conciseness	0	Lacked Conciseness	=	—	% of Total Utterances
Communication Style	0	Lacked Stylistic Variation	=	—	% of Total Utterances

Adult's Total Utterances 114

CONVERSATIONAL MOVES

INITIATING MOVES	2	New Topic Introduction	=	1.8	% of Total Utterances
	0	Restarting Old Topic	=	—	% of Total Utterances
	88	Eliciting Verbal Response	=	77.2	% of Total Utterances
	0	Intruding	=	—	% of Total Utterances
RESPONDING MOVES	8	Acknowledging	=	7	% of Total Utterances
	1	Yes/No Responses	=	.9	% of Total Utterances
	0	One-Word Answers	=	—	% of Total Utterances
	2	Repeating	=	1.8	% of Total Utterances
	2	Sustaining Topic	=	1.8	% of Total Utterances
	11	Extending Topic	=	9.6	% of Total Utterances
FALSE STARTS	0		=	—	% of Total Utterances

APPROPRIATENESS JUDGMENTS

Referent Specificity	0	Lacked Specificity	=	—	% of Total Utterances
Contributional Conciseness	0	Lacked Conciseness	=	—	% of Total Utterances
Communication Style	0	Lacked Stylistic Variation	=	—	% of Total Utterances

© 2019 by PRO-ED, Inc.

APPENDIX F   UNANALYZED TRANSCRIPTS (PAUL AND LUIS)

PAUL'S TRANSCRIPT 196

LUIS'S TRANSCRIPT 206

TRANSCRIPT (PAUL)

Name of Child	Paul		Chronological Age	4-0
Type of Situation	free play; book reading		Date	5-8
Length of Recording	55 minutes	Length of Transcript 100 utterances	Time of Day	morning
Materials Present	box containing bubbles, flag, puppet; books from home			
People Present	P = Paul; C = Chloe; student clinician; M = Mother			

ADULT	CONTEXT	CHILD	
	(Paul and the clinician are blowing bubbles in a clinic room)		
	(C blows bubbles)		
		there it goes/	1
	(C laughs)		
	(P waves the flag in the bubbles)		
Hvo ho/			
		/baɪ fwɛg/ [bye flag]	2
Lots of bubbles/			
		/fwɛg/ [flag]	3
	(P pops all of the bubbles)		
		/ədʌd/ [all done]	4
All done?			
		/ʌpɑp/ [pop]	5
More?			
		more/	imitation
Okay/			
	(C blows bubbles)		
More bubbles/			
		/ədʌd/ [all done]	6
More bubbles/			
	(P holds up a flag)		
		/ʌ fwɛg/ [a flag]	7
		/ɑ gɑ fwɛg/ [I got flag]	8
You've got the flag?			
		/keɪ/ [okay]	9
Okay/			
	(C prepares to blow bubbles)		
		/bɪg bwo/ [big blow]	10
Okay big blow/			
	(C blows bubbles)		

ADULT	CONTEXT	CHILD	
		/keɪ/ [okay]	imitation
		oh oh/	11
Whoa/			
	(P waves flag in bubbles)		
		/ʌ fwɛg/ [a flag]	12
Oh/			
		/ʌgɪ fwɛg/	uninterpretable
Look at the flag go/			
The flag is popping the bubbles/			
		/bwo bʌboʊz/ [blow bubbles]	13
	(C and P jump on bubbles)		
		pop pop/	14
Let's jump/			
		XXX jump/	unintelligible
		pop/	15
Jump on the bubbles/			
		pop/	16
	(P pops all bubbles)		
Okay/			
Here's some more/			
		/u/	uninterpretable
	(C blows more bubbles)		
	(C blows the bubbles high)		
Okay we're really high/			
		/wu/	uninterpretable
Ooh the bubbles are high/			
	(P laughs)		
		/uʌ/	uninterpretable
	(P waving flag in bubbles)	/fwɛg/ [flag]	17
The flag/			
Oh the flag is popping bubbles/			
	(P jumping on bubbles)	/bum bu/ [boom boom]	18
		/ədʌd/ [all done]	19
All done with bubbles?			
	(P grabs the bubble jar)		
		/ɑvə hiɝ/ [over here]	20

ADULT	CONTEXT	CHILD	
	(P puts bubbles in the box)		
Okay/			
		XXX/	unintelligible
	(P takes a puppet out of the box and then drops it)		
Oh/			
	(P makes a monster sound)		
		uh oh/	21
		/ʊmə/	uninterpretable
Oh/			
A monster/			
		/ʌm it↑/ [him eat?]	22
He'll eat?			
		/keɪ/ [okay]	23
Okay/			
	(P picking up the puppet)	uh oh/	24
	(P shaking the puppet)	/wʌtzæt↑/ [what's that?]	25
		/hi du gi ti/ XXX	unintelligible
He's going to eat/			
		/keɪ/ [okay]	26
The monster's going to eat/			
		XXX/	unintelligible
		/ʌm it/ [him eat]	27
	(P makes the monster move toward the flag)		
Oh/			
There he goes/			
		there he go/	imitation
		XXX/	unintelligible
		ow/	28
	(P makes the puppet eat the flag)		
The monster is eating the flag/			
		/fwɛg/ [flag]	imitation
		/gɪdɪt/ [get it]	29
		/u bu/ XXX	uninterpretable
		/fwɛg/ [flag]	30
The flag/			

ADULT	CONTEXT	CHILD	
	(the puppet hits P's head)		
		ow!/	31
Oh no/			
The monster bumped his head/			
		ow/	32
		XXX/	unintelligible
		/dʌ fwɛg/ [the flag]	33
We'll hug him/			
	(P lays his head on top of the flag on the floor)		
		XXX/	unintelligible
		night-night/	34
Oh no/			
	(P singing)	XXX/	unintelligible
	(the object sticks to the flag)		
It's stuck/			
Look/			
Ick/			
	(P sings)		
		funny/	35
	(P waves the flag)		
		/fwɛg/ [flag]	36
I'm going to eat the flag/	(C making the monster talk)		
	(the puppet grabs the flag)		
		/fwɛgən/ [flag]	37
	(the puppet waves the flag)		
		/uh oh/	38
The monster is waving the flag/			
	(P laughs)		
		/ʌ fwɛg/ [a flag]	39
		/ʌm it/ [him eat]	40
Eat?			
	(C makes the puppet eat the flag)		
		/keɪ/ [okay]	41
		ow/	42
What happened?			
		/ʌmə mɑnθu/ [the monster]	43

ADULT	CONTEXT	CHILD	
		eat↑/	44
The monster _____ /			
		/keɪ/ [okay]	45
The monster ate the flag/			
	•		
	•		
	•		
	(clinician leaves the room; mom and Paul are reading books)		
What's that baby doing?	(M pointing to a picture)		
		huh↑/	46
What's he doing?	(M pointing to another picture on the next page)		
		/ʌm it/ [him eat]	47
He's eating/			
What's this baby doing?			
		huh↑/	48
What's she doing?			
		doing cups/	49
Stacking her cups/			
Yes/			
		XXX/	unintelligible
What's she doing?			
What's she doing?	(M pointing to the page)		
	(P pointing to the page)	this is baby/	50
Baby/			
	(M pointing to a baby on the page)		
She's taking the baby for a walk?			
		XXX/	unintelligible
	(P points to a picture)		
She's watering the flowers/			
See she's pouring water in/	(M pointing to flowers in the book)		
All the pretty flowers/			
	(P flips the page)		
		swing/	51
He's swinging/			

ADULT	CONTEXT	CHILD	
		wee/	52
What color are his boots?	(M pointing to boots in the book)		
		huh↑/	53
What color are his boots?			
	(P signing blue)	/bwu/ [blue]	54
No/			
	(P signing yellow)	/jeɪjoʊ/ [yellow]	55
Yellow good/			
What's this one doing?			
What's that boy doing?	(M pointing to a picture in the book)		
		/ʌgə bʊks/ [lookit books]	56
He's reading books/			
Yes/			
He's reading books/			
		uh oh/	57
Uh oh/			
		/goʊɪŋ swip↑/ [going sleep]	58
He's going to sleep/			
What do you say when you go to sleep?			
	(P pointing to a picture in the book)	her going bath/	59
He's taking a bath/			
And what does he have here?	(M pointing to a boat in the book)		
		a boat/	60
A boat/			
What do you say when you go night-night?			
		huh↑/	61
	(M points to a picture in the book)		
Do you have to sing a song?			
		/keɪ/ [okay]	62
Can you sing rock-a-bye?			
		/keɪ/ [okay]	63
Sing rock-a-bye baby/			
	(P pounding on the book)	bye Momma/	64
Rock-a-bye/			
		Momma/	65

ADULT	CONTEXT	CHILD	
Momma?			
In the tree/			
	(P slapping the book)	top bye-bye/	66
Bye-bye/			
When the wind/			
	(P closes the book)		
		/bwoz/ [blows]	67
The cradle will/			
		/rɑ/ [rock]	68
When the bow/			
	(P pointing to pictures in the back of book)	two/ (wh)	69
What's up here?			
What what are those?			
How many?	(M pointing to pictures)		
Can you count?			
Can you count?			
Wait you count these/	(M pointing to pictures one at a time)		
Count/			
	(P pointing)	one↗ two/	70
Three:/			
		four/	71
Four/			
	(P picking up another book)	/ʌzæt?/ [what's that]	72
What's that?			
		purple/	73
Another book/			
	(P puts the book in M's lap)		
		her book/	74
What are they s/c what is she doing?	(M pointing to the object on the front of the book)		
		/pweɪŋ sænd/ [playing sand]	75
She's playing in the sand/			
What's this?	(M pointing to objects on the cover of the book)		
		a cup/	76
A big cup/			
A bucket/			
		/ʌkət/ [bucket]	imitation

ADULT	CONTEXT	CHILD	
A bucket/			
		oh oh boo/	77
Peek-a-boo/			
Can you say peek-a-boo/			
		XXX	unintelligible
		/ʌŋə pɑdɪ/ [having a party]	78
They're going ₛ/c they're having a party a party/			
What do you sing when you have a party?			
	(P points to a clown in the book)		
		/aʊn↑/ [clown]	79
	(M points to a clown in the book)		
A clown?			
You sing Happy Birthday when you have a party?			
		/əkeɪ/ [okay]	80
	(P pounds on the book and sings)		
	(P singing)	XXX/	unintelligible
Then you what?			
What do you do then?			
You blow out the/			
	(P points to a bear in the book)		
		/ʌp ʌbɝ/ [a bear]	81
	(P turns the page)		
A bear?			
You blow out the candles then/			
		/pweɪ ʌ bwoks/ [play a blocks]	82
Playing with the blocks/			
What's this boy doing?	(M pointing to a boy in the book)	XXX/	unintelligible
		XXX/	unintelligible
What are those?			
	(P points to a boy in the book)		
		huh↑/	83
What are these?			
	(M points to crayons in the book)		
		/keɪɑnz/ [crayons]	84
Crayons okay/			

ADULT	CONTEXT	CHILD	
		/goʊ sweɪd/ [go slide]	85
She's going down the slide/			
What do you say when you go down the slide?			
		oh a ball/	86
That's a ball/			
What do you say when you go down the slide?			
		/ʌ sweɪd/ [a slide]	imitation
You say wee/			
		wee/	imitation
Wee/			
What's this boy doing?	(M pointing to a boy in the book)		
		a ball/	87
He's playing with his ball/			
Is he tumbling?			
He's doing a somersault/			
	(P turns the page)		
		xxx	unintelligible
	(P pointing to a picture in the book)	/ʌzɪs?/ [what's this]	88
He's playing in the sand/			
What's this girl?	(M pointing to a girl in the book)		
		/bʌboʊz/ [bubbles]	89
Bubbles/			
What's her bear doing?	(M pointing to a bear in the book)		
		huh↑/	90
Is he blowing the bubbles?			
	(P turns the page)		
		uh oh/	91
		/gəno/ [snow]	92
Can you say snow?			
		/gəno/ [snow]	imitation
Snow/			
	(P pointing to a picture)	/ʌzɪs?/ [what's this]	93
That's snow/			
		/this snow↑/	94
That's snow/			
Has hat on/			

ADULT	CONTEXT	CHILD	
	(M pointing to a hat on the boy in the book)		
		hat on/	imitation
Keep his ears warm/			
Where are your ears?			
		huh ↑/	95
Where are Paul's ears?			
	(P points to a dog's ears in the book)		
		ear/	imitation
That's his ear/			
Where are Paul's ears?			
	(P pointing to his own ears)	there/	96
Ears/			
	(P closes the book and puts it aside)		
		/ədʌd/ [all done]	97
All done?			
Is there anything else?			
	(P picking up another book)	/o wʌzɪs?/ [oh what's this]	98
What's that book?			
		/ʌnə/ [I don't know]	99
		a book/	100

TRANSCRIPT (LUIS)

Name of Child	Luis		Chronological Age	4-9
Type of Situation	waterplay and cars		Date	7-1
Length of Recording	1 hour	Length of Transcript 100 utterances	Time of Day	morning
Materials Present	tub with water, wind-up frog, dolls, cars, trucks, village mat			
People Present	L = Luis; C = clinican; D = Dad			

ADULT	CONTEXT	CHILD	
	(Luis and clinician are putting food coloring in water that will be added to a tub of water for a swimming pool)		
Oh · my fingers are all blue/			
Oh · your fingers are gonna get blue now too/			
		and after this us have go wash our hands/	1
		right/	2
Yeah/			
	(L drops food coloring container in water)		
Oh/			
You even got it on your leg/			
	(L takes food coloring bottle out of a container and claps hands)		
Ha ha/			
Oh/			
	(L holding hands in air)		
		better go wash our hands/	3
We can probably just grab a tissue and wipe them off and wash 'em later/			
Oh should I get a tissue?			
	(L pointing to the box of tissues)		
	(C and L wiping off hands on the tissue)	no watch on my hands/	4
Yeah/			
	(C throws tissue toward wastebasket and misses)		
Whoop/			
I missed/			
Hmmm/			
What next?			
	(C gesturing)		
		hum/	5

Unanalyzed Transcripts (paul and luis)

ADULT	CONTEXT	CHILD	
	(C opens the surprise box)		
	(L pulling the frog out)	little froggie/	6
		how you do this/	7
	(L turning the frog over)	how/	8
Huh/			
		what you do with this?/	9
What do frogs do?			
	(L manipulates frog)		
		they jump/	10
They jump/			
		I wanna XXX him out/ *unintelligible*	
	(C pulls string on frog and frog paddles)		
Ha ha/			
	(L pulling string on frog)	pull it out/	11
Wind it up?			
Ha · he's swimmin'/			
Wonder where frogs like to swim the most?			
		over in · in Florida/	12
In Florida?			
	(L pulls string)		
		XXX mom went there/ *unintelligible*	
You did?			
What did you do there?			
		I didn't go there/	13
		just my mom and dad/	14
Oh/			
	(L picking up frog)	silly froggie/	15
It was?			
They must have gone to Disney World/			
	(L pulls string on frog)		
		not me/	16
No?			
Ha ha/			
Well I bet a frog likes to swim in a pool/			

Guide to Analysis of Language Transcripts

ADULT	CONTEXT	CHILD	
And look what I have/			
	(C shows L a tub of water)		
		some more water↑/	17
Yeah/			
A pool for the frog to swim in/			
		want me XXX out↑/ unintelligible	
	(L pulls string on frog and puts it in the water)		
Oh ha ha/			
	(L takes the frog out of the water)		
		should we go see froggie↑/	18
Oh/			
That's a hard one/			
	(L pulls the string on the frog and puts it in the water)		
Oh ha ha/			
		should we go see↑/	19
You know what else we need?	(C pulling the surprise box closer)		
We need _____ /			
We're gonna have a pool party/			
	(L looks in the surprise box)		
We've got _____ /			
	(C puts a slide in the water)		
		a slide↑/	20
		slide/	21
		a pool party↑/	22
	(L takes doll out of the box and slides it down the slide)		
Yeah/			
Ha ha/			
		how?/	23
		holy we going like this↑/	24
	(L gets another doll out of the box)		
		we put this guy in↑/	25
Oh yeah · I suppose he needs his shoes off doesn't he?			
	(L takes shoes off the doll)		

ADULT	CONTEXT	CHILD	
We'll pull his shirt off too/			
He can swim in his pants/			
	(L slides second doll down the slide)		
Oh · he can just swim in his shirt/			
	(L takes the frog out of the water and water drips on the floor)		
		we need frog out/	26
Oop/			
You need the frog out?			
He'll rest on his lily pad over here/	(C laying a tissue on the floor and putting the frog on it)		
Pool party/			
		pool party/	imitation
She's going to sit over here/	(C sitting the doll in the water)		
		XXX where's the guy/	unintelligible
Whoop/			
He's right there/			
		why him don't wanna go in?/	27
	(L puts male doll in water)		
		him $_{s/c}$ why him don't wanna go in?/	28
Oh no/			
		cool!/	29
		watch in here/	30
	(L dipping the doll in and out of the water)	cool/	31
Wow/			
	(L handing the doll to C to take the shirt off)	take him shirt off/	32
Okay/			
I tried that once before and it didn't work/			
	(C takes the doll's shirt off)		
		now I'm goin' down the slide/	33
	(L making another doll go down the slide)	land in the pool/	34
Oh no/			
Down the slide/			
	(L taking girl dolls out of the water)	take these girls out then gonna do↑/	35
		try that frog again/	36

ADULT	CONTEXT	CHILD	
Okay/			
We'll put the girls on their towels/			
	(L gives the dolls to C and C puts them on the tissue)		
		on towel/	37
There/			
	(L puts the male doll in the water)		
		okay/	38
		this boy wanna go in/	39
Ha ha/			
		look at him/	40
I can slide/			
You can hold this/			
Now he can probably slide down pretty well/			
	(C holds up slide and L attempts to slide the male doll down it)		
Up/			
	(the male doll falls off the slide and lands on the floor)		
	(L sliding male doll down)	try • try girls do it/	41
		try girls/	42
		do it to girls/	43
	(L picks up a girl doll and slides her down the slide)		
	(L picks a girl doll out of the water)		
		take her ponytail out/	44
		XXX take ponytails out/	unintelligible
	(C takes the ponytail out of the water)		
	(C slides the girl doll down the slide)		
There we go/			
		try this girl/	45
Oh no/			
	(L picking up the girl doll)	here I'll do it/	46
	(the tissue sticks to the doll)		
		here I'll do it/	repeat

ADULT	CONTEXT	CHILD	
	(L having the doll walk upstairs and sliding the doll down the slide)	oh they walk up a stairs/	47
Ha ha head first/			
		and let's try a frog/	48
Okay/			
	(L getting a tissue to lay the dolls on)	XXX get/	unintelligible
		here/	49
	(C left the room; Dad and Luis are playing with small cars and trucks)		
	(L holding up a truck)	wanna get this one↑/	50
		right here↑/	51
Yeah/			
Get 'em both/			
Here doesn't that thing slide out?	(D pulling a tray out of the box)		
	(L pointing to the truck)	Daddy I didn't know thems have this truck↑/	52
Yeah · we never seen that one before/			
		uh um/	53
	(L pulling a truck out of the box)	look at this/	54
Hum?			
Remember what we did with this one?	(D picking up the truck)		
		yep/	55
What?			
		put cars in 'em/	56
Yep/			
	(L pointing to another place in the room)	put 'em right over here/	57
		put 'em right over here/	repeat
Well don't we want to load that up like that?			
		just put 'em here/	58
	(L picking up a truck)	XXX gonna do/	unintelligible
Hmm?			
		XXX gonna do/	unintelligible
We're going to get into a little race or what?			
	(L arranging cars)	um hum/	59

ADULT	CONTEXT	CHILD	
Huh?			
	(L nods head)		
Okay/			
Which ones do you want here?			
	(L picks out a car)		
That one?			
Why do you want that one?			
		cause it's cooler/	60
It has a big engine in it?			
	(L nods his head)		
		where your car?/	61
I'll have this one/	(D picking up a car)		
		wait/	62
	(L picking out a car for D)	no this one/	63
Burnhart?			
		ya/	64
I wish it was black/			
		what?/	65
I wish it was black/			
Here's what we'll do/			
		XXX/	unintelligible
Make a little bit of a jump okay?	(D putting a Matchbox car case under mat to make a ramp)		
		see can go over it↑/	66
Yeah/			
		see who can go over it↑/	67
	(L pushes a car)		
Yup/			
Well that's too steep/	(D adjusting the ramp)		
That's kinda neat/			
	(L pushes his car and D pushes his)		
		on your mark • get set/	68
		my guy can't go up it very good/	69
You didn't wait till _____ /			
You took off before I said go/			

ADULT	CONTEXT	CHILD	
	(L retrieves the cars)		
		on your mark· get set · go/	70
	(L and D push the cars)		
		haw haw/	
	(L retrieves the cars)		
Huh?			
	(L letting go)	go/	71
Wait you have to say on your mark · get set/			
	(L retrieves car)		
		on your mark/	72
		get set/	73
	(L pushing a car)	go/	74
	(D pushes a car)		
You won that one so let's put the _____ /			
You have one win/			
	(L looking through the cars)	now I need a different car/	75
Okay · put that over to the side/			
	(L pushing a car)	lookit that one/	76
	(L making a car jumping sound effect)	him just XXX/	unintelligible
	(L gestures to show D how car jumped over the ramp)		
What'd he do?			
		him jumped/	77
Did he?			
		you try it/	78
	(L holding up a car)	you hafta get a roof one/	79
		you hafta get a roof one/	repeat
Why I think this guy'll go/			
Well that one you _____ /			
You threw that one/	(L and D pushing cars)		
	(L gesturing jumping motion with his hand and making car jumping sound effect)	XXX that second one went (sound effect)/	unintelligible
Well · that one took off from about here because it hit the wall over there/			
Let's get uh that truck over here with the flat bed and then we'll tow these cars around/	(D pointing across play area)		

© 2019 by PRO-ED, Inc.

ADULT	CONTEXT	CHILD	
	(L picking up a car)	this are mine/	80
	(L picks up a truck)		
		pull cars/	81
What do you call that buddy?			
		what?/	82
Towing?			
		towing/	imitation
Is that what Daddy does with the wrecker from work?			
Huh?			
	(L puts a trailer on the truck)		
		what?/	83
Towing ₛ/c tow cars			
		uh huh/	84
Here we'll put this guy/			
	(D puts cars on the trailer truck while L puts cars in the trailer truck)		
		I can put lots on/	85
We got ₛ/c we can put a lot of/			
We can put on a lot more if you put these littler ones in there/			
These flat ones?			
Oh look at that/			
	(L holding up a truck)	I wanna try this one/	86
Oh ya/			
That one there has a _____ /			
Looks like it has wings like a firebird on it/			
	(L puts more cars in the trailer)		
Remember that car we drove?			
That white one?			
		ya↑/	87
At work?			
	(L trying to put car in trailer)	this one can't get in/	88
	(L hands D a car that doesn't fit in the trailer)		
This thing doesn't turn/	(D putting the trailer on the truck)		
There/			

ADULT	CONTEXT	CHILD	
		this one can't get it/	89
	(L trying to put a car in)	cuz 'em have big wheels/	90
It won't fit in there?			
		un huh/	91
There/	(D putting a car in)		
		mine can put lots in mine/	92
Huh?			
		mine can put lot over a top/	93
Can you put a lot in there?			
	(L picking up the trailer full of cars)	mine have a heavy truck/	94
Huh?			
		mine is a heavy truck/	95
		XXX *unintelligible*	
		that's what XXX Earnhardt car/ *unintelligible*	
Earnhardt car?			
That is pretty quick/			
See these things drag on the bottom/	(D looking at the bottom of the car)		
Do you have all your stuff in there?			
All your cars?			
	(D hands the car to L; L pushes it)		
See that right here?	(D showing L the bottom of the car)		
Those things are dragging on that carpet and it's slowing it down/			
Feel how sharp they are/	(L feels the bottom of the car)		
Feel 'em?			
		they not sharp/	96
Yeah they are right on the edge/			
Go like that/			
Feel it?			
	(L tries to push the car on carpet)		
That's why that car is dragging/			
		these are on a carpet too/	97
Yeah?			

ADULT	CONTEXT	CHILD	
See they are made for hard floor like what's out in the hallway/			
Then they'd really fly/	(D pushing the car)		
Ooh that one's pretty quick/	(D showing L the car)		
Look at where the engine is on that one/			
		want me try it out quick↑/	98
Huh?			
		can we try it out quick↑/	99
No • not outside/			
Ooh/			
	(L pushing the car)	ooh come watch this/	100

GLOSSARY

ADJECTIVE: A word that describes, identifies, or qualifies a noun, pronoun, or gerund by specifying size, color, number, or other attributes.

ADVERB: A word that describes a verb, an adjective, or other adverbs by specifying time, manner, location, degree, number, or quality.

ARTICLE: Indefinite *a* or *an*, or definite *the*.

AUXILIARY VERB: A verb that has no independent existence in a sentence except to support the main verb (e.g., "He is going home"); auxiliary verbs are typically called "helping verbs" because they help the main verb by adding mood, voice, or tense; simple auxiliaries include *be, can, do, have, may, must, shall, will,* and sometimes *get;* the acquisition of the auxiliary *be* is the only auxiliary that is considered one of Brown's (1973) 14 grammatical morphemes. (See Chapter 3 for a list of Brown's 14 grammatical morphemes.)

BE, FORMS OF: *Am, are, is, was, were, be, being, been.*

CATENATIVE VERB: An early semiauxiliary verb form (e.g., *gonna, wanna, hafta*) without an auxiliary that results from a syllabic reduction of the main verb and an infinitive verb form (e.g., *gonna go = going to go*); Brown (1973) contended that children tend to be partial toward certain catenatives in the early stages of linguistic production and only later use a full range of semiauxiliaries (e.g., *"I gonna go"* versus *"I'm gonna go"*).

CLAUSE: A group of words that includes a subject and a predicate; main or independent clauses may stand alone as a sentence; subordinate or dependent clauses are incomplete and must be used with main clauses to express related ideas.

COMPLEX SENTENCE: A sentence that contains more than one verb phrase; the additional verb phrase may be a full sentence proposition (compound sentence) or assumed within a clause.

CONJUNCTION: A word used to join words, phrases, clauses, or sentences; coordinating conjunctions join words, phrases, or clauses of equivalent value and include *and, but, for, or, nor, either, neither, yet, so,* and *whereas;* subordinating conjunctions are used to join two clauses (a main clause and a dependent clause) and include *although, because, since, while, until, whenever, as, as if,* and others that place a condition on a sentence.

CONTINGENT SPEECH: Speaking turns that are linked to preceding turns by topic (e.g., "I like dogs" [Response] "Me too") and/or other conversational conventions (e.g., "How ya doing?" [Response] "Pretty good. And you?").

DEICTIC: The adjective form of *deixis* (see below).

DEIXIS: The process of using the perspective of the speaker as the reference; the use of spatial, temporal, and/or interpersonal features to mark relationships; deictic pronouns include *this, that, me, you;* deictic verbs include *come, go, bring, take.*

DEMONSTRATIVE: *This, that, these,* or *those,* each of which refers to a specific antecedent and can function as a pronoun (e.g., *that* tastes good) or an adjective (e.g., *that* shirt is green).

DISCOURSE: A unit of language that is larger than the utterance, encompassing at the very least adjacency pairs (e.g., request-response) and including several speaker changes that are linked by a common topic.

DUMMY *DO*: The auxiliary form of the verb *do* that doesn't add meaning to a sentence. Often used to form negative or interrogative sentences. To negate a sentence like "I like cookies," the dummy *do* is inset to create the negative element (i.e., I don't like cookies). In yes/no and *wh-* questions, *do* permits inversion of the auxiliary and noun phrase (e.g., "I like raisins" becomes "Do you like raisins?"). Children "invent" and use the dummy *do* in question forms with rising intonation (e.g., "You do like raisins?") before they invert it in question forms.

ECHOLALIA: The repetition of vocalizations made by another person.

ELABORATED NOUN PHRASE: A noun phrase that has more than two modifiers preceding the noun (e.g., the big black cat) or that has qualifiers such as prepositional phrases or relative clauses following the noun (e.g., the cat with the green eyes).

ELICITED SPEECH: Speech that is drawn out either through imitation by request (e.g., "This is a doggie. Say *doggie*" [Response] "Doggie") or through fill-in-the-blank (e.g., "This is a ____" [Response] "Doggie").

ELLIPSIS: A conversational convention that shortens an utterance based on information from a preceding utterance (e.g., "Who likes raisins?" [Response] "I do" [instead of "I like raisins"]).

EMBEDDED CLAUSE: A clause that is subordinated into a full sentence; see subordinate clause.

FORMAL ASSESSMENT PROCEDURE: A test, format, or inventory that has been standardized on specific populations of individuals.

GERUND: A verb ending in *-ing* that functions as a noun in a sentence (e.g., *jogging* is good for your health); it can be distinguished from the present participle by the fact that the gerund may be preceded by *the* and followed by *of* (e.g., "The making of the movie *Jaws* was on TV").

GERUND PHRASE: A gerund and its modifiers; a gerund phrase can function as the subject of a verb (e.g., "*Counting sheep* puts me to sleep"), the object of a verb (e.g., "I fell asleep *counting sheep*"), or the object of a preposition (e.g., "The monotony of *counting sheep* puts me to sleep").

GRAMMATICAL MORPHEME: A morpheme that adds to the grammatical structure of a word or phrase, including the 14 free and bound morphemes Brown (1973) studied primarily because of the obligatory context each possesses. (See Chapter 3 for a list of Brown's 14 grammatical morphemes.)

ILLOCUTIONARY FORCE: The intended interpretation of an utterance or speech act; the illocutionary force must be combined with a proposition for the speech act to be conveyed.

IMITATIVE SPEECH: Speech that repeats all or part of previous utterances (e.g., "This is a doggie" [Response] "Doggie").

INDEFINITE PRONOUNS: *Anybody, anyone, anything, each, either, everybody, everyone, everything, neither, nobody, no one, nothing, one, somebody, someone, something, both, few, many, several.*

INFINITIVE: A form of the verb that consists of *to* plus a verb; infinitives typically are used as nouns and thus function as subjects or objects of verbs (e.g., *To know* him is *to love* him); infinitives can also be used as adjectives (e.g., "He ran out of places *to hide*") or adverbs ("She was unable *to go*").

INFINITIVE PHRASE: An infinitive plus its modifiers and subject or object; it may be used as an adjective, an adverb, or a noun (e.g., "I wanted *to eat the biggest cookie*").

INFINITIVE PHRASE WITH SUBJECT DIFFERENT FROM THAT OF THE MAIN SENTENCE: An infinitive form of a verb that has a subject that is not the subject of the main verb (e.g., in the sentence "I wanted the train to go chug-chug," the subject of the sentence is *I*, but the subject of the infinitive is *the train*).

INFORMAL ASSESSMENT PROCEDURE: A descriptive analysis procedure based on the techniques used in collecting and interpreting data from research designs.

IRREGULAR PAST TENSE: The form of an irregular verb indicating that an action has already taken place; there is no consistent device for marking the past tense of irregular verbs (e.g., "She *hit* the ball," "She *ran* to first base," "She *struck* out").

IRREGULAR THIRD-PERSON SINGULAR PRESENT TENSE: The irregular form of the third-person singular form of the present tense of a verb (e.g., "She *has* a cold" or "He *does* the dishes after dinner").

LANGUAGE COMPREHENSION: The process of understanding language.

LANGUAGE PRODUCTION: The process of expressing language.

MEAN LENGTH OF UTTERANCE (MLU): The average number of morphemes per utterance.

MODAL AUXILIARY: An auxiliary verb that carries its own meaning and influences the meaning of the main verb; modal auxiliaries include *can, could, may, might, must, ought, shall, should, will,* and *would*; typical meanings are ability (*can*), intent (*will*), obligation (*must*), permission (*may*) and possibility (*might*).

MORPHEME: The smallest unit of meaning in a language, typically root words, but also all prefixes and suffixes in a language.

MULTIPLE EMBEDDINGS: Sentences that contain more than one type of embedding; may include sentences with relative clauses and infinitives or semiauxiliaries (e.g., "I think *we need to pour some water in it*") and infinitives plus relative clauses (e.g., "We looked all over *to find jellies what's my size*").

MULTITERM UTTERANCE: An utterance that contains more than one semantic role or grammatical category (e.g., Agent-Action-Object); there is not a one-to-one relationship between semantic roles or grammatical categories and words in an utterance (e.g., "The boy kicked the ball" has five words and three terms: Agent-Action-Object).

NARRATIVE: A story or description of actual or fictional events; narratives may consist of one of four basic types: recounts, event casts, accounts, or stories.

NEGATIVE SENTENCE: A sentence that contains *no* or *not* within the sentence proposition (e.g., "He is *not* sleeping" or "She wants *no* part of this").

NONCONTINGENT SPEECH: Speaking turns that are not linked to preceding utterances.

NOUN: The name of a person, place, or thing; nouns can be common (e.g., *girl, tree, house, rock*) or proper (*Bridget, Mama, Sara*).

NOUN PHRASE: A noun, or a phrase functioning as a noun, that fulfills the role of subject or object of a verb in a sentence; the only obligatory component of this sentence constituent is a noun or pronoun.

NOUN PHRASE COMPLEMENTS: Words, phrases, or clauses that complete the meaning of a noun or noun phrase; can be a prepositional phrase (e.g., His fear *of flying* is a problem) or a noun clause (e.g., the claim *that the bill was paid* was true). Also see object noun phrase complement.

OBJECT NOUN PHRASE: A phrase that functions as the object of the verb, or predicate, of a sentence; the form of object noun phrases changes developmentally (e.g., "eat *cookie*," or "I ate the *chocolate-chip cookie*").

OBJECT NOUN PHRASE COMPLEMENT: A part of the predicate, or verb phrase, that serves to complement by stating in a different way the object of the verb or noun phrase (e.g., "She made his room a *mess*").

OBLIGATORY CONTEXT: The grammatical obligation of a structure for meaning to be clear; in relation to Brown's (1973) 14 grammatical morphemes, use was judged to be obligatory rather than optional, so that absence of the morpheme would indicate nonacquisition, not choice. (See Chapter 3 for a list of Brown's 14 grammatical morphemes.)

PERFECT TENSES: Pairs of simple tenses (e.g., "I *have written* four letters to the president") and progressive tenses (e.g., "I *have been writing* every week") of verbs indicating that action *was*, *is*, or *will be* completed within a given time.

PERSONAL PRONOUN: A word that takes the place of a noun, including *I*, *you*, *she*, *them*, *his*, and *ours*, among others; order of acquisition in production by Brown's (1973) Stages: I = *I, mine*; II = *my, it, me*; III = *you, your, she, them, he, yours, we, her*; IV = *they, us, him, hers, his*; V = *its, our, ours, myself, yourself, their, theirs*; V+ = *herself, himself, itself, ourselves, yourselves, themselves.*

PHRASE: A group of words that functions as a single part of speech but does not have both a subject and a verb; phrases may be used as a noun ("*The red bird* flew away"), a verb ("I *could have eaten* more cookies"), an adjective ("The cat *with brown stripes* ran away"), or an adverb ("The sun came out *in the afternoon*").

PRAGMATICS: The study of language use independent of language structure; rules and principles that relate the structure of language to its use; a level of linguistic analysis.

PREDICATE OF A SENTENCE: The verb phrase of the sentence; the explanation of the action, condition, or effect of the subject of a sentence (e.g., The little puppies *wagged their tails*).

PREPOSITION: A word that shows how a noun or pronoun is related to another word in a sentence; most prepositions are simple (i.e., consist of one word: *at, in, over, of, to, under, up, from, with*) and introduce a phrase (e.g., *at the store; in the box*); a preposition may be considered a verb particle; in relation to Brown's (1973) 14 grammatical morphemes, only the prepositions in and on are considered. (See pages Chapter 3 for a list of Brown's 14 grammatical morphemes.)

PRESENT PROGRESSIVE *-ING*: The present tense form of a verb with an *-ing* ending indicating ongoing action; the present tense, progressive aspect of a verb (e.g., *going*) that when used in a sentence requires the use of an auxiliary verb (e.g., "She *is kicking* the ball").

PRONOUN: A word that takes the place of a noun.

PROPOSITION OR PROPOSITIONAL COMPLEMENT: The conceptual information contained within an utterance or a speech act; the proposition of a speech act is the speaker's meaning; the proposition must be combined with an intention for the speech act to be conveyed.

PROPOSITIONAL CONTENT: The meaning of a speech act expressed most simply as the noun–verb relationship.

REFERENT: A word that stands for a concrete thing (e. g., the word *ball is* the referent for a real ball; the word *bounces* stands for the activity of bouncing).

REGULAR PAST TENSE: The form of a regular verb indicating that an action has already taken place; the past tense form of a regular verb requires the addition *of -ed* to the verb (e.g., "She *kicked* the ball").

REGULAR THIRD-PERSON SINGULAR PRESENT TENSE *-S*: The regular form of the third-person singular form of the present tense of a verb; the regular third-person singular present tense requires the addition of -s to the verb (e.g., "She *hits* the ball").

RELATIVE CLAUSE: A subordinate clause that is introduced by a relative pronoun (i.e., *who, which, that*, and sometimes the agrammatical *what*; e.g., "My shoes have these holes *what your toes come out*") (see subordinate clause).

RELATIVE PRONOUNS: *Who, which, that*, and sometimes the agrammatical *what*.

SEMANTIC RELATION: A combination of two or more individual semantic roles and/or residual grammatical categories; typically, semantic relations express meanings in addition to the meanings expressed by individual words (e.g., the semantic relation agent-action expresses the relationship between the noun and verb in addition to the meaning expressed by the noun and verb).

SEMANTICS: The study of language content; rules and principles for the expression and understanding of meaning; a level of linguistic analysis.

SEMIAUXILIARY: A word such as *gonna, gotta, wanna,* and *hafta* used with a verb that appears to be the main verb of a sentence (e.g., "He *gonna* go")—including catenatives; the term *semiauxiliary* is really incorrect in that semiauxiliaries are actually semi-infinitives because they are reduced forms of infinitives that appear to function as auxiliaries in sentences (e.g., *gonna* is a reduction of *going to* in relation to a verb).

SEMIAUXILIARY (NOUN PHRASE) COMPLEMENT: A noun phrase that is the complement of the infinitive within the semiauxiliary verb phrase (e.g., "I wanna *pour the water*").

SENTENCE: A subject, or noun phrase (NP), and a predicate, or verb phrase (VP), that together express a complete thought; a sentence can be either simple (i.e., contains only one verb phrase) or complex (i.e., contains more than one verb phrase); in sentence notation, S = sentence; S → NP + VP.

SIMPLE INFINITIVE: The form of a verb consisting of *to* plus the verb; see infinitive.

SIMPLE INFINITIVE CLAUSE: The form of a verb consisting of *to* plus the verb used in a sentence without other sentence constituents (e.g., "I wanted *to go*").

SPEECH ACT: A linguistic unit of communication consisting of a proposition (meaning) and illocutionary force (intention); also considered when analyzing speech acts is the listener's interpretation of the speaker's meaning and intention.

SPONTANEOUS SPEECH: Speech that does not repeat part of preceding utterances.

SUBJECT NOUN PHRASE: A phrase that functions as the subject of the verb (or predicate) of a sentence; the form of subject noun phrases changes developmentally (e.g., "*boy go*" and "*The little boy is* going to school").

SUBJECT OF A SENTENCE: A person, thing, or idea—expressed as a single noun, pronoun, or noun phrase—being described in a sentence.

SUBORDINATE CLAUSE: A group of words, consisting of at least a noun and a verb, that cannot stand alone because it is introduced by a subordinating conjunction (e.g., *although, because, since, while, until, whenever, as, as if*) or a relative pronoun (e.g., *who, which, that,* and sometimes the agrammatical *what*).

SYNTAX: The study of language forms; rules and principles for combining grammatical elements and words into utterances and sentences; a level of linguistic analysis.

THIRD-PERSON SINGULAR PRESENT TENSE: See regular third-person singular present tense and irregular third-person singular present tense.

TOPIC: An aspect of conversation that holds conversation together; a topic may be viewed as old or new in relation to previous utterances; may be manipulated using a variety of linguistic devices (e.g., a comment, a question, a repetition).

TYPE-TOKEN RATIO (TTR): A measure of vocabulary diversity obtained by dividing the number of different words in a sample of 50 utterances by the total number of words.

UNCONTRACTIBLE AUXILIARY OF THE VERB *BE*: The uncontractible form of the verb *be* as an auxiliary verb; uncontractible forms are uncontractible because they cannot be pronounced as a contraction without dropping the syllable (e.g., "The mouse *is* sleeping"), cannot be pronounced as a contraction without losing tense or number information (e.g., "They *were* sleeping"), or cannot be reduced further because they are elliptical (e.g., "Who is going to the picnic?" [Response] "I *am*"); keep in mind that this grammatical morpheme deals with the *uncontractible* auxiliary, not the *uncontracted* auxiliary, so caution should be used in identifying uncontractible forms.

UNCONTRACTIBLE COPULA OF THE VERB *BE*: The uncontractible form of the verb *be* as a main verb; uncontractible forms are uncontractible because they cannot be pronounced as a contraction without dropping a syllable (e.g., "The mouse *is* dead"), cannot be pronounced as a contraction without losing tense or number information (e.g., "She *was* sick"), or cannot be reduced further because they are elliptical (e.g., "Who is hungry?" [Response] "I *am*"); keep in mind that this grammatical morpheme deals with the *uncontractible* copula, not the *uncontracted* copula, so caution should be used in identifying uncontractible forms.

UNMARKED INFINITIVE CLAUSE: An infinitive clause in which the *to* is not stated but is implied from the sentence structure (e.g., "Help me [*to*] pick these up"); usually introduced by *let, help, watch, make, need, see, hear,* or *feel*.

VERB: A word that depicts action or state of being; verbs typically function as the predicate of a sentence and explain the action, condition, or effect of the subject of that sentence.

VERB PARTICLE: A relational word (e.g., slow *down*, wake *up*, turn *off*) that is associated with a verb; verb particles can be differentiated from prepositions by transposing the word in question to the right of the object noun and judging grammaticality (e.g., "She *put on* the hat" → "She *put* the hat *on*" = verb particle; "She danced *on* the table" → "She danced the table *on*" = preposition); also referred to as particle.

VERB PHRASE: The verb plus any additional words or phrases that are needed to complete the verb; the only obligatory component of this sentence constituent is a verb; object noun phrases are considered to be part of the verb phrase.

VERB PHRASE COMPLEMENT: Words and phrases that complete the meaning of a verb or verb phrase; can be a prepositional phrase (e.g., the man talked *about his journey*); or a verb phrase, often in the form of an infinitive (e.g., The child came *to play*).

WH- CLAUSE: A subordinate clause that is introduced by *a wh-* word and provides adjectival information (e.g., "I know *where he is*"); typical *wh-* words that introduce *wh-* clauses and not relative clauses include *who, where, when, why, how,* and sometimes *what*.

WH- INFINITIVE CLAUSE: An infinitive that is introduced by *a wh-* word, therefore subordinated to the main verb (e.g., "You know *how to make this*" or "Show me *what to do*").

WH- QUESTION: A question form that requests specific information characterized by one of the following *wh-* words: *who, what, what-doing, where, why, when,* and *how.*

YES/NO QUESTION: A question form that requires a yes or no response (e.g., "More?" or "Do you want a cookie?").

REFERENCES

Adams, C., Lockton, E., Gaile, J., Earl, G., & Freed, J. (2012). The social communication intervention project: A randomized controlled trial of the effectiveness of speech and language therapy for school-age children who have pragmatic and social communication problems with or without autism spectrum disorder. *International Journal of Language and Communication Disorders, 47*, 233–244.

American Psychiatric Association. (2013). *Diagnostic and statistical manual of mental disorders* (5th ed.). Washington, DC: Author.

American Speech-Language-Hearing Association. (2004). Knowledge and skills needed by speech-language pathologists and audiologists to provide culturally and linguistically appropriate services [Knowledge and skills]. Retrieved from http://www.asha.org/policy/KS2004-00215.htm

American Speech-Language-Hearing Association. (2017). *ASHA practice portal*. Retrieved from https://www.asha.org/Practice-Portal

Anderson-Wood, L., & Smith, B. (1997). *Working with pragmatics*. Oxon, UK: Winslow Press.

Barenbaum, E., & Newcomer, P. (1996). *Test of children's language*. Austin, TX: PRO-ED.

Bates, E. (1976). *Language and context*. New York, NY: Academic Press.

Bedrosian, J. L. (1985). An approach to developing conversational competence. In D. N. Ripich & F. M. Spinelli (Eds.), *School discourse problems* (pp. 231–255). San Diego, CA: College Hill Press.

Beilin, H. (1975). *Studies in the cognitive basis of language development*. New York, NY: Academic Press.

Benedict, H. (1979). Early lexical development: Comprehension and production. *Journal of Child Language, 10*, 321–335.

Berko Gleason, J. (1973). Code switching in children's language. In T. E. Moore (Ed.), *Cognitive development and the acquisition of language* (pp. 159–167). New York, NY: Academic Press.

Bernstein, M. H., & Haynes, O. M. (1998). Vocabulary competence in early childhood: Measurement, latent construct, and predictive validity. *Child Development, 69*, 654–671.

Betz, S. K., Eickhoff, J. R., & Sullivan, S. F. (2013). Factors influencing the selection of standardized tests for the diagnosis of specific language impairment. *Language, Speech, and Hearing Services in Schools, 44*, 133–146. doi:10.1044/0161-1461(2012/12-0093)

Beveridge, M., & Conti-Ramsden, G. (1987). *Children with language disabilities*. Milton Keynes, UK: Open University Press.

Bishop, D., & Edmundson, A. (1987). Language-impaired 4-year-olds: Distinguishing transient from persistent impairment. *Journal of Speech and Hearing Disorders, 52*, 156–173.

Bloom, L. (1973). *One word at a time: The use of single-word utterances before syntax*. The Hague, The Netherlands: Mouton.

Bloom, L., & Lahey, M. (1978). *Language development and language disorders*. New York, NY: Wiley.

Bloom, L., Lightbown, P., & Hood, L. (1975). Structure and variation in child language. *Monographs of the Society for Research in Child Development, 40*(2, Serial No. 160).

Bloom, L., Rocissano, L., & Hood, L. (1976). Adult-child discourse: Developmental interaction between information processing and linguistic knowledge. *Cognitive Psychology, 8*, 521–552.

Boehm, A. (2001). *Boehm test of basic concepts* (3rd. ed.). New York, NY: Psychological Corporation.

Bowers, L., Huisingh, R., Orman, J., & LoGiudice, C. (1998). *The expressive language test*. East Moline, IL: LinguiSystems.

Bray, C., & Wiig, E. (1985). *Let's talk inventory for children*. San Antonio, TX: Psychological Corporation.

Brinton, B. (1990). Peer commentary on "Clinical pragmatics: Expectations and realizations," by Tanya Gallagher. *Journal of Speech-Language Pathology and Audiology, 14*(1), 7–8.

Brinton, B., & Fujiki, M. (1984). Development of topic manipulation skills in discourse. *Journal of Speech and Hearing Research, 27*, 350–358.

Brinton, B., & Fujiki, M. (1989). *Conversational management with language-impaired children: Pragmatic assessment and intervention*. Rockville, MD: Aspen.

Brinton, B., Fujiki, M., Loeb, D., & Winkler, E. (1986). The development of conversational repair strategies in response to requests for clarification. *Journal of Speech and Hearing Research, 29*, 75–81.

Brinton, B., Fujiki, M., & Powell, J. M. (1997). The ability of children with language impairment to manipulate topic in a structured task. *Language, Speech, and Hearing Services in Schools, 28*, 3–11.

Brinton, B., Fujiki, M., & Sonnenberg, E. (1988). Responses to requests for clarification by linguistically normal and language-impaired children in conversation. *Journal of Speech and Hearing Research, 53,* 383–391.

Brinton, B., Fujiki, M., Spencer, J. C., & Robinson, L. A. (1997). The ability of children with specific language impairment to access and participate in an ongoing interaction. *Journal of Speech, Language, and Hearing Research, 40,* 1011–1025.

Brinton B., Robinson L., & Fujiki M. (2004). Description of a program for social language intervention: "If you can have a conversation, you can have a relationship." *Language, Speech, and Hearing Services in Schools, 35,* 283–290.

Brown, R. (1973). *A first language: The early stages.* Cambridge, MA: Harvard University Press.

Brown, R., & Bellugi, U. (1964). Three processes in the child's acquisition of syntax. *Harvard Educational Review, 34,* 133–151.

Brownell, R. (2000). *Expressive one-word picture vocabulary test.* Novato, CA: Academic Therapy.

Bruinsma, Y., Koegel, R., & Koegel, L. (2004). Joint attention and children with autism: A review of the literature. *Mental Retardation and Developmental Disabilities, 10,* 169–175.

Bruner J. (1975). The ontogenesis of speech acts. *Journal of Child Language, 2*(1), 1–19.

Bruner, J. (1981). The social context of language acquisition. *Language and Communication, 1,* 155–178.

Carpenter, L. (1991, November). *Narrative discourse in language minority and language learning disabled children.* Paper presented at the annual convention of the American Speech-Language-Hearing Association, Atlanta, GA.

Carrow-Woolfolk, E. (2011). *Oral and written language scales* (2nd edition). San Antonio, TX: Pearson.

Carrow-Woolfolk, E. (2017). *Comprehensive assessment of spoken language* (2nd ed.). Circle Pines, MN: American Guidance Service.

Carrow-Woolfolk, E. (2014). *Test for auditory comprehension of language* (4th ed.). Austin, TX: PRO-ED.

Carrow-Woolfolk, E., & Allen, E. (2014). *Test of expressive language.* Austin, TX: PRO-ED.

Casby, M.W. (2011). An examination of the relationship of sample size and mean length of utterance of children with developmental language impairment. *Child Language Teaching and Therapy, 27,* 286–293. doi:10.1177/0265659010394387

Cazden, C. (1968). The acquisition of noun and verb inflections. *Child Development, 39,* 433–438.

Chapman, R. (1981). Exploring children's communicative intents. In J. Miller (Ed.), *Assessing language production in children: Experimental procedures* (pp. 111–136). Baltimore, MD: University Park Press.

Chapman, R., Paul, R., & Wanska, S. (1981). *Syntactic structures in simple sentences* (Unpublished raw data).

Chase, K. B., & Johnston, J. R. (2013). Testing local: Small-scale language sample databases for ESL assessment. *Canadian Journal of Speech-Language Pathology and Audiology/Revue Canadienne d 'Orthophonie Et d'Audiologie, 37*(1), 42–56.

Coggins, T., & Carpenter, R. (1981). The communicative intention inventory: A system for observing and coding children's early intentional communication. *Applied Psycholinguistics, 2,* 235–251.

Colozzo, P., Gillam, R., Wood, M., Schnell, S., & Johnston, J. (2011). Content and form in the narratives of children with specific language impairment. *Journal of Speech, Language, and Hearing Research, 54,* 1609–1627.

Condouris, K., Meyer, E., & Tager-Flusberg, H. (2003). The relationship between standardized measures of language and measures of spontaneous speech in children with autism. *American Journal of Speech-Language Pathology, 12,* 349–358.

Cook-Gumperz, J., & Corsaro, W. (1977). Social-ecological constraints on children's communication strategies. *Sociology, 11,* 411–434.

Craig, H., & Washington, J. (2000). An assessment battery for identifying language impairments in African-American children. *Journal of Speech, Language, and Hearing Research, 43,* 366–379.

Craig, H. (1991). Pragmatic characteristics of the child with specific language impairment: An interactionist perspective. In T. Gallagher (Ed.), *Pragmatics of language: Clinical practice issues* (pp. 163–198). San Diego, CA: Singular.

Crais, E., Watson, L., Baranek, G., & Reznick, J. R. (2006). Early identification of autism: How early can we go? *Seminars in Speech and Language, 27*(3), 143–160.

Cross, T. (1984). Habilitating the language-impaired child: Ideas from studies of parent-child interaction. *Topics in Language Disorders, 4*(4), 1–14.

Crystal, D. (1992). *Profiling linguistic disability* (2nd ed.). San Diego, CA: Singular.

Crystal, D., Fletcher, P., & Garman, M. (1976). *The grammatical analysis of language disability: A procedure for assessment and remediation.* London, UK: Edward Arnold.

Crystal, D., Fletcher, P., & Garman, M. (1991). *The grammatical analysis of language disability: A procedure for assessment and remediation* (2nd ed.). San Diego, CA: Singular.

Damico, J. (1991). Clinical discourse analysis: A functional approach to language assessment. In C. Simon (Ed.), *Communication skills and classroom success: Assessment and therapy methodologies for language and learning disabled students* (pp. 165–206). Eau Claire, WI: Thinking Publications.

Dawson, G., Toth, K., Abbott, R., Osterling, J., Munson, J., Estes, A., & Liaw, J. (2004). Early social attention impairments in autism: Social orienting, joint attention, and attention to distress. *Developmental Psychology, 40*(2), 271–283.

de Villiers, J., & de Villiers, P. (1973). A cross-sectional study of the acquisition of grammatical morphemes. *Journal of Psycholinguistic Research, 2,* 267–278.

Donahue, M., & Bryan, T. (1983). Conversational skills and modeling in learning disabled boys. *Applied Psycholinguistics, 4,* 251–278.

Dore, J. (1974). A pragmatic description of early language development. *Journal of Psycholinguistic Research, 4,* 343–350.

Dore, J. (1978). Variation in preschool children's conversational performances. In K. Nelson (Ed.), *Children's language: Vol. 1* (pp. 397–444). New York, NY: Gardner Press.

Dotson, W., Leaf, J., Sheldon, J., & Sherman, J. (2010). Group teaching of conversational skills to adolescents on the autism spectrum. Research in *Autism Spectrum Disorders, 4*(2), 199–209.

Duchan, J. F. (1984). Language assessment: The pragmatics revolution. In R. C. Naremore (Ed.), *Language science* (pp. 147–180). San Diego, CA: College Hill.

Dunn, T., & Dunn, L. (2007). *Peabody picture vocabulary test* (4th ed.). Circle Pines, MN: American Guidance Service.

Dunn, M., Flax, J., Silwinski, M., & Aram, D. (1996). The use of spontaneous language as criteria for identifying children with specific language impairment: An attempt to reconcile clinical and research incongruence. *Journal of Speech and Hearing Research, 39,* 643–654.

Ebert, K. D., & Scott, C. M. (2014). Relationships between narrative language samples and norm-referenced test scores in language assessments of school-age children. *Language Speech and Hearing Services in Schools, 45,* 337–350. doi:10.1044/2014_LSHSS-14-0034

Eisenberg, S. L., Fersko, T. M., & Lundgren, C. (2001). The use of MLU for identifying language impairment in preschool children: A review. *American Journal of Speech-Language Pathology, 10,* 323–342. doi:10.1044/1058-0360(2001/028)

Ervin-Tripp, S. (1970). Discourse agreement: How children answer questions. In J. R. Hayes (Ed.), *Cognition and the development of language* (pp. 79–107). New York, NY: Wiley.

Ervin-Tripp, S., & Mitchell-Kernan, C. (1977). *Child discourse.* New York, NY: Academic Press.

Evans, J. (1996). Plotting the complexities of language sample analysis: Linear and non-linear dynamical models of assessment. In K. Cole, P. Dale, & D. Thal (Eds.), *Assessment of communication and language* (p. 257). Baltimore, MD: Paul H. Brookes.

Fey, M. (1986). *Language intervention with young children.* San Diego, CA: College Hill Press.

Fey, M., & Leonard, L. (1983). Pragmatic skills of children with specific language impairment. In T. Gallagher and C. Prutting (Eds.), *Pragmatic assessment and intervention issues in language* (pp. 65–82). San Diego, CA: College Hill Press.

Fujiki, M., Brinton, B., McCleave, C. P., Anderson, V. W., & Chamberlain, J. P. (2013). A social communication intervention to increase validating comments by children with language impairment. *Language, Speech, and Hearing Services in Schools, 44,* 3–19.

Gallagher, T. (1983). Pre-assessment: A procedure for accommodating language use variability. In T. Gallagher & C. Prutting (Eds.), *Pragmatic assessment and intervention issues in language* (pp. 1–15). San Diego, CA: College Hill Press.

Gallagher, T. (1991). Language and social skills: Implications for clinical assessment and intervention with school-age children. In T. Gallagher (Ed.), *Pragmatics of language: Clinical practice issues* (pp. 11–41). San Diego, CA: Singular.

Garvey, C. (1975). Requests and responses in child speech. *Journal of Child Language, 2*(1), 41–63.

Gerber, S., Brice, A., Capone, N., Fujiki, M., & Timler, G. (2012): Language use in social interactions of school-age children with language impairments: An evidence based systematic review of treatment. *Language, Speech, and Hearing Services in Schools, 43,* 235–249.

Gleitman, L., Gleitman, H., & Shipley, E. (1972). The emergence of the child as grammarian. *Cognition, 1,* 137–164.

Golinkoff, R., & Ames, G. (1979). A comparison of fathers' and mothers' speech with their children. *Child Development, 50,* 28–32.

Greenfield, P., & Smith, J. (1976). *The structure of communication in early language development.* New York, NY: Academic Press.

Grice, H. P. (1975). Logic and conversation. In P. Cole & J. Morgan (Eds.), *Syntax and semantics. Volume 3: Speech acts* (pp. 41–58). New York, NY: Academic Press.

Griffith, P. L., Ripich, D. N., & Dastoli, S. L. (1986). Story structure, cohesion and propositions in story recalls by learning-disabled and nondisabled children. *Journal of Psycholinguistic Research, 15*(6), 539–555.

Guo, L.-Y., & Eisenberg, S. (2014). The diagnostic accuracy of two tense measures for identifying 3-year-old children with language impairment. *American Journal of Speech-Language Pathology, 23,* 203–212. doi:10.1044/2013_AJSLP-13-0007

Guo, L.-Y., & Eisenberg, S. (2015). Sample length affects the reliability of language sample measures in 3-year-olds: Evidence from parent-elicited conversational samples. *Language, Speech and Hearing Services in Schools, 46,* 141–153. doi:10.1044/2015_LSHSS-14-0052

Hale, C., & Tager-Flusberg, H. (2005). Brief report: The relationship between discourse deficits and autism symptomatology. *Journal of Autism and Developmental Disorders, 35*(4), 519–524.

Hall, W., & Cole, M. (1978). On participants' shaping of discourse through their understanding of the task. In K. Nelson (Ed.), *Children's language: Vol. 1* (pp. 445–465). New York, NY: Gardner Press.

Halliday, M. (1977). *Learning how to mean: Explorations in the development of language.* New York, NY: Elsevier.

Hammill, D. D., & Newcomer, P. L. (2019). *Test of language development: Primary* (5th ed.). Austin, TX: PRO-ED.

Heilmann, J. (2010). Myths and realities of language sample analysis. *SIG 1 Perspectives on Language Learning and Education, 17,* 4–8.

Heilmann, J., Nockerts, A., & Miller, J. (2010). Language sampling: Does the length of the transcript matter? *Language, Speech, and Hearing Services in Schools, 41,* 393–404.

Hendrick, D., Prather, E., & Tobin, A. (1975). *Sequenced inventory of communication development–Revised.* Torrance, CA: WPS.

Hodson, B. (2010). *Evaluating and enhancing children's phonological systems.* Wichita, KS: PhonoComp.

Hoerning, H. (2007). *Type-token ratio scores: Establishing norms for preschool-aged children* (Unpublished masters thesis). University of Wisconsin, Eau Claire.

Horgan, D. (1979, May). *Nouns: Love 'em or leave 'em*. Address to the New York Academy of Sciences, New York.

Hoskins, B., & Noel, K. (2011). *Conversations framework*. Chippewa Falls, WI: The Cognitive Press.

Hresko, W., Reid, D., & Hammill, D. (2018). *Test of early language development* (4th ed.). Austin, TX: PRO-ED.

Huddleston, R. (1988). *Introduction to the grammar of English*. New York, NY: Cambridge University Press.

Hughes, D., McGillivray, L., & Schmidek, M. (1997). *Guide to narrative language: Procedures for assessment*. Eau Claire, WI: Thinking Publications.

Huttenlocher, J. (1974). The origins of language comprehension. In R. L. Solso (Ed.), *Theories in cognitive psychology* (pp. 331–368). New York, NY: Halsted.

Ingram, D. (1972). The development of phrase structure rules. *Language Learning, 22,* 65–77.

Ingram, D. (1981). *Assessing communication behavior: Procedures for the phonological analysis of children's language (Vol. 2)*. Baltimore, MD: University Park Press.

Keenan, E., & Schieffelin, B. (1976). Topic as a discourse notion: A study of topic in the conversation of children and adults. In C. L. (Ed.), *Subject and topic* (pp. 337–383). New York, NY: Academic Press.

Klee, T. (1992). Developmental and diagnostic characteristics of quantitative measures of children's language production. *Topics in Language Disorders, 12*(2), 28–41.

Klima, E., & Bellugi, U. (1966). Syntactic regularities in the speech of children. In J. Lyons & R. Wales (Eds.), *Psycholinguistic papers* (pp. 183–208). Edinburgh, UK: Edinburgh University Press.

Koegel, L., Koegel, R., & Smith, A. (1997). Variables related to differences in standardized test outcomes for children with autism. *Journal of Autism and Developmental Disorders, 27,* 233–242.

Klee, T. (1985). Clinical language sampling: Analysing the analyses. *Child Language Teaching and Therapy, 1,* 182–187.

Kramer, C., James, S., & Saxman, J. (1979). A comparison of language samples elicited at home and in the clinic. *Journal of Speech and Hearing Disorders, 44,* 321–330.

Landra, R. J., Holman K.C., & Garrett-Mayer, E. (2007). Social and communication development in toddlers with early and later diagnosis of autism spectrum disorders. *Archives of General Psychiatry, 64*(7), 853–864.

Larson, V. Lord, & McKinley, N. (1998). Characteristics of adolescents' conversations: A longitudinal study. *Clinical Linguistics and Phonetics, 12*(3), 183–203.

Lee, L. (1966). Developmental sentence types: A method for comparing normal and deviant syntactic development. *Journal of Speech and Hearing Disorders, 31,* 311–330.

Lee, L. (1974). *Developmental sentence analysis*. Evanston, IL: Northwestern University Press.

Leinonen, E., & Smith, B. (1994). Appropriacy judgements and pragmatic performance. *European Journal of Disorders of Communication, 29*(1), 77–84.

Leonard, L. (1976). *Meaning in child language*. New York, NY: Greene and Stratton.

Leonard, L., & Fey, M. (1991). Facilitating grammatical development: The contribution of pragmatics. In T. Gallagher (Ed.), *Pragmatics of language: Clinical practice issues* (pp. 333–355). San Diego, CA: Singular.

Liiva, C. A., & Cleave, P. L. (2005). Roles of initiation and responsiveness in access and participation for children with specific language impairment. *Journal of Speech, Language, and Hearing Research, 48,* 868–883.

Liles, B. (1985a). Cohesion in the narratives of normal and language-disordered children. *Journal of Speech and Hearing Research, 28,* 123–133.

Liles, B. (1985b). Production and comprehension of narrative discourse in normal and language-disordered children. *Journal of Communication Disorders, 18,* 409–427.

Liles, B. (1987). Episode organization and cohesion conjunctions in narratives of children with and without language disorder. *Journal of Speech and Hearing Research, 30,* 185–196.

Limber, J. (1973). The genesis of complex sentences. In T. Moore (Ed.), *Cognitive development and the acquisition of language* (pp. 169–185). New York, NY: Academic Press.

Long, S. H., Fey, M. E., & Channel, R. W. (2003). Computerized profiling. (Version 9.70) [Computer software, Windows only]. Cleveland, OH: Case Western Reserve University.

Longhurst, T., & File, J. (1977). A comparison of developmental sentence scores from head start children collected in four conditions. *Language, Speech, and Hearing Services in Schools, 8,* 54–64.

Maljaars, J., Noens, I., Jansen, R. Scholte, E., & van Berkelaer-Onnes. (2011). Intentional communication in nonverbal and verbal low-functioning children with autism. *Journal of Communication Disorders, 44*(6), 601–614.

Martlew, M. (1980). Mothers' control strategies in dyadic mother/child conversations. *Journal of Psycholinguistic Research, 9*(4), 327–346.

Martlew, M., Connolly, K., & McCleod, C. (1978). Language use, role, and context in a five-year-old. *Journal of Child Language, 5,* 81–99.

Mayer, M. (1973). *Froggie on his own*. New York, NY: Dial Books.

McCord, J., & Haynes, W. (1988). Discourse errors in students with learning disabilities and their normally achieving peers: Molar versus molecular views. *Journal of Learning Disabilities, 21,* 237–243.

McLean, J., & Snyder-McLean, L. (1978). *Transactional approach to early language training.* Columbus, OH: Merrill.

McNeill, D. (1970). *The acquisition of language: The study of developmental psycholinguistics.* New York, NY: Harper and Row.

McTear, M. (1985). *Children's conversation.* Oxford, UK: Blackwell.

McTear, M., & Conti-Ramsden, G. (1991). *Pragmatic disability in children.* San Diego, CA: Singular.

Meline, T., & Brackin, S. (1987). Language-impaired children's awareness of inadequate messages. *Journal of Speech and Hearing Disorders, 52,* 263–270.

Merrison, S., & Merrison, A. J. (2005). Repair in speech and language therapy interaction: Investigating pragmatic language impairment of children. *Child Language Teaching & Therapy, 21*(2), 191–211.

Merritt, D. D., & Liles, B. Z. (1987). Story grammar ability in children with and without language disorder: Story generation, story retelling, and story comprehension. *Journal of Speech and Hearing Research, 30,* 539–552.

Miller, J. (1981). *Assessing language production in children: Experimental procedures.* Baltimore, MD: University Park Press.

Miller, J. (1991). Quantifying productive language disorder. In J. Miller (Ed.), *Research on child language disorders: A decade of progress* (pp. 211–220). Austin, TX: PRO-ED.

Miller, J. F., Andriacchi, K., & Nockerts, A. (2015). *Assessing language production using SALT software* (2nd ed.). Middleton, WI: SALT Software.

Miller, J. F., & Chapman, R. S. (1981). The relation between age and mean length of utterance in morphemes. *Journal of Speech and Hearing Research, 24,* 154–161.

Miller, J. F., & Chapman, R. S. (2000). SALT: A computer program for the systematic analysis of language transcripts [Computer software]. Madison, WI: Language Analysis Laboratory, Waisman Center, University of Wisconsin.

Montgomery, J. (2008). *MAVA: Montgomery assessment of vocabulary acquisition.* Greenville, SC: SuperDuper.

Mosher, J. R. (1968). *English grammar.* Lincoln, NE: Cliff's Notes.

Mundy, P., Sigman, M., & Kasari, C. (1990). A longitudinal study of joint attention and language development in autistic children. *Journal of Autism and Developmental Disorders, 20*(1), 115–128.

Muller, E., Cannon, L., Kornblum, C., Clark, J., & Powers, M. (2016). Description and preliminary evaluation of a curriculum for teaching conversational skills to children with high-functioning autism and other social cognition challenges. *Language, Speech, and Hearing Services in Schools, 47,* 191–208.

National Institute on Deafness and Other Communication Disorders (NIDCD). (2010). *Language benchmarks in children with autism spectrum disorder (ASD).* Retrieved from https://www.nidcd.nih.gov/workshops/language-benchmarks-children-autism/2007

Nelson, K. (1973). Structure and strategy in learning to talk. *Monographs of the Society for Research in Child Development, 38*(1–2, Serial No. 149).

Nisswandt, B. (1983). *The effects of situational variability on the grammatical speech forms of three-year-olds* (Unpublished master's thesis). University of Wisconsin, Eau Claire.

Norris, J., & Damico, J. (1990). Whole language in theory and practice: Implications for language intervention. *Language, Speech, and Hearing Services in Schools, 21,* 212–220.

Oetting, J. B. (1999). Children with SLI use argument structure cues to learn verbs. *Journal of Speech, Language, and Hearing Research,42,* 1261–1274.

Olswang, L., & Carpenter, R. (1978). Elicitor effects on the language obtained from young language-impaired children. *Journal of Speech and Hearing Disorders, 43,* 76–88.

Owens, R. (1992). *Language development: An introduction.* Columbus, OH: Merrill.

Owens, R. (2014). *Language disorders: A functional approach to assessment and intervention* (6th ed.). Upper Saddle River, NJ: Pearson.

Owens, R., & Pavelko, S. (2015, November). *Bye-bye Roger: Rethinking Dr. Brown's language sample collection and analysis.* A presentation at the annual convention of the American Speech-Language-Hearing Association, Denver, CO.

Owens, R., & Pavelko, S. (2017). Relationships among conversational language samples and norm-referenced test scores. *Clinical Archives of Communication Disorders, 2*(1), 43–50. doi:http://dx.doi.org/10.21849/cacd.2017.00052

Paul, R. (1981). Analyzing complex sentence development. In J. Miller (Ed.), *Assessing language production in children.* Baltimore, MD: University Park Press.

Paul, R., & Norbury, C. (2012). *Language disorders from infancy through adolescence: Assessment and intervention* (4th ed.). St. Louis, MO: Mosby/Elsevier.

Pavelko, S. L., & Owens, R. E. (2017). Sampling utterances and grammatical analysis revised (SUGAR): New normative values for language sample analysis measures. *Language, Speech, and Hearing Services in Schools, 48*(3), 197–215.

Pavelko, S., Owens, R., Ireland, M., & Hahs-Vaughn, D. (2016). Use of language sample analysis by school-based SLPs: Results of a nationwide survey. *Language, Speech, and Hearing Services in Schools, 47,* 246–258. doi:10.1044/2016_LSHSS-15-0044

Pavelko, S., Owens, R., & Johnson, V. (2016, November). *The new normal: New norms for school-age children and adolescents.* Presentation at the annual convention of the American Speech-Language-Hearing Association, Philadelphia, PA.

Penn, C. (1988). The profiling of syntax and pragmatics in aphasia. *Clinical Linguistics and Phonetics, 2,* 179–207.

Phelps-Terasaki, D., & Phelps-Gunn, T. (2007). *Test of pragmatic language* (2nd ed.). Austin, TX: PRO-ED.

Price, L., Hendricks, S., & Cook, C. (2010). Incorporating computer-aided language sample analysis into clinical practice. *Language, Speech, and Hearing Services in Schools, 41,* 205–222. doi:10.1044/0161-1461 (2009/08-0054)

Prutting, C., & Kirchner, D. (1983). Applied pragmatics. In T. Gallagher & C. Prutting (Eds.), *Pragmatic assessment and intervention issues in language* (pp. 29–64). San Diego, CA: College Hill Press.

Prutting, C., & Kirchner, D. (1987). A clinical appraisal of pragmatic aspects of language. *Journal of Speech and Hearing Disorders, 52,* 105–119.

Quirk, R., Greenbaum, S., Leech, G., & Svartvik, J. (1972). *A grammar of contemporary English.* New York, NY: Seminar Press.

Ratner, N. B., & Brundage, S. (2016). *A clinician's complete guide to CLAN and PRAAT.* Retrieved from http://talkbank.org/manuals/Clin-CLAN.pdf

Ratner, N. B., Fromm, D., & MacWhinney, B. (2017). *Child language sample analysis (LSA): How to make it faster, more accurate, and more informative!* Presentation 1199 at the annual conference of the American Speech-Language-Hearing Association, Los Angeles, CA.

Renfrew, C. (1969). *The bus story: A test of continuous speech.* (Available from the author at North Place, Old Headington). Oxford, UK.

Retherford, K. (1980). *Appropriateness judgments* (Unpublished class materials). University of Wisconsin, Eau Claire.

Retherford, K. S. (1987). *Guide to analysis of language transcripts.* Eau Claire, WI: Thinking Publications.

Retherford, K., & Hoerning, H. (2006, November). *Type-token ratio scores: Establishing norms for preschool-aged children.* Presentation at the annual convention of the American Speech-Language-Hearing Association, Miami Beach, FL.

Retherford, K., Schwartz, B., & Chapman, R. (1977, September). *The changing relationship between semantic relations in mother & child speech.* Paper presented at the Second Annual Boston University Conference on Language Acquisition, Boston, MA.

Retherford, K., Schwartz, B., & Chapman, R. (1981). Semantic roles in mother & child speech: Who tunes into whom? *Journal of Child Language, 8,* 583–608.

Rice, M. L., Smolik, F., Perpich, D., Thompson, T., Rytting, N., & Blossom, M. (2010). Mean length of utterance levels in 6-month intervals for children 3–9 years with and without language impairments. *Journal of Speech, Language, and Hearing Research, 53,* 333–349. doi:10.1044/1092-4388(2009/08-0183)

Rice, M., Sell, M., & Hadley, P. (1990). The social interactive coding system (SICS): An on-line, clinically relevant descriptive tool. *Language, Speech, and Hearing Services in Schools, 21,* 2–14.

Rizzo, J., & Stephens, M. (1981). Performance of children with normal and impaired oral language production on a set of auditory comprehension tests. *Journal of Speech and Hearing Disorders, 46,* 150–159.

Roth, F. P. (1986). Oral narrative abilities of learning-disabled students. *Topics in Language Disorders, 7*(1), 21–30.

Roth, F., & Spekman, N. (1984). Assessing the pragmatic abilities of children: Part I. Organizational framework and assessment parameters. *Journal of Speech and Hearing Disorders, 49,* 2–11.

Sachs, J., & Devin, J. (1976). Young children's use of age-appropriate speech styles in social interaction and role playing. *Journal of Child Language, 3,* 81–98.

Schlesinger, I. (1971). Learning grammar: From pivot to realization rule. In R. Huxley & E. Ingram (Eds.), *Language acquisition: Models and methods* (pp. 79–89). New York, NY: Academic Press.

Schneider, P., & Hayward, D. (2010). Who does what to whom: Introduction of referents in children's storytelling from pictures. *Language, Speech, and Hearing Services in Schools, 41,* 459–473.

Schwartz, A. (1985). Microcomputer-assisted assessment of linguistic and phonological processes. *Topics in Language Disorders, 6*(1), 26–40.

Scott, C., & Taylor, A. (1978). A comparison of home and clinic gathered language samples. *Journal of Speech and Hearing Disorders, 43,* 482–495.

Scott, C. M., & Windsor, J. (2000). General language performance measures in spoken and written narrative and expository discourse of school-age children with language learning disabilities. *Journal of Speech, Language, and Hearing Research, 43,* 324–339. doi:10.1044/jslhr.4302.324

Searle, J. (1969). *Speech acts.* Cambridge, MA: Cambridge University Press.

Semel, E., Wiig, E., & Secord, W. (2004). *Clinical evaluation of language fundamentals: Preschool* (2nd ed.). San Antonio, TX: Pearson.

Shatz, M., & Gelman, R. (1973). The development of communication skills: Modifications in the speech of young children as a function of listener. *Monographs of the Society for Research in Child Development, 38*(1–2, Serial No. 149).

Shertzer, M. (1986). *The elements of grammar.* New York, NY: Macmillan.

Shriberg, L., & Kwiatkowski, J. (1980). *Natural process analysis (NPA): A procedure for phonological analysis of continuous speech samples.* New York, NY: Wiley.

Shumway, S., & Wetherby, A. (2009). Communicative acts of children with autism spectrum disorders in the second year of life. *Journal of Speech, Language, and Hearing Research, 52,* 1139–1156.

Smedley, M. (1989). Semantic-pragmatic language disorder: A description with some practical suggestions for teachers. *Child Language Teaching and Therapy, 5,* 174–190.

Smith, P., & Daglish, L. (1977). Sex differences in parent and infant behavior in the home. *Child Development, 48*(4), 1250–1254.

Smith, B., & Leinonen, E. (1992). *Clinical pragmatics: Unravelling the complexities of communicative failure.* London, UK: Chapman and Hall.

Spaulding, T. J., Plante, E., & Farinella, K. A. (2006). Eligibility criteria for language impairment: Is the low end of normal always appropriate? *Language, Speech and Hearing Services in the Schools, 37,* 61–72.

Stalnaker, L., & Craighead, N. (1982). An examination of language samples obtained under three experimental conditions. *Language, Speech, and Hearing Services in Schools, 13,* 121–128.

Stein, N., & Glenn, C. (1979). An analysis of story comprehension in elementary school children. In R. Freedle (Ed.), *New directions in discourse processing* (Vol. 2, pp. 53–120). Norwood, NJ: Ablex.

Stiegler, L. (2015). Examining the echolalia literature: Where do speech-language pathologists stand? *American Journal of Speech-Language Pathology, 24,* 750–762.

Stone, W., Ousley, O., Yoder, P., Hogan, K., & Hepburn, S. (1997). Nonverbal communication in two- and three-year-old children with autism. *Journal of Autism and Developmental Disorders, 27*(6), 677–696.

Strong, C. (1998). *The Strong narrative assessment procedure.* Eau Claire, WI: Thinking Publications.

Templin, M. (1957). *Certain language skills in children: Their development and interrelationships* (Institute of Child Welfare Monograph Series No. 26). Minneapolis, MN: University of Minnesota Press.

Thorne, J., & Coggins, T. (2016). Cohesive referencing errors during narrative production as clinical evidence of central nervous system abnormality in school-aged children with fetal alcohol spectrum disorders. *Journal of Speech-Language Pathology, 25,* 532–546.

Thorne, J., Coggins, T., Carmichael Olson, H., & Astley, S. (2007). Exploring the utility of narrative analysis in diagnostic decision making: Picture-bound reference, elaboration and fetal alcohol spectrum disorders. *Journal of Speech, Language, and Hearing Research, 50,* 458–474.

Toe, D., Rinaldi, P., Caselli, M., Paatsch, L., & Church, A. (2016). The development of pragmatic skills in children and young people who are deaf and hard of hearing. In M. Marschark, V. Lampropoulou & E. K. Skordilis (Eds.), *Diversity in deaf education* (pp. 247–270). New York, NY: Oxford University Press.

Tomasello, M. (1992). The social bases of language acquisition. *Social Development, 1*(1), 67–87.

Tyack, D., & Ingram, D. (1977). Children's production and comprehension of questions. *Journal of Child Language, 4*(2), 211–224.

Ukrainetz, T., & Blomquist, C. (2002). The criterion validity of four vocabulary tests compared with a language sample. *Child Language Teaching and Therapy, 18,* 59–78.

van Balkom, H., Verhoeven, L., & van Weerdenburg, M. (2010). Conversational behavior of children with developmental language delay and their caretakers. *International Journal of Language & Communication Disorders, 45*(3), 295–319.

Wallace, G., & Hammill, D. (2013). *Comprehensive receptive and expressive vocabulary test* (3rd ed.). Austin, TX: PRO-ED.

Watkins, R., Kelly, D., Harbers, H., & Hollis, W. (1995). Measuring children's lexical diversity: Differentiating typical and impaired language learners. *Journal of Speech and Hearing Research, 38,* 1349–1355.

Watson, M., Murthy, J., & Wadhwa, N. (2003). Phonological analysis practice [Computer software]. Eau Claire, WI: Thinking Publications.

Weiner, F. (2000). Parrot easy language sample analysis 2000 (PELSA) [Computer software]. State College, PA: Parrot Software.

Wells, G. (1981). *Learning through interaction: The study of language development.* Cambridge, MA: Cambridge University Press.

Wetherby, A., Cain, D., & Yonclas, D. (1988). Analysis of intentional communication of normal children from the prelinguistic to multiword stage. *Journal of Speech & Hearing Research, 31,* 240–252.

Wetherby, A., & Prizant, B. (1992). Profiling young children's communicative competence. In S. Warren & J. Reichle (Eds.), *Causes and effects in communication and language intervention* (pp. 217–253). Baltimore, MD: Brookes.

Wetherby, A., & Prizant, B. (1998). Communicative, social/affective, and symbolic profiles of young children with autism and pervasive developmental disorders. *American Journal of Speech-Language Pathology, 7*(2), 79–91.

Wetherby, A., & Prizant, B. (2002). *Communication and symbolic behavior scales developmental profile. First normed edition.* Baltimore, MD: Brookes.

Wetherby, A., & Prutting, C. (1984). Profiles of communicative and cognitive-social abilities in autistic children. *Journal of Speech and Hearing Research, 27,* 364–377.

Wetherby, A., Watt, N., Morgan, L., & Shumway, S. (2007). Social communication profiles of children with autism spectrum disorders late in the second year of life. *Journal of Autism and Developmental Disorders, 37,* 960–975.

Wetherby, A., & Woods, J. (2006). Early social interaction project for children with autism spectrum disorders beginning in the second year of life. *Topics in Early Childhood Education, 26*(2), 67–82.

Wilkinson, L., Hiebert, E., & Rembold, K. (1981). Parents' and peers' communication to toddlers. *Journal of Speech and Hearing Research, 24,* 383–388.

Wilson, M., & Fox, B. (2015). *LanguageLinks to Literacy: Expressive syntax assessment.* Verona, WI: Attainment.

Woods, J., & Wetherby, A. (2003). Early identification of and intervention for infants and toddlers who are at risk for autism spectrum disorder. *Language, Speech, and Hearing in Schools, 34*(3), 180–193.

Zimmerman, I., Steiner, V., & Pond, R. (2011). *Preschool language scale-5.* New York, NY: Psychological Corporation.

ABOUT THE AUTHORS

Kristine S. Retherford, PhD, CCC-SLP, currently serves as Dean of the College of Allied Health and Nursing at Minnesota State University, Mankato. Prior to returning to her alma mater to accept this position, she was on the faculty at the University of Wisconsin-Eau Claire for 32 years, where she taught a variety of courses including Normal Communication Development, Childhood Language Disorders, and Facilitating Communication in Preschool Children. The first edition of this textbook/resource guide was completed just weeks after the birth of her first child, who is now 30 years old.

Linda R. Schreiber, MS, CCC-SLP, ASHA Fellow, Board Certified Specialist in Child Language and Language Disorders, is CEO of Linda R. Schreiber & Associates and The Cognitive Press. She is also Clinical Assistant Professor at the University of Wisconsin–Eau Claire. Linda has extensive experience in the school setting as a speech–language pathologist, a program administrator, and a liaison between the department of public instruction and local districts. She has authored and coauthored numerous publications and articles in the area of phonology, language, literacy, phonological awareness, and adolescent language disorders.

Becca Jarzynski, MS, CCC-SLP, received her Master of Science degree in Communication Disorders from the University of Wisconsin–Eau Claire (UWEC) in 2000. She is a Clinical Instructor at UWEC, where she provides clinical supervision to graduate and undergraduate students and teaches a variety of courses, including Normal Communication Development, Clinical Procedures, Facilitating Communication in Preschool Students, Birth-to-Three Methods, and Childhood Apraxia of Speech. Becca has also worked as a pediatric speech–language pathologist for 16 years and currently owns a small private practice, Child Talk Speech Therapy, L.L.C., in Eau Claire.